CAMBRIDGE

active GRAMMAR

LEVEL 2

Without answers

Fiona Davis and Wayne Rimmer
Series editor: Penny Ur

Shaftesbury Road, Cambridge CB2 8EA, United Kingdom

One Liberty Plaza, 20th Floor, New York, NY 10006, USA

477 Williamstown Road, Port Melbourne, VIC 3207, Australia

314–321, 3rd Floor, Plot 3, Splendor Forum, Jasola District Centre, New Delhi – 110025, India

103 Penang Road, #05–06/07, Visioncrest Commercial, Singapore 238467

Cambridge University Press & Assessment is a department of the University of Cambridge.

We share the University's mission to contribute to society through the pursuit of education, learning and research at the highest international levels of excellence.

www.cambridge.org
Information on this title: www.cambridge.org/9780521153591

First published 2011

22

Printed and bound by CPI Group (UK) Ltd, Croydon, CR0 4YY

A catalogue record for this publication is available from the British Library

ISBN 978-0-521-17599-9 Paperback with answers and CD-ROM
ISBN 978-0-521-15359-1 Paperback without answers and CD-ROM

Introduction

What is Active Grammar?

Active Grammar is a grammar reference and practice series for secondary students and university students. It is divided into three levels, corresponding to the levels of *The Common European Framework of Reference for Languages* (CEF). Level 1 corresponds to A1–A2, Level 2 to B1–B2, and Level 3 to C1–C2. The books give comprehensive coverage of grammar at each level, while also covering reading, composition and discussion. The books are suitable for students who are preparing for Cambridge ESOL exams.

How are the books organised?

Each unit includes

- a short **presentation** text which shows the grammar in context and provides authentic content in areas such as geography, history, social studies and science.
- easy-to-understand **grammar explanations** with plenty of examples.
- **Tip** boxes which highlight common errors or other interesting facts about the grammar.
- graded grammar **practice exercises**, many of which are in the style of Cambridge ESOL exams, aimed at building students' confidence.
- a **My Turn** activity, where students can actively apply the grammar to their own experiences, opinions and personal preferences.
- a **My Test** section which allows students to check their understanding of key points.

Also included in the book

- regular **Review** units which provide contrastive practice of previous units.
- the **Appendices**, which include a **Glossary** with definitions for all highlighted words in the units.

The CD-ROM includes

- extra activities for all the grammar covered in the book.
- printable progress tests.

How do I use the book?

You can work through the book unit by unit from Unit 1. Alternatively, you can use any unit or group of units separately if you want to focus on a particular area of grammar.

The book can be used for self-study, or in the classroom. For teachers, a comprehensive online teacher's guide gives practical tips on how to use the material in class.

www.cambridge.org/elt/activegrammar

Contents

Present simple and present continuous

I'm holding my breath.

blogspot blogspot blogspot blogspot blogspot blogspot

new post

posts | view blog | info | about

Friday night

It's midnight and **I'm holding** my breath.

I feel so scared that I can't move.

There it is again – a noise downstairs. **I think** there's someone in the house.

'Don't be silly!' **I say** to myself. (**I'm** always **lying** awake at night and listening to noises. Usually **I find out** it's the fridge or someone next door or … just nothing.)

I'm staying at my friend's house. Round here all the houses **have got** two floors. My friend **doesn't live** in a safe part of town and sometimes burglars **come in** through the downstairs windows.

I've prepared for this moment. This is what you do:

1 You **lock** the door as quietly as you can. 2 You **phone** the police on your mobile. 3 You **talk** to the police very loudly.

There's the noise again … and it**'s getting** closer.

I **don't want** to do this. I **get** slowly out of bed. But then I **stop**. Two round eyes **are looking** at me.

I **scream**.

The neighbour's cat **runs** back the way it came. How did it get in? Probably through the downstairs window.

But that **means** the downstairs window is open …

?

1 Where is the writer of the story?
2 What is making the noise?

Answers: 1 The writer is at his or her friend's house. The writer is in bed upstairs.
2 The neighbour's cat

Present simple and present continuous

Present simple

1 Add an *-s* for third person forms in present simple statements. All other forms stay the same.
*I / you / we / they **run**.*
*He / she / it **runs**.*

2 Make negative forms of regular verbs with *don't* and *doesn't*.
*I **don't want** to do this.*
*My friend **doesn't live** in a safe part of town.*
NOT ~~*… doesn't lives …*~~

3 Use the present simple for things that are always or usually true.
*He **doesn't live** in a safe part of town.*

4 Use the present simple for regular or repeated events and habits.
*I **visit** my friend every month.*

5 **We often use the present simple with adverbs of frequency, e.g. *always, never, usually.***

__Usually__ I __find out__ it's the fridge or someone next door ... or just nothing.

6 **We often use the present simple to give instructions or directions.**

1 You __lock__ the door as quietly as you can.
2 You __phone__ the police on your mobile.

7 **We often use the present simple to tell a story, or to describe a series of events as they happen.**

I __get__ slowly out of bed. But then I __stop__.

8 **We often use the present simple for a review (of a book or a film, for example).**

The film __tells__ the story of a boy who lives in the poorest part of the city. It __has__ an unexpected ending.

TIP

***Have got* means the same as *have*.**
***Have got* is more common in informal and British English.**

I've __got__ three brothers. = I __have__ three brothers.
I __haven't got__ any sisters. = I __don't have__ any sisters.
A: __Have__ you __got__ any children?
B: Yes, I __have__. / No, I __haven't__.
= A: __Do__ you __have__ any children? B: Yes, I __do__. / No, I __don't__.

Present continuous

9 **Make present continuous sentences with *am / is / are* + verb + *-ing*.**

__I'm__ always __lying__ awake.
__It's getting__ closer.
Two round eyes __are looking__ at me.

10 **Use the present continuous to describe an activity in progress now or around now.**

Two round eyes __are looking__ at me.
__I'm studying__ two languages: English and Spanish.

11 **Use the present continuous to talk about unfinished or temporary actions.**

__I'm staying__ at my friend's.

TIP

Note the difference:

He __lives__ in a beautiful flat. (The speaker doesn't think this situation will change soon.)
__He's living__ in the north of the city at the moment. (The speaker thinks this is a temporary situation.)

12 **Use the present continuous with *always, constantly* or *forever* to criticise.**

__I'm__ always __hearing__ noises.

13 **Use the present continuous to talk about situations which are gradually changing.**

The noise __is getting__ louder.

14 **We often use the present continuous to describe the background to a story. We use the present simple to describe the events.**

It's midnight and __I'm holding__ my breath.
'Don't be silly!' I __say__ to myself.

15 **We don't usually use the present continuous with state verbs (which describe states, not actions), e.g. *want, sound, believe, mean, promise.***

I __don't want__ to do this.
That __means__ the downstairs window is open.

16 **We can use some state verbs in the continuous form to describe actions. The verb then has a different meaning. Some common verbs we use like this are: *appear, expect, feel, have, imagine, look, think, see, smell, taste, weigh.***

I __think__ there's someone there.
(*think* = talking about a belief)
__I'm thinking__ what to do next.
(*think* = talking about a process)

We often use the present simple in formal letters and emails.

I __write__ to inform you that ...
I __look__ forward to meeting you.

We often use the present continuous in more informal letters and emails.

I'm writing to let you know that ...
I'm looking forward to seeing you.

▶ See Unit 8 for the present simple and present continuous with future meaning.

Practice

A Underline the correct option.

It's the middle of the afternoon. In a quiet neighbourhood a burglar [1]*tries / is trying* to break into a house. He [2]*creeps / is creeping* round the house when he [3]*hears / is hearing* a voice.
'Spider-Man [4]*watches / is watching* you!'
The burglar [5]*turns / is turning* round quickly but he [6]*doesn't see / isn't seeing* anything. So he [7]*starts / is starting* creeping across the garden again.
'Spider-Man [8]*watches / is watching* you!'
The burglar [9]*hears / is hearing* the voice again and this time he [10]*sees / is seeing* a parrot. The parrot [11]*sits / is sitting* by the side of the house.
[12]'*Do you talk / Are you talking* to me?' [13]*asks / is asking* the burglar.
'Yes,' [14]*says / is saying* the parrot. 'How do you do? I'm Batman.'
'That's a silly name,' [15]*laughs / is laughing* the burglar. 'Why [16]*does your owner call / is your owner calling* you that?'
'I have no idea,' [17]*replies / is replying* the parrot, 'and [18]*I don't know / I'm not knowing* why the rottweiler's name is Spider-Man.'
'I [19]*don't want / am not wanting* to find out!' the burglar [20]*says / is saying*.
And he [21]*runs / is running* away!

C Match the pairs.

1 At last the sun —— a is coming out.
2 The sun —— b always comes after rain.

3 They're not staying — a at home in the evenings.
4 They don't usually stay — b in the country for very long.

5 The sea level on Earth — a is rising.
6 The sun — b rises early.

7 In the mountains — a it's getting cold.
8 Come and have your dinner – b it gets cold.

9 I'm looking forward — a to meeting you at the interview tomorrow.
10 We look forward — b to seeing you in town tomorrow.

D Complete the sentences using the verbs from the box in the present simple or present continuous. Each verb is used twice.

not have not look think weigh

1 The child ...weighs... 21 kilos.
2 He .... all the ingredients for a cake.
3 They .... any pets.
4 Alex .... breakfast this morning.
5 What .... about?
6 What .... of this photo?
7 You .... very happy.
8 You won't find it. You .... in the right place.

B Match each text 1–5 to a description a–e. Then complete the texts using the words in brackets and either the present simple or the present continuous.

1 [c]

You ...go... (go) along this street and you ...turn... (turn) left at the end. The shop is on your right.

2 [ ]

As oil prices rise, the cost of air travel .... (increase). Reports show that as a result more and more people .... (stay) at home for their holidays and .... (not travel) abroad.

3 [ ]

What annoys me about my sister? Well, she .... (always talk) to her friends on the phone! And she .... (always lose) things.

4 [ ]

I .... (work) at the garage until September.

5 [ ]

I enjoyed this. It's about a guy who .... (go) round the world and .... (travel) on as many different forms of transport as possible.

a a description of change
b a book review
c directions
d criticism
e temporary situation

E Complete the questions using the verbs in brackets in either the present simple or present continuous.

1 A: Do you know ………… that woman? (know) B: No, I've never met her before.
2 A: When ………… ? (get home) B: Usually at about 4.
3 A: Where ………… she ………… ? (go) B: To the shop, I think.
4 A: ………… you ………… ? (agree) B: Yes, I think you are right.
5 A: Why ………… ? (laugh) B: I just heard a funny joke.
6 A: ………… his name ? (remember) B: I think it began with B.
7 A: What ………… ? (read) B: It's a novel by a new young writer.
8 A: Why ………… ? (cry) B: It's a really sad film.

F Complete the sentences in an appropriate way.

1 First of all, the oven has to be hot and then you put the cake in for 20 minutes.
2 ………… because he's a vegetarian.
3 On Saturday I work in a café all day but ………… .
4 ………… but she wants to be a doctor one day.
5 Hurry up – ………… .
6 Look – ………… .
7 I'm an only child – ………… .
8 He makes me angry – ………… .

MY TURN!

Complete the descriptions by inventing answers to the questions.

1 Where are you? And what are you doing? I'm in bed and I'm sleeping.
What happens next? The alarm rings. I turn it off and go back to sleep.
How do you feel? I feel tired.

2 When is it? And where are you? …………
What happens next? I see my brother.
How do you feel? …………

3 When is it? And where are you? …………
What happens next? The lights go out.
How do you feel? …………

4 Where are you? And what are you doing? …………
What happens next? I see someone famous and I go up to her.
How do you feel? …………

5 When is it? And what are you doing? …………
What happens next? The car breaks down.
How do you feel? …………

6 When is it? And what are you doing? …………
What happens next? A stranger comes up to me.
How do you feel? …………

MY TEST!

Circle the correct option.

1 The Pyrenees ………… on the border between France and Spain. a lie b lies c are lying
2 This bag ………… to me. a doesn't belongs b doesn't belong c isn't belonging
3 We sometimes ………… the car racing in the holidays. a watch b watches c are watching
4 It's Sunday and I'm bored. It ………… heavily. a rain b rains c is raining
5 This film is great – I ………… it! a really like b am really like d am really liking

My Test! answers: 1a 2b 3a 4c 5a

2 Past simple and past continuous

He was driving on a dark night.

Casey Jones (1863–1900) **was** an American railway driver. He **became** a hero when he **died** because he **saved** the lives of many passengers in a terrible accident.

On 30 April 1900 Casey **was driving** his train back to the station during a dark and wet night. He was with another driver, his friend Webb. The train **was going** fast because Casey **wanted** to get back quickly but this **wasn't** the problem. There **was** another train on the same railway. Casey and Webb **didn't know** about this train.

As Casey was coming around a bend, he saw the other train. Casey realised the danger. 'Jump!' he shouted to his friend. Webb **jumped** from the train while Casey **was trying** to stop. Webb **fell** 100 metres but he **didn't die**. While **he was falling**, he **heard** Casey. Casey **was shouting**, 'Help!' The train **was going** fast, so it **couldn't stop** quickly. Casey **slowed** the train down but it still **crashed**. Casey **was killed** but the passengers **didn't** die.

Casey **became** very famous after this and his friend **wrote** a very popular song, *The Ballad of Casey Jones*, about him.

? Underline the correct options:

1 Casey is a hero because he *saved many lives / wrote a song.*

2 Webb was a *driver / passenger.*

Answers: 1 saved many lives 2 driver

Past simple and past continuous

Past simple

1 **Add *-ed* to make the past simple (regular) for all persons. Use *did not* with the infinitive without *to* to make the negative and use *did* to make a question.**

	statement ✓	negative ✗
I / You / He / She / It / We / They	**started.**	**did not (didn't) start.**

question ?	short answer ✓✗
Did I / you / he / she / it / we / they **start**?	Yes, (I) **did.** No, (I) **did not (didn't).**

2 **Many common verbs have irregular forms for past simple statements, e.g. *go* → *went*, *see* → *saw*, *be* → *was* / *were*.**
*Casey **went** to the station.*
*We **saw** the crash.*

▶ See page 203 for a list of irregular verbs.

3 **Use the past simple for past actions, states and facts.**
*Casey **lived** in the USA.*
*Millions of immigrants **moved** to the USA in the nineteenth century.*

4 **We usually use the past simple for repeated or usual actions or situations.**
*While I was on the train, Mike **called** twice.*
*Casey **walked** to work every day.*

Past continuous

5 **Make the past continuous using the verb *was* / *were* + verb + *-ing*.**

	statement ✓	negative ✗
You / We / They	**were working.**	**were not (weren't) working.**
He / She / It	**was working.**	**was not (wasn't) working.**

Make questions and short answers as follows:

question ?		short answer ✓✗
Were you / we / they	**working?**	Yes, (we) **were.** No, (we) **weren't.**
Was I / he / she / it	**working?**	Yes, (he) **was.** No, (he) **wasn't.**

6 **Use the past continuous (e.g. *was walking, were living,* etc.) to talk about events which were in progress at a particular time in the past.**
*On 30 April Casey **was driving** his train back to the station.*
*What **was he doing** the day before?*

7 **Use the past continuous for a description of simultaneous ongoing situations.**
*It **was raining**, so we **weren't driving** fast.*
*What **were** the passengers **doing** while this **was happening**?*

Past simple and past continuous

8 **We can use the past simple with the past continuous in the same sentence. The past simple is a shorter action / event that happens in the middle of, or interrupts, a longer past continuous action / event.**
*My dad **phoned** while I **was having a shower**.*

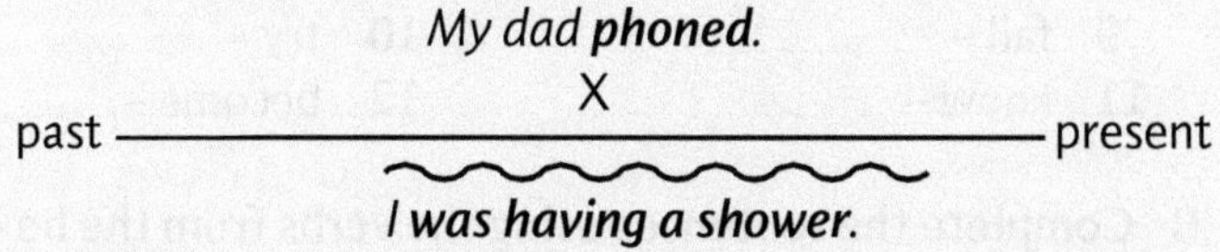
My dad **phoned.**
X
past
present
I **was having a shower.**

9 **Use the past continuous to give the reason for a past event, or to set the background to a story – to talk about what was going on when an event happened.**
*The train **was going** fast, so it **couldn't stop** quickly.*
*I **was listening** to the radio when I **heard** the news.*

When, while and *as*

10 **Use *when, while* or *as* to link past simple and past continuous verbs. Use *when* before the past simple or the past continuous verb. Use *while* before the past continuous verb.**
***While** he **was falling**, he **heard** Casey.*
*I **didn't say** anything **when** / **while** the police **were asking** questions.*

11 **Use *when* to join past simple events that are consecutive.**
*The train **stopped when** it **arrived** at the station.*
***When** the phone **rang**, Jack **answered** it.*

12 **We usually use *when* with states, e.g. ages.**
*They left America **when** they were children.*
*Casey died **when** he was 37.*

13 **We usually use *as* to describe two short events that happen simultaneously, or two events that change together.**
***As** the train **crashed**, everyone **screamed**.*
***As** the train **went** faster, Casey **worked** harder.*

TIP

Use *during* to say when something happened.
Use *for* to say how long something went on.
*The train crashed **during** the night.*
*He was a train driver **for** 10 years.*
*I was working **during** my holidays and didn't see her **for** three weeks.*

Practice

A Write the past simple forms of these verbs.

1 drive – drove
2 do – ....
3 have – ....
4 get – ....
5 open – ....
6 eat – ....
7 swim – ....
8 shout – ....
9 fall – ....
10 try – ....
11 know – ....
12 become – ....

B Complete the sentences using the verbs from the box in the past continuous.

cry dream ~~drive~~ have live not play not snow wait watch not work

1 Max was driving his car to work when it happened.
2 The baby .... very loudly, so I couldn't hear.
3 .... you .... TV all night?
4 I couldn't call you because our phone ....
5 While we .... for the bus, it started to rain.
6 .... John .... in London when you met him?
7 My mum and dad .... a coffee in the kitchen.
8 It .... but it was very cold.
9 Did it really happen or .... I only ....?
10 Glenn and Kirsten .... in the game last Saturday.

C Match the pairs.

1 When I got home, —— a I made dinner. / b I was making dinner.
2 The bottle smashed — a as it fell on the floor. / b while it was falling on the floor.
3 After the teacher finished, — a the students asked some questions. / b the students were asking some questions.
4 What music did you like — a while you were 11 years old? / b when you were 11 years old?
5 I wasn't working — a during two years. / b for two years.
6 Clare was working in Oxford — a as Mike studied at night school. / b while Mike was studying at night school.
7 We started — a when everything was ready. / b while everything was ready.
8 Was Susan wearing the same dress — a when she came in? / b when she was coming in?

D This accident happened yesterday. Write what the people were doing at the time of the accident.

When the accident happened ...

1 Joy was eating an ice cream.
2 ....
3 ....
4 ....
5 ....
6 ....
7 ....
8 ....

E Someone stole a picture from the museum last night. Read the detective's notebook with information from three museum workers, then use the notes to write sentences. Every sentence should have one verb in the past simple and one in the past continuous.

Tom Higgins: leave museum / hear noise
remember his car keys / walk to his car
come back / see a woman with a picture
shout / the woman run away

Martha Wilkins: clean the room / lights go out
look for some matches / lights come on
notice glass on the floor / look around

Sam Smith: sit at his desk / the phone ring
he pick up the phone / a strange woman come in
he speak / the woman go out

1 Tom was leaving the museum when he heard a noise.
2 ....
3 ....
4 ....
5 ....
6 ....
7 ....
8 ....
9 ....
10 ....

F Circle the correct option.

Dick Whittington (1358–1423) was a famous mayor of London. The story says that Dick was a poor boy who [1]... to London to become rich. Dick [2]... his cat with him for company. Life was very hard in London. Dick worked as a servant [3]... some months but he got very little money and all he had was his cat. Finally, Dick decided to give his cat to a merchant and leave London. As he [4]... down the street, he [5]... a voice in his head. The voice said, 'Come back, Dick, you will be Mayor of London three times!' Dick came back. At the same time, the merchant and his men [6]... by ship to another country. It was a good ship but there was a big problem: rats! Rats [7]... everywhere on the ship and no one [8]... them. Luckily, Dick's cat was very good at catching rats. The merchant was very happy with the cat and gave Dick a nice present when he [9]... home.

Dick now had some money and he started his own business. He also married a rich woman. Dick [10]... mayor of London three times and [11]... he died he left a lot of money. The story does not say what [12]... to his cat.

1 a was coming (b) came c has come d comes
2 a was taking b were taking c took d taken
3 a for b during c in d at
4 a walks b is walking c has walked d was walking
5 a hear b heard c was hearing d were hearing
6 a travels b travelled c was travelling d were travelling
7 a is running b are running c was running d were running
8 a has caught b could catch c did catch d didn't catch
9 a get b got c gotten d was getting
10 a did become b become c was becoming d did becoming
11 a as b while c when d since
12 a happens b happened c did happen d was happening

MY TURN!

Complete the sentences to make them true for you.

1 When I got home yesterday, my sister was playing a computer game.
2 .... during the summer.
3 While I was having breakfast, ...
4 It was very late when ....
5 .... as I was going to my friend's.
6 When I was 10, ...

MY TEST!

Circle the correct option.

1 .... the train stopped, all the passengers got off. a When b While c As
2 I didn't interrupt Casey because he .... to Webb. a spoke b was speaking c were speaking
3 Webb was a driver .... a long time. a during b since c for
4 What .... Casey's wife .... when she heard the news? a was ... saying b did ... say c has ... said
5 Casey's friend never .... by train again. a didn't travel b travelled c was travelling

My Test answers: 1a 2b 3c 4b 5b

3 *Used to* and *would*

They used to pay soldiers in salt.

Before there was money, people **used to** exchange things. They **would** give each other things they both wanted; for example, you'd give a sheep and get a knife.

Traders **used to** prefer metals, like gold and silver, because, unlike a sheep, they **would** last a long time. The Egyptians **used to** exchange gold bars.

The Lydians, people who **used to** live in part of modern Turkey, invented coins about 2,600 years ago. The Lydians **would** put a picture on their coins to show where the money came from.

The Romans **used to** pay their soldiers partly in salt. Salt **used to** be very valuable and soldiers **would** sell it for other things. The word 'salary' means 'salt money' and the expression 'worth your salt' (= good at your job) comes from this.

The Chinese made the first paper money about 1,500 years ago. In some parts of China they didn't have enough metal for coins so they **would** print paper money for the same value. However, paper money **didn't use** to be very common in Europe until about 1700.

? True or False?

1 The Lydians lived in Egypt.

2 Coins came before paper money.

Answers: 1 False 2 True

Used to and *would*

Used to

1 ***Used to*** **is followed by an infinitive without *to.***
Used to **has no present or continuous forms.**
*Salt **used to be** very valuable.*

2 **Make *used to* questions with *Did* + noun / pronoun + *use to* ...?**
***Did the Egyptians use to** buy gold?*
***Did you use to** eat a lot of sweets when you were young?*

3 **Make the negative of *used to* with *did not* (*didn't*) *use to* or *never used to.***
*Paper money **didn't use to** be very common.*
*We **never used to** spend much.*

The negative *didn't used to* is also common.
***Used not to* is also possible in formal language.**

4 ***Used to*** **is for habits and activities which are no longer happening today. *Used to* often contrasts the past and the present. *Used to* usually comes without a time expression.**
*The Romans **used to** pay soldiers in salt.*
*I **used to** work in a bank but now I'm a teacher.*

Would

5 ***Would*** **is followed by an infinitive without *to*, and the negative is *would not*. The affirmative short form is *'d* and the negative short form is *wouldn't*.**
*For example, you**'d give** a sheep and get a knife.*
*They **wouldn't work** on Sundays.*

6 ***Would*** **is similar in meaning to *used to* but it is less common. In a text, *would* usually follows *used to* or a past time expression.**
*That summer we **would** go swimming every morning.*
*Jack **used to** love books. He **would** read two books every week.*

In this meaning, *would* is very rarely used in questions.

Used to vs. *would*

7 ***Used to*, not *would*, is for past states.**
*The Lydians **used to** live in Turkey.* NOT ~~... *would live* ...~~
*My sister **used to** know him.* NOT ~~... *would know* ...~~

Used to and *would* vs. the past simple

8 **We can use the past simple instead of *used to* and *would*.**
*We **used to** watch / **watched** too much TV.*
*The soldiers **would** sell / **sold** the salt for other things.*

9 **Use the past simple, not *used to* or *would*, when talking about single events, how long they took or how many times they happened.**
*I **went** to the market yesterday.*
NOT ~~*I used to go to the market yesterday.*~~
*We **didn't eat** for two days.*
NOT ~~*We didn't use to eat for two days.*~~
*Jane **visited** me in hospital twice.*
NOT ~~*Jane used to visit me in hospital twice.*~~

Be / get used to **means to know something so that it is not strange or new. A noun or verb + *-ing* can come after *be / get used to*.**
*After three weeks, I **was used to my new home**.*
*It's difficult to **get used to working** at night.*

▶ See Units 14, 35, 36 and 37 for other uses of *would*.

Practice

A Underline the correct option.

1. The Romans *used to* / *didn't use to* have paper money.
2. George Bush *used to* / *didn't use to* be president of America.
3. Thirty years ago, we *used to* / *didn't use to* have mobile phones.
4. English *used to* / *didn't use to* be an international language.
5. Robin Hood *used to* / *didn't use to* help poor people.
6. Space travel *used to* / *didn't use to* be impossible.
7. Children *used to* / *didn't use to* go to school.
8. December *used to* / *didn't use to* be the tenth month of the year.
9. There *used to* / *didn't use to* be any hospitals.
10. France *used to* / *didn't use to* have a king and queen.

B Joe used to be in prison but now he is a free man! Write about the changes in Joe's life with *used to* and *didn't use to*.

Now	Then
1 He gets up at 9.00.	~~6.00~~
2 He is a mechanic.	✗ ~~mechanic~~
3 He works in a garage.	the prison kitchen
4 He likes his neighbours	✗ his neighbours
5 He writes emails	letters
6 He wears nice clothes	a prison uniform
7 He sees his friends.	✗ see his friends
8 He goes to bed late.	early
9 He feels happy.	sad
10 He is free.	✗ free

1 He used to get up at 6.00.
2 He didn't use to be a mechanic.
3 ....
4 ....
5 ....
6 ....
7 ....
8 ....
9 ....
10 ....

C Change the past simple into *would* in this text, if possible.

I remember my childhood very well. Every summer, we ~~went~~ would go to the seaside. I was ten years old and I loved the sea. I played on the beach and my father bought me an ice cream. Sometimes we went on a boat. Some people swam around the boat, others fished, others watched. One trip my sister fell into the sea! Luckily, she was a good swimmer. That was very funny. In the evenings, we walked around the town. My mother told us stories about all the places and we listened very carefully. At night I fell asleep feeling very happy. A wonderful time!

D Underline the correct option. Sometimes more than one option is possible.

1. My best friend *used to have* / *would have* a mountain bike.
2. That summer we *used to spend* / *would spend* all day on the beach.
3. Yesterday I *would phone* / *phoned* Jill.
4. When I lived in France I *used to speak* / *spoke* French very well.
5. On long car journeys we *used to play* / *would play* cards.
6. Sheila *didn't use to know* / *wouldn't know* Charles then.
7. *Did it use to be* / *Would it be* a rich country?
8. When we got to the airport, the strongest boys *used to carry* / *would carry* the bags.
9. Last April, they *didn't use to work* / *didn't work* for a week.
10. In those days, I *never used to worry* / *would never worry* about my future.
11. Maggie *used to be* / *would be* the best student in her class.

E Complete each sentence b so that it has a similar meaning to sentence a. Use two to four words including the word in brackets.

1 a My Dad was an engineer. (be)
b My Dad used to be an engineer.
2 a People did more exercise then. (do)
b People .... more exercise then.
3 a We wouldn't go to the cinema much. (used)
b We .... to the cinema much.
4 a Was Mike in your team? (be)
b .... in your team?
5 a When I was a teenager, I used to get up at 11.00. (would)
b When I was a teenager, I .... at 11.00.
6 a The prices weren't so expensive in the 1990s. (never)
b The prices .... so expensive in the 1990s.
7 a His sister always used to shout at me. (would)
b His sister .... at me.
8 a Jennifer drank coffee for breakfast every morning. (have)
b Jennifer .... coffee for breakfast.

F Complete the text using the words in brackets and, where possible, *used to* or *would*.

From 1921–1923, there [1] was (be) very high inflation in Germany: the cost of things increased very dramatically. The reason for this was the bad political and financial situation after the First World War. The national currency in Germany [2] .... (be) the Mark. At the beginning of 1921, one American dollar [3] .... (cost) 60 Marks. By the end of 1922, one dollar [4] .... (get) you 8,000 Marks. The effect on ordinary German people was terrible. In 1922, a loaf of bread cost three billion Marks. People [5] .... (buy) something in the morning and find the price much higher a few hours later. There is a story that once someone [6] .... (leave) a big bag of money outside a shop. When she [7] .... (come) back, the bag wasn't there but the money was on the floor! Money [8] .... (become) worthless, so people [9] .... (exchange) things. Finally, the government [10] .... (make) some new money, the Rentenmark, and the inflation stopped.

MY TURN!

Write five things you used to do or be when you were younger. Use *used to* and *would*.

1 I used to collect coins.
2 ....
3 ....
4 ....
5 ....

Write four sentences about your friend.

6 Maria used to live in Barcelona.
7 ....
8 ....
9 ....

MY TEST!

Circle the correct option.

1 He .... be a millionaire. **a** used to **b** are used to **c** used
2 Jack .... sometimes give them some money for sweets. **a** used **b** use **c** would
3 Last Saturday I .... a lot of money. **a** used to spend **b** spent **c** have spent
4 .... collect coins when you were young? **a** Did you use to **b** Would you **c** Did you used
5 Money never .... important to me. **a** used to be **b** would not be **c** wouldn't be

My Test! answers: 1a 2c 3b 4a 5a

4 Present perfect, past simple, present simple

Many famous people have studied at Harvard.

HARVARD UNIVERSITY

Harvard University **is** the oldest university in the USA. The university **started** in 1636 and it **got** its name two years later when John Harvard **died** and **gave** a library to the university. Since then, the university **has grown** and Harvard **has become** one of the most famous universities in the world. Now people all over the world **have heard** about Harvard. Many famous people **have studied** at Harvard, including the poet T.S. Eliot, the president Barack Obama and the actress Natalie Portman. Many Harvard students **have won** Nobel Prizes.

Education at Harvard **has changed** a lot over its history. Charles Eliot, president of Harvard from 1869–1909, **made** the biggest changes. For example, before Eliot **was** president, students **didn't take** entrance exams. Today, thousands of students **want** to study at Harvard but only about 10% of them **pass** the entrance exams.

Harvard **is** not all about education. Sport and culture **are** also very important. Twenty-first-century students **work** hard and **play** hard.

?
1 What year did John Harvard die?
2 Who was Charles Eliot?

Answers: 1 1638 2 President of Harvard from 1869–1909

Present perfect, past simple, present simple

Present perfect

1 Make the present perfect using the verb *have* + past participle.

	statement ✓	negative ✗
I / You / We / They	**have ('ve) visited**	**have not (haven't / 've not) visited**
He / She / It	**has ('s) visited**	**has not (hasn't / 's not) visited**

Make questions and short answers as follows:

question ?			short answer ✓✗
Have	I / you / we / they	**visited** ...?	Yes, (I) **have.** No, (I) **haven't.**
Has	he / she / it	**visited** ...?	Yes, (he) **has.** No, (he) **hasn't.**

2 Use the present perfect to talk about recent events or a past event which the speaker feels is connected with the present.

Kurt is very happy that he ***has graduated****.*
A: ***Have*** *they* ***arrived****? B: Yes, they're here.*

Past simple

3 Use the past simple to talk about a finished action in the past.

John Harvard ***died****.*
Matt Damon ***went*** *to Harvard.*

Present simple

4 Use the present simple to talk about present facts or events.

I ***study*** *Mathematics at Harvard.*
There ***are*** *15 students in my class.*

Present perfect vs. present simple

5 Use the present perfect, not the present simple, for an event or a situation which began in the past and continues in the present, when we want to say how much time it has been going on.

Harvard ***has been*** *a university since 1636.*
NOT ~~*... was a university ...*~~
Natalie, how long ***have you worked*** *in the movie business?*
NOT ~~*... did you work ...*~~
It ***hasn't rained*** *for months now.* NOT ~~*... didn't rain ...*~~

6 *Go* has two past participles: *gone* and *been*. There is a difference in meaning.

My brother ***has gone*** *to America.*
(= My brother is travelling to America or is there now.)
My brother ***has been*** *to America.*
(= My brother went to America but he is back home now.)

Present perfect vs. past simple

7 Use the present perfect when we do not know exactly when the past event took place, or it is not important. Use the past simple to give details later.

Have *you* ***seen*** *my book?*
Bill ***has come*** *back from university. He* ***arrived*** *on Tuesday.*
President Obama ***has arrived*** *in India. He* ***met*** *Indian business men and* ***visited*** *...*

8 With the present perfect, we use words which mean 'at a time up to now', e.g. *already, ever, for, lately, never, recently, since, yet*. With the past, we use words and expressions which mean a finished period of time, e.g. *ago, in 2003, last week, on my birthday, then, when, yesterday*.

Teresa ***has already graduated****.*
I've never been *to America.*
The university ***started in 1636****.*
Last Saturday *we* ***had*** *a party.*

9 With *today* and *this* + time word, e.g. *this afternoon, this year*, we can use the present perfect or the past simple. Use the present perfect to mean the complete time period up to now. Use the past simple to mean a finished part of that time period.

I've phoned *John this morning.*
(It is still the morning.)
I ***phoned*** *John this morning.*
(It is now the afternoon.)

TIP

In conversation, we can often use either the past simple or the present perfect.
Did *you* ***speak*** *to Jim?*
OR ***Have*** *you* ***spoken*** *to Jim?*
Brenda ***bought*** *a hat.*
OR *Brenda* ***has bought*** *a hat.*

Practice

A Complete these news stories with the present perfect and the past simple.

1 John Bruce ....has won.... (win) three million euros in a lottery. He ....bought.... (buy) the lottery ticket last Saturday and ...
2 Princess Lola and Sir John Falstaff .... (marry). They .... (meet) at a party at Windsor Castle in 2009.
3 Cameron Bowie .... (break) the 800 m record in Oslo. He .... (run) 1.40.23, the fastest time in the world.
4 Farmer Bo Peep .... (lose) all her sheep. She .... (call) the police last night but they ...
5 Pop star Donna Ma .... (go) to live in Greenland. The pop star .... (say) that ...
6 Builders Hansel and Gretel Sweet .... (build) a house out of sugar. Work on the house .... (start) two years ago and ...

B <u>Underline</u> the correct option.

1 Let's go out. The rain *stops* / *<u>has stopped</u>*.
2 Alice *lives* / *has lived* in Newcastle for three years.
3 It *is* / *has been* my birthday today.
4 Tony *doesn't speak* / *hasn't spoken* German.
5 Tony *doesn't speak* / *hasn't spoken* to me for years.
6 *Do you ever see* / *Have you ever seen* my school photos?
7 I *play* / *have played* it twice.
8 This cake *doesn't taste* / *hasn't tasted* very nice.
9 England *has* / *has had* a king or queen for more than 1,000 years.
10 Who *thinks* / *has thought* he knows the answer?

C Match the pairs.

1 Leo Tolstoy — a has written many books.
2 That woman next to you — b wrote many books.

3 Mark watched the film — a yesterday.
4 Mark has watched the film — b today.

5 He's been to Berlin. — a He will be back next Monday.
6 He's gone to Berlin. — b He got back last night.

7 I really need it — a now.
8 I really needed it — b then.

9 It hasn't rained for months, — a so there wasn't much water.
10 It didn't rain for months, — b so there isn't much water.

11 Kangaroos live — a in Australia.
12 Kangaroos have lived — b in Australia for a long time.

13 Sheila bought a bike — a when she was on holiday.
14 Sheila has bought a bike — b but she never uses it.

15 'What happened next?' — a 'Let's wait and see.'
16 'What happens next?' — b 'Look in the newspaper.'

D Complete the dialogue using the verbs in brackets in the present perfect, past simple or present simple.

Susan: I'm not happy! It [1] ....has been.... (be) a hard week and it [2] .... (have not) finished yet!
Lorraine: What [3] .... ? (happen)
Susan: Well, after training on Monday Mr Jones [4] .... (phone) me and [5] .... (tell) me I couldn't be in the handball team.
Lorraine: Oh no, you always tell me that handball [6] .... (be) your favourite sport.
Susan: That isn't true any more. It [7] .... (be) my favourite, but not now! I never want to play again.
Lorraine: This is terrible. [8] .... you .... (speak) to the other players?
Susan: No, I [9] .... (not see) them all week. They are probably hiding!
Lorraine: When [10] .... you .... (start) playing handball?
Susan: Three years ago, My dad [11] .... (take) me to a handball club. I [12] .... (not miss) a single training session since then.
Lorraine: Don't worry, Susan, you will get on the team again.

E Circle the correct option.

The University of Bologna is the oldest university in the world. It [1]... a university since 1088. (The oldest university in England, Oxford University, [2]... in 1167.) Bologna, in the north of Italy, [3]... a beautiful town and many tourists [4]... the university each year to understand its history and traditions. The first students at Bologna only [5]... law but now the university [6]... over a hundred different types of courses, from agriculture to zoology. Many famous people [7]... from Bologna, especially in law and science. Perhaps the most important scientist is Copernicus (1473–1543). Copernicus was an astronomer (someone who studies the planets and stars). He [8]... that the earth went round the sun at a time when everyone [9]... that the earth was the centre of the universe. Since 2000, Bologna [10]... 'Alma Mater Studiorum', which means 'Dear mother of studies' in Latin.

	a	b	c	d
1	a was	b is	(c) has been	d have been
2	a started	b starts	c has started	d have started
3	a was	b is	c has been	d have been
4	a visited	b visit	c has visited	d have visited
5	a studied	b study	c has studied	d have studied
6	a taught	b teaches	c has taught	d have taught
7	a graduated	b graduates	c has graduated	d have graduated
8	a thought	b thinks	c has thought	d have thought
9	a believed	b believes	c has believed	d have believed
10	a was called	b is	c has been called	d have been called

F You are interviewing the DJ at a hotel in Greece. Write questions to match his replies, using the present perfect, past simple or present simple.

1 'For fifteen years.'
How long have you been a DJ? How long have you worked in this hotel?

2 'When I was a boy, it was always my dream to be a DJ.'
....?

3 'The sea is great and the people are so friendly.'
....?

4 'In 1976. It was the first hotel on the island.'
....?

5 'Yes, lots of famous people have stayed here.'
....?

6 'No, we are open 365 days a year.'
....?

7 'I've never thought about it – I love my job!'
....?

MY TURN!

Make questions with the present perfect, past simple or present simple, using words and expressions from the box and write them below. Then answer them.

the weather you your best friend your parents your English teacher your dog / cat	be do give have go play want	recently this week now today yesterday last year

1 *Has your best friend had a party recently?*
No, she hasn't.

2 ....?
....

3 ....?
....

4 ....?
....

5 ....?
....

6 ....?
....

MY TEST!

Circle the correct option.

1 John Harvard .... from England. a comes b came c has come
2 Lesley .... a student for two years now. a is b was c has been
3 Obama .... president in 2009. a becomes b became c has become
4 Women .... at Harvard for about the last 100 years. a study b studied c have studied
5 My brother needs good marks because he .... to go to Harvard. a wants b wanted c has wanted

My Test! answers: 1b 2c 3b 4c 5a

Present perfect simple and present perfect continuous

She's been living here for 30 years.

Villageradio

We went to Saffron Walden, a beautiful English village, and asked people some questions about life there.

'How long have you been living in Saffron Walden, Paula?'

'Oh, only three months. My mum and dad moved here from London. They**'ve always liked** the country and they wanted a quieter life. It's difficult for my dad as he still works in London and he**'s been travelling** from here to London every day. I prefer London but **I've** already **made** some nice friends here. They**'ve been helping** me a lot, so it **hasn't been** too bad. Look, why don't you speak to Mrs Black over there by the bus stop; she**'s been living** here for 30 years.'

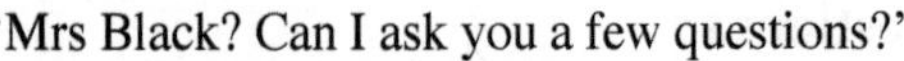

Saffron Walden maze

'Mrs Black? Can I ask you a few questions?'

'Sure, **I've been waiting** for a bus for 20 minutes, so I've got some time.'

'Has life here changed much in the last 30 years?'

'Yes and no. The buses are still always late. They**'ve been promising** to improve the bus service for years, but nothing **has happened**. Seriously, the village centre is still the same. We**'ve kept** all the beautiful houses and historical places, and the maze of course. The village **has been growing** as young people like Paula and her family **have moved** here from towns. One thing I don't like … . Sorry, I need to go, my bus **has come**!'

Next we visited the village of Inkpen.

1 Who goes to London very often?
  a Paula b Paula's dad c Mrs Black

2 What do you do in a maze?
  a walk around b have a picnic c wait for a bus

Answers: 1b 2a

Present perfect simple and present perfect continuous

Present perfect simple

1 Use the present perfect simple to talk about events and situations which started in the past and continue into the present, or have only just stopped.

*I **have moved** to Saffron Walden and I'm very happy there now.*

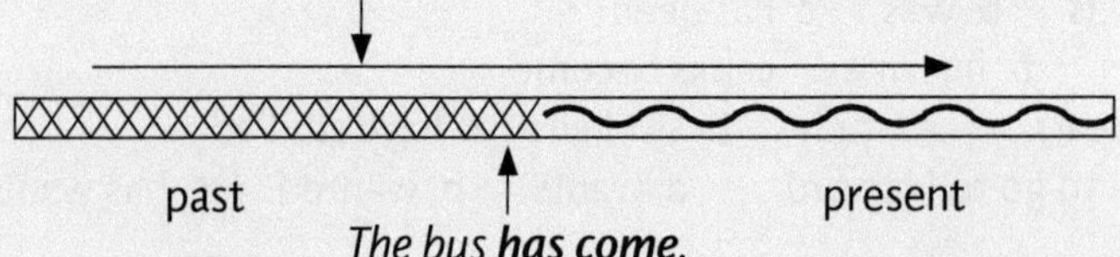

▶ See Unit 4 for how to form the present perfect.

Present perfect continuous

2 Make the present perfect continuous using *have* + *been* + verb + *-ing*.

	statement ✓	negative ✗
I / You / We / They	have ('ve) been working.	have not (haven't / 've not) been working.
He / She / It	has ('s) been working.	has not (hasn't / 's not) been working.

Make questions and short answers as follows:

question ?			short answer ✓✗
Have	I / you / we / they	been working?	Yes, (I) **have.** No, (I) **haven't.**
Has	he / she / it	been working?	Yes, (he) **has.** No, (he) **hasn't.**

3 We use the present perfect continuous (or sometimes the present perfect simple) for a situation or activity that is still going on or has only just ended, when we want to talk about how long something has been going on. We do not use the present tense in these examples.

*She's **been living** in the village for 30 years.*
NOT ~~*... lives in the village ...*~~
***I've been waiting** for a bus for 20 minutes.*
NOT ~~*... am waiting ...*~~
*Professor X, who is leaving us today, **has taught** here for many years.* NOT ~~*... teaches here ...*~~

Use *for* with a period of time, e.g. ***for an hour, for a few days, for ages*** (= for a long time); use *since* to emphasise when a situation began, e.g. ***since Monday, since last year, since she got married.***

*I've been standing here **for** half an hour / **since** 12 o'clock.*

4 We usually use the present perfect continuous for changes.

*The village **has been growing**.*
*Their music **has been getting** more popular.*

Present perfect simple vs. present perfect continuous

5 We usually use the present perfect simple for longer permanent situations and the present perfect continuous for shorter temporary situations.

*People **have spoken** English for 1,500 years.*
*Victor **has been studying** English for three months.*

6 We usually use the present perfect simple for facts or events and the present perfect continuous for activities.

*Mrs Black **has gone** home.*
*She **has been working** and is very tired.*

TIP

We can use ***still ... not*** with the present perfect simple when we want to emphasise that a past situation is not finished. ***Still*** goes before ***have.***

*The bus **still hasn't** come!*

7 Use the present perfect simple, not the present perfect continuous, with state verbs, e.g. ***understand, have*** and ***like.***

*Saffron Walden **has had** a church for 1,000 years.*
NOT ~~*Saffron Walden has been having ...*~~

8 Use the present perfect simple, not the present perfect continuous, to talk about how often you have done something.

***I've done** the washing twice.*
NOT ~~*I've been doing ...*~~

9 Do not use the present perfect simple and present perfect continuous with past time expressions. Use the past simple and past continuous with past time expressions.

*We **visited** Saffron Walden **last summer.***
NOT ~~*We've visited ...*~~
*It **was raining last night**.*
NOT ~~*It's been raining ...*~~

TIP

Often there is no difference in meaning between the present perfect and the present perfect continuous, but the present perfect is more common.

*I **have lived** here for 20 years = I **have been living** here for 20 years.*

Practice

A Make present perfect continuous sentences from the words.

1 been / it / day / raining / has / all
It has been raining all day.

2 have / looking / for / I / everywhere / been / you
....

3 been / well / hasn't / Mike / feeling
....

4 giving / her / been / we / have / advice
....

5 eating / my / has / been / chocolate / who
.... ?

6 my / been / has / me / helping / dad
....

7 haven't / the / working / phones / been
....

8 doing / crossword / been / have / you / that
.... ?

B Underline the correct option.

1 It <u>*has been*</u> / *has been being* a difficult day.
2 Trevor, have you *listened* / *been listening* to me?
3 Pete *hasn't come* / *hasn't been coming* back from London.
4 She *has sung* / *has been singing* for two hours, so she needs a rest.
5 Has Sam *taken* / *been taking* my pen again?
6 Louise *has read* / *has been reading* the same book for two months.
7 The match *has finished* / *has been finishing* and Liverpool are champions!
8 I *have thought* / *have been thinking* about you all day.
9 He *hasn't understood* / *hasn't been understanding* what to do.
10 He can't drive home because he *has drunk* / *has been drinking*.

C Write these time expressions under *for* or *since*.

ages a long time February it happened I got home midnight my whole life she was two years old the rest of the year two months Christmas

for	since
ages	

D Write present perfect continuous sentences to match the pictures.

1 She's been running.
2 ....
3 ....
4 ....
5 ....
6 ....

E Complete the sentences about changes in a village using the present perfect continuous.

	2000	Now
Cars	300	500
Winter temperature	3°	5°
Working day	8 hours	9 hours
Population (= people who live there)	800	700
Tourists visiting every year	6,000	8,000
How much money each tourist spends	50$ a day	70$ a day

1 People have been buying more cars.
2 Winters .... warmer.
3 People .... harder.
4 The population ....
5 More tourists ....
6 The tourists .... more money.

F Write one new sentence using the verb in brackets and the present perfect or present perfect continuous.

1 John came to the bus stop 20 minutes ago. There is still no bus. (wait)
John has been waiting for a bus for 20 minutes.

2 I didn't speak German at all three years ago. I know it perfectly now. (learn)

....

3 Shelly is driving to Newcastle. She left at 13.00 and it is now 15.00. (drive)

....

4 The window is broken. The children did it. (break)

....

5 They are playing tennis. The match started at 12.00 and is still going on. (play)

....

6 I don't have my keys. I left them at home. (forget)

....

7 My sister started to tell me a joke. The joke is not finished yet. (tell)

....

8 Ed saw the film at the cinema and then watched it again at home. (watch)

....

G Complete the dialogue using the verbs from the box in the present perfect or present perfect continuous.

not be ~~come~~ decide freeze get have leave not sell stand think

Journalist: I [1] have come to the village of Inkpen to interview some more village people. Oh, hello, could I ask you a few questions? Are you all right, you look very cold!

Villager: Hello. I am cold, I [2] .... here in the market all day. I think my feet [3] ....!

Journalist: Well, have some tea with me. What do you do in the market?

Villager: I sell fruit and vegetables. Today [4] .... a great day. I [5] .... much. In fact, recently business [6] .... worse and worse.

Journalist: Don't people buy fruit and vegetables now?

Villager: Of course they do, but in supermarkets outside the village. My wife and I [7] .... about it and we [8] .... to close our business and do something new.

Journalist: Really?

Villager: We're not the only ones. A lot of people, especially young people, [9] .... the village in the last few years. It's very sad.

Journalist: [10] .... you .... any ideas about your future?

Villager: Yes. I want to work in a supermarket.

MY TURN!

Write possible explanations for the events or situations, using the present perfect and present perfect continuous.

1 His eyes are red.
He has been crying. / He hasn't been sleeping.

2 She is hiding behind the sofa.

....

3 My mobile phone isn't working.

....

4 I can't find my pen.

....

5 My friend wants to speak to me. It's 2 o'clock in the morning!

....

6 My hands are very dirty.

....

MY TEST!

Circle the correct option.

1 The Blacks .... in Saffron Walden for thirty years and they still like it. **a** lived **b** has lived **c** have been living
2 Stephanie .... Saffron Walden three times. **a** has visited **b** have visited **c** has been visiting
3 I'm sorry, Paula, ... for me long? **a** do you wait **b** did you wait **c** have you been waiting
4 Saffron Walden .... a lot in the last five hundred years. **a** has grown **b** grew **c** is growing
5 .... that book about English villages yet? **a** Have you finished **b** Do you finish **c** Are you finishing

My Test! answers: 1c 2a 3c 4a 5a

Past perfect simple and past perfect continuous

Scientists had been studying a hurricane.

On 28 August 2005, the US government told everyone in New Orleans to leave the city. Scientists **had been studying** a hurricane in the Gulf of Mexico. It was moving towards the city.

The US government **had been preparing** for a hurricane in New Orleans for a number of years and **had** already **decided** on a plan to get people out. People were able to leave the city quickly by using both sides of certain roads.

When Hurricane Katrina hit the city on 29 August, many people **had** already **left**. However, the government **had** not **been** ready for the large number of people who could not, or did not, leave. More than 1,800 people died and tens of thousands of people lost their homes when winds of 125 miles per hour hit the city. It was one of the worst disasters in the history of the United States.

After the hurricane, around 80% of New Orleans was under water.

?

1 How strong was Hurricane Katrina?
2 What damage did it cause?

Answers: 1 Hurricane Katrina had winds of 125 miles per hour.
2 More than 1,800 people died and tens of thousands of people lost their homes.

Past perfect simple and past perfect continuous

Past perfect simple

1 **Make the past perfect simple using *had* + past participle.**
*They **had** already **left** / **'d** already **left**.*
*The government **had not been** / **hadn't been** ready.*
*What **had** they **decided**?*

2 **Use the past perfect to talk about an event which happened before another event in the past.**
*When Hurricane Katrina hit the city on 29 August, many people **had** already **left**.*

Note the difference:

When I turned on the TV,

*I **heard** the news.*

(= I turned on the TV and immediately heard the news.)

When my friend phoned,

*I **had heard** the news.*

(= I heard the news before my friend phoned.)

3 **Use the past perfect to talk about things that did not happen as you expected or wished.**
*I **had intended** to visit New Orleans that summer.*

4 **The past perfect is common in indirect speech.**
*I told her what I **had seen**.*

▶ See Unit 38 on indirect statements.

5 **In sentences with the time expressions *after, as soon as, by the time* or *when*, we can often use either the past perfect or the past simple.**
***As soon as** I (**had**) **sat** down, somebody knocked on the door.*
*It was half past ten **by the time** they (**had**) **finished**.*

Past perfect continuous

6 **Make the past perfect continuous using *had been* + *-ing*.**
*They **had been studying** / **'d been studying** a hurricane.*
*I **had not been listening** / **hadn't been listening**.*
*How long **had** they **been studying** it?*

Like the present perfect, we often use the past perfect with the adverbs *ever, never, just* and *already*.
*The US government **had already decided** on a plan to get people out.*

7 **The past perfect continuous is not as common as the past perfect simple. Use the past perfect continuous to describe an activity or situation in the past which began before something else happened and continued during it or finished just before. Use the past perfect simple to talk about completed events or past states. Sometimes both forms are acceptable.**
*The US government **had been preparing** for a hurricane in New Orleans for a number of years.*
(= These preparations continued up until the hurricane.)
*The government **had decided** on an evacuation plan.*
(= The decision and the plan were complete.)

The past perfect is not used on its own to talk about the past. We use the past perfect only in relation to another event or time in the past.
✗ *~~She had got up at ten to seven.~~*
✓ *She left the house at seven o'clock. She had got up at ten to seven.*

Practice

A **Match the sentence beginnings to the correct endings.**

1 We had become friends
2 I had been waiting for an hour
3 They had been enjoying the picnic
4 I was bored with piano classes; I had been going
5 He'd had an accident
6 My best friend had already been at the school

a for as long as I could remember.
b for a year when I came.
c by the time the bus finally arrived.
d when he was on his way to work.
e when it started to rain.
f a few years earlier on holiday.

B What do these sentences mean? Tick a or b.

1 The film had started when we sat down.
   a We sat down, then the film started.
   b The film started, then we sat down. ✓
2 When I arrived, everyone had left.
   a Everyone left, then I arrived
   b I arrived, then everyone left.
3 By the time I got his letter, I had forgiven him.
   a I got the letter, then I forgave him.
   b I forgave him, then I got the letter.
4 We had just been talking about my cousin when she phoned us.
   a My cousin phoned and then we talked about her.
   b We talked about my cousin and then she phoned us.
5 She went to her friend's house. She'd made a cake for her.
   a She made a cake, then she went to her friend's house.
   b She went to her friend's house, then she made a cake.
6 When they had given me the medicine, I felt ill.
   a I felt ill, then they gave me the medicine.
   b They gave me the medicine, then I felt ill.
7 When I started school, I had learnt to read.
   a I started school, then I learnt to read.
   b I learnt to read, then I started school.
8 She'd taken the wrong turning, so she got lost.
   a She took the wrong turning, then she got lost.
   b She got lost, then she took the wrong turning.

C Read the story and number the pictures in order 1–8.

One Monday evening in September, Grant put up his tent on a campsite on the edge of a mountain lake. The next morning Grant started a 15-mile walk through the mountains. A ranger had driven him to the start of the walk.

That evening a snowstorm started after he had put up his tent for the night. In the morning there was snow on the ground, but it was sunny and clear, so Grant continued his walk. Grant could not see the path very well and he slipped and fell down some steep rocks. He landed on a flat rock, but he could not move. He had lost his glasses and broken his arm.

On Saturday morning Grant's friend, Ed, waited for him at the end of the trail. When he did not arrive, Ed phoned the rescue team. But Grant was lucky, a helicopter had already found him.

a ☐

b 1

c ☐

d ☐

e ☐

f ☐

g ☐

h ☐

D Underline the correct option.

1 She was surprised to see him at work so early. She *had told* / *had been telling* him not to arrive before 9.00.
2 I couldn't believe it when I saw the exam question. It was just what I *had been hoping* / *had hoped* for.
3 He*'d been coming* / *had come* to the station to pick her up.
4 He wanted to see the dentist, but she *had been going* / *had gone* on holiday.
5 It was great to hear from her. I *had been waiting* / *had waited* for her call.
6 She fell over and hit her head. She didn't know how she *had been doing* / *had done* it.
7 The children were very dirty. They *had been playing* / *had played* in the woods.
8 I *hadn't been hearing* / *hadn't heard* of Louis de Bernières before I read *Captain Corelli's Mandolin*.

E Complete the sentences using the words in brackets. Use one verb in the past simple and the other in the past perfect simple or continuous.

1 I ...found... (find) the letter in my bag – I ...had forgotten... (forget) to post it.
2 I .... (already make) some new friends by the time my first day .... (end).
3 I .... (visit) Mallorca twice before, so I .... (know) the best hotel to stay at.
4 I .... (thank) my aunt for the book – but she .... (give) me the same one the year before!
5 I .... (just finish) my lunch when Jemma .... (arrive).
6 Toby .... (come) home late last night – he .... (watch) the football with his friends.
7 I .... (think) that my friends .... (not be) very kind.
8 I .... (not be) ready for the exams. I .... (intend) to study more for them.

F Complete the text using the verbs in brackets in either the past simple, past perfect simple or past perfect continuous.

On 26 December 2004 a very large earthquake [1] ...took place... (take place) off the west coast of Sumatra in Indonesia. The earthquake [2] .... (cause) one of the worst tsunami in history. More than 200,000 people [3] .... (die) in 11 countries on the Indian Ocean. In all these countries, survivors [4] .... (tell) similar stories of that morning's events. Many were tourists who [5] .... (travel) to the area for their Christmas holiday. Many of them [6] .... (begin) their day with a morning swim or [7] .... (run) on the beach when the wave suddenly [8] .... (arrive). They [9] .... (not have) any warning. Some [10] .... (see) the sea disappear from the beach before it [11] .... (return) a few minutes later as a wall of water. Many local fishermen also [12] .... (lose) their lives in the tsunami. They [13] .... (be fishing) at sea but they [14] .... (not come) home again.

MY TURN!

Complete the sentences with your own ideas. Use the past perfect simple or continuous.

1 When I woke up, I was in hospital. I didn't remember what ...had happened... .
2 I saw the water on the ground and I thought ....
3 By the time I arrived, ...
4 When I saw my friend's face, I knew ....
5 When I got home, the door was open. Maybe ....
6 I was very tired when I got off the bus. It ....
7 Nobody understood why ....
8 In the morning I could still remember my dream. I ....

MY TEST!

Circle the correct option.

1 We .... long when we saw her. a didn't wait b don't wait c hadn't been waiting
2 When Jack .... the next morning, the bean plant had grown in the night. a get up b gets up c got up
3 Esther put on the music very loud and everyone .... a jump b jumped c had jumped
4 When my mum came home, I still .... up. a not tidied b tidy c hadn't tidied
5 I had been looking for my mobile phone all morning when I .... it ring! a hear b heard c had heard

My Test! answers: 1c 2c 3b 4c 5b

Will and *be going to*

What will the future be like?

What will the future be like?

We asked you for your ideas.

Meili

I'm **going to** be an architect. I'm interested in making buildings more green. In the future we **won't** need electricity power stations. Each house **will** produce enough energy from the sun for heating and lights.

I think we'll spend too much time in virtual worlds. Even when we travel – the car **will** drive itself and we **will** sit inside and play computer games. We'll probably even forget to look out of the window. Maybe the computer **will** send you a message saying 'It's sunny today, did you know?' or 'Look out! You're **going to** crash!'

Seb

Boris

Your fridge **will** be 'intelligent'. When you **don't have** any food, the supermarket **will** automatically send you your favourite things.

?

1 Who is worried about the future?
2 Who is hoping to do less shopping?

Answers: 1 Seb 2 Boris

Will and *be going to*

Will

1 **Use *will* with the infinitive without *to*. The short form *'ll* is used mainly with pronouns and in conversation. The negative is *will not* + infinitive without *to*. We often use the negative short form: *won't*.**

*We'**ll** spend too much time in virtual worlds.*
*We **won't** need electricity power stations.*

2 ***Will* is the most usual way to talk about the future in English. We use it to give information about the future.**

*The holidays **will** start soon.*

However, we don't use *will* to talk about plans, arrangements or schedules.

▶ See below for *be going to* for future plans.
▶ See Unit 8 for the present continuous and present simple for future schedules and arrangements.

3 **Use *will* for instant decisions made at the time of speaking. We often use *'ll* in this context.**

A: I haven't done the washing-up.
*B: Don't worry! I'**ll** do it for you.*

4 **Use *will* for predictions based on your opinion. We often use words like *think, hope* and *be sure* with *will*.**

*Maybe your computer **will** send you a message.*
*I hope she **will** write soon.*

> TIP
>
> **We often use *will* with the adverbs *certainly, definitely, probably, possibly*. Use these adverbs after *will* but before *won't*.**
>
> *I'll **definitely go** to the party.*
> *Sam **probably won't** go.*

> TIP
>
> **After *when, as soon as, until, after, before, if, unless,* we often use the present simple to express the future and not *will*.**
>
> *When you **don't have** any food, the supermarket will automatically send you your favourite things.*
> NOT ~~*When you won't have any food ...*~~

▶ See Unit 35 for the use of *will* in the first conditional.

Be going to

5 **Use *am / is / are* (*not*) *going to* + infinitive without *to*.**

*I **am** (I'**m**) **going to** be an architect.*
*He **is** (He'**s**) **going to** crash.*
*They **aren't** (They'**re not**) **going to** run out of food.*

> **When we are speaking, we often pronounce *going to* as *gonna*. Sometimes we spell it as *gonna* in informal writing too, especially in American English.**

6 **Use *be going to* for plans and intentions.**

*She's **going to** be an architect.*
***Are** you **going to** clean your shoes?*

7 **Use *be going to* for predictions based on present evidence.**

*A large storm is coming towards the east coast of the USA. It'**s going to** reach Florida soon.* (We can see that this is going to happen.)

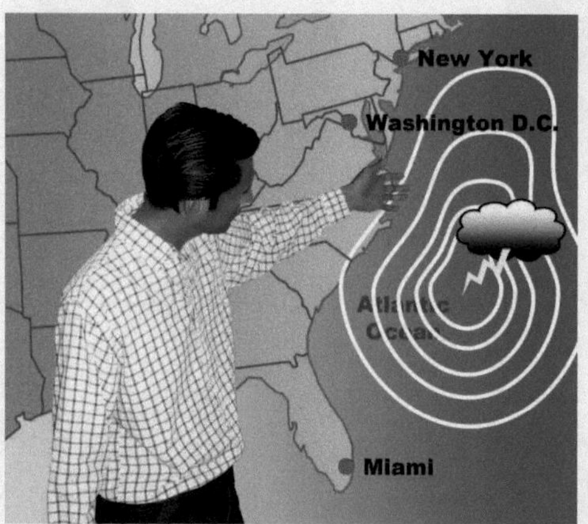

We also use *be going to* for something which has already started to happen or will happen very soon.

*I'**m going to** be sick.*

Will and *be going to*

8 **We use both *will* and *be going to* for predictions about the future, with slightly different meanings.**

*They'**re going to** crash.* (Something I can see now tells me this.)
*I think they'**ll** crash.* (This is my opinion.)

▶ See Unit 14 for other uses of *shall* and *will*.

Practice

A Complete the predictions using the verbs in brackets and either *will certainly, will probably, will possibly, probably won't* or *definitely won't*.

50 years from now ...

1. There *will possibly be* a city on Mars. (be)
2. People .... through the air and not on roads. (travel)
3. There .... a vaccine for colds. (be)
4. We .... all our classes at home. (have)
5. Robots .... think like a human. (be able to)
6. There .... a lot of oil in the world. (be)
7. We .... coins any more. (have)
8. We .... live forever. (be able to)

B Write predictions with *be going to* and the words in the box.

break burn do some exercise drop them fall over ~~win~~

1 Number 1 is *going to win* ....

2 He ....

3 She ....

4 They ....

5 It ....

6 He ....

C Add one missing word to each sentence.

1. I feel really hungry. I *'ll* make a sandwich.
2. This will the runner's last race.
3. What they going to do when they leave school?
4. The film finishes quite late. My dad's going pick me up afterwards.
5. Don't be scared of the dog. It not bite you.
6. I've bought some paint. I going to paint my room.
7. What do you think he do now?
8. Oh no! My phone has stopped working. I take it to the shop.

D Complete the sentences by putting the verbs in brackets in the correct places. One verb should be in the present simple and one should be with *will / won't*.

1. I *'ll have* a cup of coffee as soon as I *get* home. (get, have)
2. I .... until I .... everything is all right. (not leave, know)
3. She .... angry when she .... (be, find out)
4. You .... an accident unless you .... more careful. (be, have)
5. After I .... my mum back, I .... any money left. (pay, not have)
6. It .... easy to find work before the summer .... (start, not be)
7. When he .... , he .... a famous writer. (be, grow up)
8. If they .... as a team, they .... (work, do well)

E <u>Underline</u> the correct option. Sometimes both options are possible.

1. Your plan <u>*won't / is not going to*</u> work.
2. Those cakes look lovely. I*'ll / 'm going to* take two.
3. The actor, Tom Dickins, has been found guilty of stealing and *will / is going to* spend one year in prison.
4. She *will / 's going to* have a baby next month.
5. They *will / are going to* get married on Saturday.
6. I hope I*'ll / 'm going to* see you later.
7. The sky is very dark. It*'ll / 's going to* rain.
8. Who *will / is going to* be there tonight?

F Complete the dialogues using the verbs in the box and *will* or *be going to*. Sometimes both forms are possible.

~~be~~ buy have land not like sell stay win

1 A: I hope the party goes well tomorrow.
B: Don't worry. Everything *'s going to be / will be* all right.

2 A: Who do you think .... the match?
B: The blue team – they've already scored two goals.

3 A: Do you have any plans for the holidays?
B: Mum and Dad have to work. I .... at my cousin's for a couple of weeks.

4 A: This is such a long flight!
B: Don't worry. We .... soon.

5 A: Would you like apple or orange juice?
B: I .... apple juice, please.

6 A: Why are you cleaning your bike?
B: I don't ride it any more – I .... it.

7 A: I forgot to get some milk!
B: Don't worry! We .... some on the way home.

8 A: I've bought Mum a new top.
B: She probably .... it. It's too bright!

MY TURN!

Make predictions about the future in your area: things that you think will happen and things that you think won't happen.

1 *I think there will be more sports centres for young people.*
2 ....
3 ....
4 ....

Write about things you have planned for tomorrow, for next week and for next year. Write about something you plan *not* to do.

5 *I'm going to visit my friends tomorrow.*
6 ....
7 ....
8 ....

MY TEST!

Circle the correct option.

1 A: Could you read this letter for me?
B: Of course. I .... read it now. a am going to b am going c 'll

2 She's got the best score. She .... win the competition. a will b isn't going to c is going to

3 We .... go on holiday this year. a probably won't b won't probably c probably

4 A: .... stay at home tonight?
B: Yes, I'm really tired. a Will you b Do you c Are you going to

5 If your team ...., you'll be really disappointed. a won't win b wins c doesn't win

My Test! answers: 1c 2c 3a 4c 5c

Present continuous and present simple for future use; future continuous

We'll be flying from Hong Kong to Bangkok.

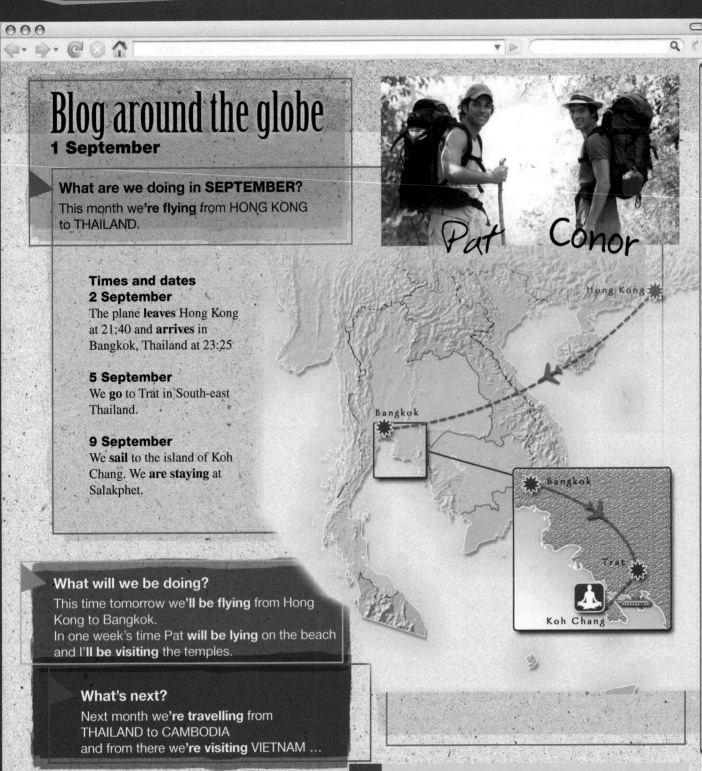

Blog around the globe

1 September

What are we doing in SEPTEMBER?

This month we**'re flying** from HONG KONG to THAILAND.

Pat Conor

Times and dates

2 September
The plane **leaves** Hong Kong at 21:40 and **arrives** in Bangkok, Thailand at 23:25

5 September
We **go** to Trat in South-east Thailand.

9 September
We **sail** to the island of Koh Chang. We **are staying** at Salakphet.

Hong Kong
Bangkok
Bangkok
Trat
Koh Chang

What will we be doing?

This time tomorrow we**'ll be flying** from Hong Kong to Bangkok.
In one week's time Pat **will be lying** on the beach and I**'ll be visiting** the temples.

What's next?

Next month we**'re travelling** from THAILAND to CAMBODIA and from there we**'re visiting** VIETNAM …

?

1 Where will Pat and Conor be in September?
2 Where will they be in October?

Answers: 1 Thailand 2 Cambodia

Present continuous and present simple for future use; future continuous

Present continuous for future use

1 **Use the present continuous form (*be* + verb + *-ing*) for plans in the future, especially when we already know the time and place.**
*Where **are** you **going** in September?*
*We're **travelling** from Hong Kong to Thailand.*

2 **Sometimes we can use either the present continuous or *be going to* for plans in the future, especially when we are talking about a decision that we have already made.**
*I'm **going to have** my first flying lesson on Friday.* = *I'm **having** my first flying lesson on Friday.* (= A plan and I know when it is taking place.)

We usually use *be going to* (not the present continuous) for intentions or plans which have not been arranged.
*One day, I'm **going to have** flying lessons.* NOT ~~*One day, I'm having flying lessons.*~~ (= A plan but I don't know when it will happen.)

▶ See Unit 7 for other uses of *be going to* for the future.

Present simple for future use

3 **We use the present simple to talk about future events which are part of a timetable or schedule.**
*On 2 September we **leave** Hong Kong.*
*On Wednesday I **have** Geography.*

After *when, as soon as, until, after, before, if, unless,* we often use the present simple to express the future and not *will*.
*When you **don't have** any food, the supermarket will automatically send you your favourite things.*
NOT ~~*When you won't have any food ...*~~

TIP

Write dates with just the number and the month.
2 September / 2nd September (UK English)
September 2 (US English)
But say:
'the second of September' or *'September the second'*

Future continuous

4 **We make the future continuous with *will / won't* + *be* + verb + *-ing*.**
*While we are having our meeting, the boss **will be talking** to the builders.*
*My course finishes at the end of May. I **won't be studying** in June.*

We occasionally use *shall / shan't* + *be* + verb + *-ing* with *I* and *we* in formal language.
*I **shall be making** a speech during the afternoon.*

5 **Use the future continuous to talk about something that will be in progress at a particular time in the future.**
*This time tomorrow we'**ll be flying** from Hong Kong to Bangkok.*

TIP

Note the difference:
*At 21.40 I'**m flying** to Bangkok.*
(= My plane takes off at 21.40.)

*At 22.00 I'**ll be flying** from Hong Kong to Bangkok.*
(= I'll be sitting on the plane on the way to Bangkok.)

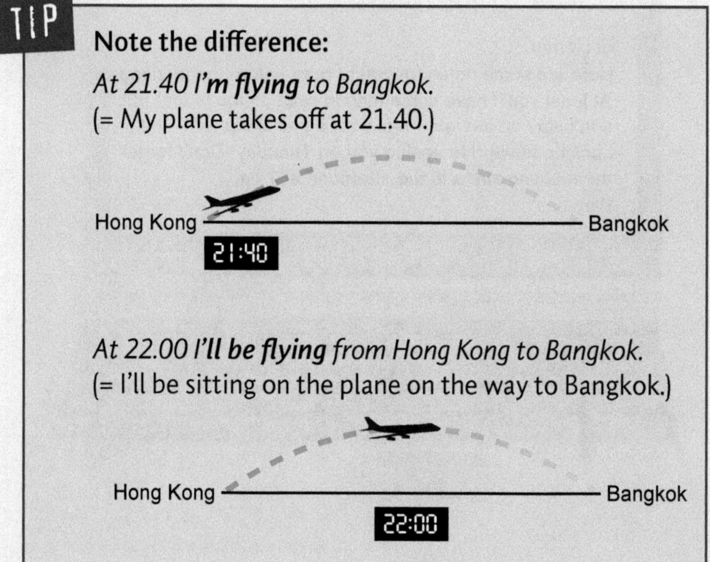

Practice

A Match the sentence beginnings to the correct endings.

1	I'm having dinner	a	I'm going to own a Porsche.
2	Tomorrow's match	b	we will be living in the new house.
3	This time next year	c	with my grandparents tonight.
4	In 50 years' time, I think	d	every month.
5	Next year the Chinese New Year	e	people will be living in cities underground.
6	He's going to save 100 euros	f	starts in January.
7	One day	g	is not taking place in the new stadium.

B Read the information about Harriet's trip next week, then complete the sentences using the present simple or the future continuous.

Sky high airlines TICKET

Date of travel: Monday 13 February
Depart: 18:25 John F Kennedy International Airport (JFK), New York, USA
Arrive: 06:35 Tuesday 14 February, Heathrow (LHR), London, UK
Depart: 08:50 Heathrow (LHR), London, UK
Arrive: 11:35 Tegel (TXL), Berlin, Germany

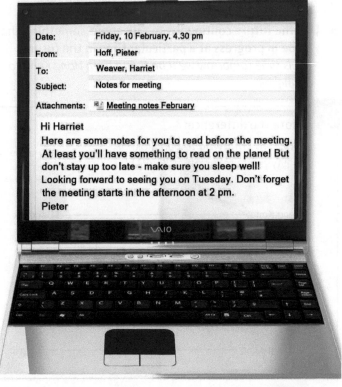

Date: Friday, 10 February. 4.30 pm
From: Hoff, Pieter
To: Weaver, Harriet
Subject: Notes for meeting
Attachments: Meeting notes February

Hi Harriet
Here are some notes for you to read before the meeting. At least you'll have something to read on the plane! But don't stay up too late - make sure you sleep well!
Looking forward to seeing you on Tuesday. Don't forget the meeting starts in the afternoon at 2 pm.
Pieter

1 At 6.25 pm on Monday Harriet leaves New York.
2 During the flight ....
3 At 1.00 am on Tuesday ....
4 At 6.35 am on Tuesday ....
5 At 7.30 am on Tuesday ....
6 At 8.50 am on Tuesday ....
7 At 11.35 am on Tuesday ....
8 At 2.30 pm on Tuesday ....

C Complete the dialogue between Pat and his friend Sam using the verbs in brackets in the present continuous (future use) or *be going to* future. Sometimes more than one answer is possible.

Sam: Hi Pat! It's good to see you! I've been reading all your news on the blog. What [1] ....are.... you ....going to do.... (do) now?
Pat: I [2] .... (get) a job. I [3] .... (meet) someone from Euroflight on Monday to talk about jobs in the company.
Sam: You [4] .... (not be able to) give up travelling!
Pat: I know. I [5] .... (find) it really difficult. But I've promised my mum and anyway I haven't got any money left!
Sam: So, no more travelling ever?
Pat: I don't think I'll ever really stop travelling. I haven't seen the Americas yet. One day [6] .... (travel) along the Pacific coast. And I've already booked a weekend away next month – I [7] .... (go) Scotland. Some friends and I [8] .... (spend) the weekend in the mountains.
Sam: You haven't stopped at all! Where [9] .... you .... (live)?
Pat: I [10] .... (rent) a flat with my friend, Conor. We [11] .... (look at) some possible places next week.

D Underline the correct option. Sometimes both options are possible.

1 Have your parents decided what they are doing / are going to do next summer?
2 The bus *leaves* / *is leaving* at 6.00 tomorrow morning.
3 When they ask you what happened, what are you *going to say* / *saying*?
4 Get better soon. We *think* / *will be thinking* of you.
5 I can't come out tonight – I'm *going to babysit* / *babysitting*.
6 *I'm helping* / *I help* at the school fair tomorrow.
7 My dad *is retiring* / *is going to retire* in the summer.
8 They*'re not arriving* / *don't arrive* until later.
9 During the next hour, I *shall be talking* / *am talking* about the effect of the Internet on shopping habits.

E Cross out all the options which are NOT possible. Cross out one or two options each time.

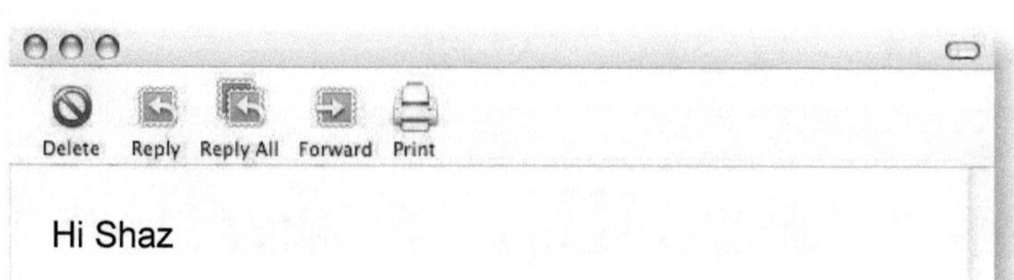

Hi Shaz

I'm so jealous of my sister! She [1]~~*takes*~~ / *is going to take / is taking* next month off work and [2]*spends / is spending / will be spending* it in the Swiss Alps. She [3]*is finally going to learn / is finally learning / will finally learn* how to ski.

This time next week she [4]*skiing / is skiing / will be skiing* down the slopes. I hope she [5]*will not be breaking / is not breaking / is not going to break* her leg or something! Her plane [6]*gets in / will get in / is getting in* on Saturday morning and the classes [7]*begin / are beginning / shall be beginning* straight away in the afternoon.

She [8]*picks up / is picking up / is going to pick up* her tickets this afternoon and talks about nothing else! And just imagine what she [9]*is going to be like / is being like / is like* when she gets back. She [10]*is not talking / won't be talking / isn't going to talk* about anything else for months!

Grrr!

Jem x

F What would you say in the following situations? Write a sentence for each one, using one of the future forms from this unit.

1 Find out if your friend has any plans to go on holiday this year.
Are you going on holiday this year?

2 You have an appointment at the dentist's tomorrow at midday. Some friends want to visit you in the morning. Tell them what time they can visit and why.

3 You are arranging an interview for a summer job in a café. Tell the interviewer how to recognise you.

4 There is a good show at your local theatre. Ring the theatre to find out the time of the show.

5 A friend invites you to dinner tomorrow evening but you don't want to go. Make an excuse.

6 It's your birthday next week. Your mum wants to take you out but you have already made plans with your friends. Tell her about these.

MY TURN!

Write questions with the words given, using the present simple, present continuous, *be going to* future or future continuous.

1 What / do / next weekend?
What are you going to do next weekend?

2 What / do / this time tomorrow?

3 When / start / your next school term?

4 Who / have / dinner with tonight?

5 In ten years' time, where / live?

6 What time / get up / tomorrow?

MY TEST!

Circle the correct option(s). Sometimes more than one option is possible.

1 My friends .... me outside the swimming pool at 5.00. a meet b are going to meet c are meeting
2 What .... your parents .... you for your next birthday? a do ... get b are ... getting c are ... going to get
3 One day they .... children. a have b are having c are going to have
4 This time tomorrow .... at the hospital. a I wait b I'm waiting c I'll be waiting
5 The boat .... until the morning. a doesn't leave b isn't leaving c isn't going to leave

My Test answers: 1 b and c 2 b and c 3c 4c 5 a, b and c

9 Future perfect and other future forms

Will they all have gone?

save our wonderful world

what do we do? | places | buildings | animals

Many places in the world are in danger. If we are to save these places, we need your help.

Zabid is a very old town in Yemen with very interesting buildings. It was once the capital of Yemen and it had an important Islamic university. The problem is that many businesses there need new roads and buildings and the town is changing. Some people say that by 2050 people **will have built** a new town and all the old places **will have gone**.

Virunga National Park is in the Congo. It has lots of different animals, like the mountain gorillas in the photograph. Virunga National Park **was going to be** a great centre for tourists and nature lovers, but everything changed in the 1990s. There were wars in countries near the Congo and many people have come to live in the park. These people are hungry and kill the animals. **Will all the animals have died** before the wars stop?

Change is possible. In 1965 Venice was **on the verge of falling** into the sea after some very heavy rain, but today, after a lot of building work, it is one of the most popular tourist places in the world. By the end of this summer, two million people **will have visited** Venice.

This building was the only building left in Hiroshima after the nuclear bomb fell in 1945. The sad history of Hiroshima tells us that we – people – are the biggest danger to this beautiful world, its places, people and animals. When we **are about to do** something bad, we should think about this.

?

True or False?

1 Zabid is the capital of Yemen.
2 Venice is a good example of how we can save interesting places.
3 Hiroshima 1945 is a bad example of what people can do.

Answers: 1 False 2 True 3 True

Future perfect and other future forms

Future perfect

1 **Make the future perfect using *will* + *have* + past participle.**

	statement ✓	negative ✗
I / You / He / She / It / We / They	**will have ('ll) have finished.**	**will not (won't) have finished.**

Make questions and short answers as follows:

question ?			short answer ✓✗
Will	I / you / he / she / it / we / they	**have** finished?	Yes, (he) **will** (have). No, (he) **won't** (have).

2 **Use the future perfect to talk about actions and situations that will be finished by a certain time in the future.**

*By the end of this summer, two million people **will have visited** Venice.*
***Will** all the animals **have died** before the wars stop?*
*This time next week I **will have finished** all my exams.*

> **TIP**
> **Don't use the future perfect for states, use *will*.**
> *You'**ll** be very tired by the time you get home.*
> NOT ~~*... will have been very tired...*~~

3 **We often use the future perfect with a time phrase about the future.**

*Do you think the tour **will have finished by 17.00**?*
*The old town **will have changed** completely **before they do anything**.*

Be + *to*-infinitive

4 **Use *be* + *to*-infinitive to talk about plans and arrangements in formal language. We don't usually use *be* + *to*-infinitive in negatives and questions.**

*The King **is to visit** Zabid tomorrow.*

5 **Use *if* + *is* / *are to* ... to show that something must happen before something else.**

***If** we **are to save** these places, we need your help.*
(= We need your help before we can save these places.)

Be about to

6 **Use *be about* + *to*-infinitive to talk about actions and situations that are going to happen very soon or immediately.**

*When countries **are about to start** a war ...*
*The match **is about to begin.***

> **TIP**
> **We can also use *be on the verge of* + *-ing* and *be on the point of* + *-ing*, to talk about actions and situations that will happen soon.**
> *The park **is on the verge / on the point of** closing.*

Present perfect

7 **We can use the present perfect to talk about actions and situations in the future that will finish before something else happens.**

*After you'**ve seen** Venice, go to Rome.*
*I'll phone you when I'**ve finished**.*

Future in the past

8 **We can use past forms of future forms, e.g. *am going to* ➜ *was going to*, *are trying* ➜ *were trying*, to talk about actions and situations in the past that were planned but did not happen, or that were planned but we don't know if they happened.**

*The park **was going to be** a great tourist centre.*
(This was a plan but it never happened because of the war.)
*We **were visiting** Yemen later that month, so we needed visas.* (This was a plan but we don't know if they went or not.)

Practice

A Ivan is thinking about his future. He is very ambitious! First, match the years to the events, then write sentences about his future using the future perfect.

2015, 2018, 2020, 2030, 2035, 2040, 2041, 2050
become a millionaire
graduate
retire to the island
start my own business
buy a 10 million dollar house
finish school
sell this house for a big profit
move to an island.

1 By 2015, he will have finished school.
2 By 2018, ...
3 By 2020, ...
4 By 2030, ...
5 By 2035, ...
6 By 2040, ...
7 By 2041, ...
8 By 2050, ...

Now do the same for your own future.

1 By next year, I will have learned to drive.
2 ....
3 ....
4 ....

B Read about Sarah's week.

Sarah eats two eggs a day, but only one on Saturday and none on Sundays.
She studies Italian for three hours on Wednesday and two hours on Thursday.
Sarah watches TV for two hours every day except for Friday.
She runs 10 km every morning except Friday, her rest day, and Sunday, when she runs 15 km.
Sarah sleeps seven hours a night, three hours more than this on Friday and Saturday.
She drives for one hour to work and one hour back. She doesn't work at the weekend.
Sarah gives £20 to 'Save the Animals' every week.

It is Monday. What will Sarah have done by the end of the week?

1 She will have eaten 11 eggs.
2 ....
3 ....
4 ....
5 ....
6 ....
7 ....

C Complete the sentences using the verbs from the box and the phrases in brackets.

burn	drink	~~fall~~	jump	sing	win

1 2
3 4
5 6

1 It's on the verge of falling. (on the verge of)
2 .... (on the point of)
3 .... (about to)
4 .... (on the verge of)
5 .... (about to)
6 .... (on the point of)

D Write a new sentence about each situation using *was / were going to*.

1 Tom wanted to buy a new bike last year, but he didn't have enough money.
He was going to buy a new bike.
2 I wanted to phone him last night but I forgot.
....
3 The sky got very dark and people opened their umbrellas.
....
4 He was hot and the window was closed. He went to the window, but it was locked.
....
5 My friends said, 'We will meet you at 5.00.' It's now 5.30, so where are they?
....
6 Louise planned to move house, then her plans changed.
....

E The Queen and the Prime Minister of Atlantis are visiting Shangri-La tomorrow. Decide which activities each will do and which they will both do, then write sentences using *be* + *to*-infinitive.

9:00	– arrive at the airport
10:00	– visit the Atlantis museum; meet journalists
12:00	– speak at a conference; give prizes to school children
13:30	– have lunch
16:00	– see the King of Shangri-La; go to a business meeting
18:00	– give a talk to Economics students
18:30	– open a theatre
21:00	– return home

1 *At 9:00, the Queen and the Prime Minister are to arrive at the airport.*
2 *At 10.00, the Queen is to visit the museum and the Prime Minister is to meet journalists.*
3 ....
4 ....
5 ....
6 ....
7 ....
8 ....

F Circle the correct option.

Siberian tigers used to live all round Asia and eastern Russia but now they only live in the north-east of Siberia. We asked Olga Alexandrovna, an expert on Siberian tigers, for some information on them. Olga [1]... go on a conference but she agreed to speak to us.
'There are not many Siberian tigers left, but it is not true that we are on the verge of [2]... these beautiful animals. The 1990s was a very bad time for the tigers because of hunters. I thought the hunters [3]... kill all the tigers; it was terrible. It is important to tell people about these problems and this is why I do a lot of travelling; I [4]... to 28 different countries by the end of this year. I'm an optimist and I think the number of tigers [5]... by, say, 2030. In the future, people [6]... more sensible and they [7]... that we need the tigers. If we [8]... change the situation, we need everyone to help. Sadly, in the future, most Siberian tigers [9]... in zoos but we [10]... them from hunters.' Olga [11]... meet the President of Russia very soon and discuss this problem with him.

1 a was on the verge of b was on the point of ⓒ was about to
2 a losing b to lose c lose
3 a were going to b were going c were to
4 a was going b will have been c am
5 a have increased b are increasing c will have increased
6 a will be b are c will have been
7 a understand b are about to understand c will have understood
8 a are to b will have c are
9 a have been b will be c will have been
10 a on the verge of saving b about to save c will have saved
11 a is b is to c was going

MY TURN!

Complete these sentences using future forms from this unit.

1 I might phone my friend, when *I've finished this exercise.*
2 Last night .... , but I changed my mind.
3 I hope I .... by the time I'm 25.
4 Maybe I .... before the weekend.
5 Someone .... by the year 2050.
6 When .... , I will be very happy.
7 At the moment, ...

MY TEST!

Circle the correct option.

1 This time tomorrow we .... on the plane to Venice. a be b are c will be
2 This time tomorrow we .... in Venice. a have arrived b has arrived c will have arrived
3 The president .... to Hiroshima next January. a came b is to come c come
4 The gorilla .... run away. a is about to b is to c is on the verge of
5 They .... a new road there but they didn't have enough money. a built b will have built c were going to build

My Test answers: 1c 2c 3b 4a 5c

R1 Review: present, past and future forms

A **Underline the correct option.**

1. At the end of the novel, the old lady *goes / is going* back to the village where she was born.
2. Magda *has / is having* a driving lesson right now, so can you call back later?
3. I'*m thinking / think* about having a party at my house next month.
4. My brother *is forever getting / forever gets* into trouble at school.
5. *Is your mum usually taking / Does your mum usually take* the train to go to work?
6. Jaime is 19 years old but *still grows / is still growing*.
7. I *am not believing / don't believe* a single word of Andrew's story.
8. My sister *is borrowing / borrows* my mobile phone until she gets a new one.
9. In the summertime in Scotland it *isn't getting / doesn't get* dark until well after 10 pm.
10. To use the website, you *are just completing / just complete* a form with your name, date of birth and email address.

B **Complete the sentences with the correct past forms of the verbs in brackets.**

1. As soon as the bell rang, everyone ......left...... the room. (leave)
2. Ben .... his jacket when a button came off. (put on)
3. Aren't you hungry? You .... anything since 7 o'clock this morning. (not eat)
4. I'm sorry. Are you OK? I .... to hurt you. (mean)
5. What nice shoes! How long .... you .... them? (have)
6. We needed to stop and have a rest because we .... for several hours. (drive)
7. The children .... that computer game for three hours now. It's time for them to stop. (play)
8. We're old friends. We .... each other for over ten years. (know)
9. Laura didn't want to watch the film with Robin because she .... it already. (see)
10. What time .... you .... this morning? (wake up)

C **Complete the text with the words from the box.**

ago during ever for ~~last~~ never recently since still then when

This time [1]......last...... year my older brother Matt was working in a special park for wild animals in Bolivia. Matt has been very interested in animals ever [2].................... he was a small boy, and he absolutely loved Inti Wara Yassi, as the park is called. It was first opened over 20 years [3].................... by two young Bolivians, Juan Carlos and Nena. [4].................... they started the park, their aim was to provide care for five monkeys which had not been well looked after by their owners, but [5].................... they realised there were lots of other wild animals in need of help. So, [6].................... the 1990s, they started to look after wild cats, bears and birds, and they now have over 700 animals in their care. People come from all round the world to help them. Matt worked there [7].................... six months. He looked after monkeys and wild cats and he said it was one of the best things he'd [8].................... done in his life. Personally, I [9].................... used to like animals very much, but [10].................... , after listening to Matt's stories, I've become interested in them and I want to visit Inti Wara Yassi myself. I [11].................... haven't decided when I'm going but I hope it's soon.

D **Complete each sentence b so that it has a similar meaning to sentence a, using two to five words including the word in brackets.**

1. a The last time I spoke to Gemma was on Saturday. (since)
   b I haven't ......spoken to Gemma since...... Saturday.
2. a It's hard to imagine now, but when he was younger, my uncle was a professional footballer. (play)
   b It's hard to imagine now, but when he was younger, my uncle .... professionally.
3. a The concert started before we got to the theatre. (already)
   b The concert .... time we got to the theatre.
4. a Katia began to learn English about three years ago. (learning)
   b Katia .... about three years.

5 a When you went to Scotland, was that your first camping holiday? (ever)
b .... on a camping holiday before you went to Scotland?
6 a This is my first visit to the science museum. (have)
b I .... the science museum before.
7 a When did you start to play chess online? (been)
b How .... chess online?
8 a Whenever I saw the postman, he always said hello with a big smile on his face. (would)
b Whenever I saw the postman, he .... hello with a big smile on his face.

E Cross out ONE incorrect option.

1 a I think it's going to rain / b I think it'll rain / c ~~I think it rains~~ } this evening.

2 a We're on the point / b We're just about / c We're on the verge } of going on holiday.

3 a If his English gets better, / b If he wants his English to get better, / c If his English is to get better, } he'll need to practise a lot.

4 a I'm meeting Louise at the beach / b I was going to meet Louise at the beach / c I was to meet Louise at the beach } but she can't now.

5 a Will you be seeing Jay / b Are you seeing Jay / c Do you see } next weekend.

6 a We'll have had dinner / b We'll be having dinner / c We're having dinner } by the time you arrive.

7 a I'm going to visit my cousin in Canada / b I'm visiting my cousin in Canada / c I'll visit my cousin in Canada } one day.

8 a The bus will have come / b The bus will come / c The bus is coming } soon – don't worry.

9 a I'm sure you're going to have a good time / b I'm sure you'll have a good time / c I'm sure you're having a good time } at the party tonight.

10 a If they will use fresh vegetables, / b If they've used fresh vegetables, / c If they use fresh vegetables, } the salad will be nice.

F Circle the correct option.

1 When Kazu ... that you're coming for the weekend, he'll be really happy.
2 Eleni doesn't feel too well, so she probably ... to school tomorrow.
3 On the television news they said ... next week.
4 Sorry, Janis, but we ... have dinner, so can I call you back later?
5 Frank ... you but he didn't have time.
6 I'll lend you the book as soon as ... reading it.
7 By the end of this course, I'm sure your English ... a lot.
8 If you're not careful, ... an accident.
9 I ... you next summer.
10 We can stay in the park until ... dark.

1 a will hear (b) hears c is hearing
2 a won't go b shan't go c doesn't go
3 a it rains b it's raining c it's going to rain
4 a will just b are just about to c are just to
5 a is to call b will have called c was going to call
6 a I've finished b I'll have finished c I'm going to finish
7 a is improving b has improved c will have improved
8 a you're having b you're going to have c you'll have had
9 a will definitely see b am on the point of seeing c am about to see
10 a it's getting b it will have got c it gets

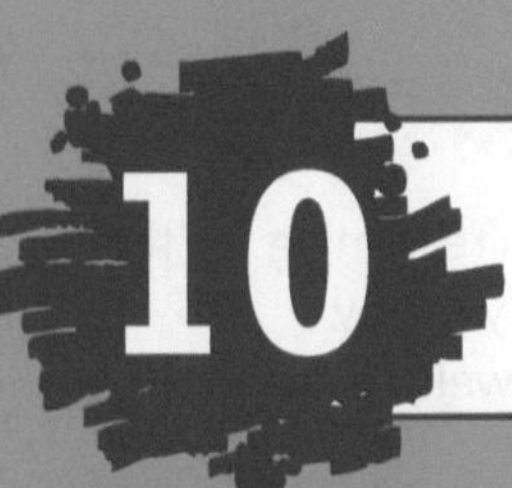

Modals of ability and obligation 1

Six astronauts can stay there.

Space stations are places for astronauts to work and study life in space. The biggest space station is the International Space Station; six astronauts **can** stay there. Astronauts **are able to** stay on space stations for a long time - the longest was 437 days - but they **need to** be strong and healthy because life is very difficult in space.

Usually, if you drop an apple, it **must** fall down: this is because of gravity. But in space there is no gravity, so astronauts **cannot** stand or walk normally. This makes it difficult for them to exercise their legs, so they **have to** do special exercises every day to keep fit.

There are no showers on the International Space Station - water **cannot** go down! - so astronauts **have to** have baths. Astronauts **have got to** be very careful with washing because they have very little water. It **cannot** rain in space.

The International Space Station

Could we live in space in the future? Not very soon. You **need to** have a lot of money to build a space city and not many countries could do this. Even if we **are able to** live in space, life wouldn't be easy there. We **should** make where we live a nicer place instead!

1 What is the longest time someone has stayed in space?
2 How do astronauts wash in space?

Answers: 1 437 days 2 They have baths.

Modals of ability and obligation 1

1 *Can, could, must* and *should* are modal verbs. Use a second verb in the infinitive without *to* after modal verbs. Make negatives with *not*. Put them before the subject in questions.

Six astronauts ***can*** *stay there.*
You ***must not*** *use too much water.*
Could *we live in space?*

Can / be able to

2 Use *can* (*not*) and *be* (*not*) *able to* for talking about present ability. *Be able to* is less common and more formal.

Can *you see the moon?*
Astronauts ***are able to*** *stay on space stations for a long time.*

3 Use *will be able to* for future ability. The negative form of the future is *will not be able to* or *won't be able to*.

One day we ***will be able to*** *live on the moon.*
She ***won't be able to*** *walk after a year in space.*

4 We can also use *can* for future ability if we are talking about a possible plan.

I ***can't*** *meet Ted today but I* ***can*** *see him tomorrow.*

5 *Could = would be able to.*

Could *people live in space in the future?*
She ***could*** *be a scientist if she wanted to.*

Must, have to, should

6 There are no past or future forms of *must*. Use forms of *have to* for obligation in the past or the future.

Yesterday I ***had to*** *do my science homework and today I* ***must*** *give it to the teacher.*
The first spaceships ***had to*** *be very small.*
Will *we* ***have to*** *live in space one day?*

7 Use *must* and *have to* to talk about rules and laws, or something that is necessary.

You ***must*** *never look at the sun through a telescope.*
Astronauts ***have to*** *be intelligent.*

8 Use *must* to talk about what the speaker thinks is necessary. *Have to* is usually about an obligation imposed on the speaker by others or the situation. Questions are more common with *have to* than *must*.

I ***must*** *phone Bill, I really want to speak to him.*
I ***have to*** *stay at home – the doctor is coming.* (The speaker can't change the situation.)
Do I ***have to*** *phone Bill?* (not usually *Must I phone Bill?*)

TIP

Have got to means the same as ***have to*** but it is more informal.

Have *you* ***got to*** *read that boring book?*

9 Use *mustn't* or *can't* (NOT ~~*don't have to*~~) to talk about things we are not allowed to do.

You ***mustn't / can't*** *park your car here.*

10 Use *don't have to* or *doesn't have to* for something which is not necessary.

You ***don't have to*** *come with me. Stay at home if you want.*

11 Use *should* to say what it is necessary to do and to give advice. *Should* is not as strong as *must*.

We ***should*** *make where we live a nicer place!*
You ***shouldn't*** *do it if you don't like it.*

Ought to, need, had better

12 *Ought to = should* but it is much less common. *Ought to* (negative *ought not to*) is very rare in questions.

Astronauts ***ought to*** *exercise every day.*

13 *Need* is usually followed by the *to*-infinitive, but sometimes it is a modal verb. The future is *will need to*.

She ***needs to*** *train more.*
Need *I go?*
Will *we* ***need to*** *go?*

14 *Do not need to*, or *need not*, means there is no obligation.

You ***don't need to*** *explain. I already understand.*
We ***needn't*** *take any money.*

TIP

We can use *There's no need to ...* when there is no obligation.

Everything is all right. ***There's no need to*** *worry.*

15 Use *had better* to give strong advice or orders. The form is always past and it is followed by the infinitive without *to*. The negative is *had better not*. The question form is not very often used.

We ***had better*** *make Earth a nicer place.*
You'd ***better*** *listen to me!*

Practice

A Match the sentence beginnings to the correct endings.

1 If you can't drive, you
2 You have to help her because she
3 They won't be able to find it without help so they
4 You have to write a story but it
5 I mustn't make her angry, so I
6 There's no need to translate, she
7 It doesn't need to be expensive but it
8 We need to finish it tomorrow, so you
9 I could run a marathon but I
10 Rich countries must understand that they

a can't do everything.
b have to help poor people.
c had better work faster.
d ought to speak nicely.
e shouldn't look cheap.
f have to walk.
g will have to train a lot.
h doesn't have to be very long.
i should take a map.
j can understand everything.

1 ...f... 2 .... 3 .... 4 .... 5 ....
6 .... 7 .... 8 .... 9 .... 10 ....

B Underline the correct option.

1 Dogs *can't / couldn't* talk.
2 It's a difficult question. I *must / can* think about it.
3 Soon you *will be able to / can* speak English well.
4 Tomorrow is Sunday, so I *mustn't / don't have to* get up early.
5 *Can / Should* you swim?
6 You *mustn't / don't have to* play football near the window.
7 *Should she / Ought she* see a doctor?
8 It's raining hard. You *should / are able to* get an umbrella.
9 Tom *could / has to* do it if he wanted.
10 I *can / have got to* phone Jane but her phone is off.
11 Actresses *don't need to / must not* be beautiful to work on the radio.
12 We *can / have to* meet tomorrow if you get some free time.

C What *can / must / should*, etc. these people do in their jobs / lives? Answer using modals.

1 A doctor
She has to work long hours. She should study hard.
She can meet a lot of different people.
....

2 A teacher
....
....
....

3 An astronaut
....
....
....

4 A model
....
....
....

5 I
....
....
....

D Rewrite each sentence so that it has a similar meaning, using modals. Sometimes more than one answer is possible.

1 It would be a good idea for Jack to go home.
Jack should go home.

2 It is necessary for Jill to eat more.
....

3 Emily cooks very well.
....

4 It would be a bad idea for us to stop.
....

5 There is no obligation for you to wait.
....

6 Jo speaks French.
....

7 Will it be possible for you to come tomorrow?
....

8 They don't want to go but it is necessary.
....

E Complete the following sentences using the correct forms of the modals in the box, then give reasons / situations.

be able to ~~can~~ have to have to
must ~~must~~ need to ought to

1 We ....must.......... speak Chinese.
You are in China.

2 I ....can't.......... swim.
You never learned at school.

3 He .... buy 15 bottles of cola.
....

4 I .... go to bed very early.
....

5 We .... visit the museum.
....

6 She .... do the test again.
....

7 I .... speak to my mum.
....

8 My friend .... ride a bike.
....

F Circle the correct option.

At the moment we [1]... travel between planets but we [2]... travel between stars. Stars are very far away from each other and our spaceships [3]... go fast enough to get there. The nearest star to the Sun is Proxima Centauri but a spaceship [4]... only get there in a few thousand years. But why [5]... we go to other stars? Well, stars are very important, so we [6]... know more about them. For example, our nearest star is the Sun – you can see it from your window, but you [7]... look too long because it can be bad for your eyes. We [8]... live without the Sun because it gives our planet energy.
We [9]... visit other stars to know about them because we have very good telescopes, but if you really want to see 'life' on stars you [10]... watch films or read books.

1 a must b should (c) can
2 a can't b don't have to c mustn't
3 a mustn't b aren't able to c shouldn't
4 a can b could c has to
5 a should b ought c can
6 a can b could c ought to
7 a have not to b mustn't c don't have to
8 a couldn't b shouldn't c mustn't
9 a mustn't b don't have to c shouldn't
10 a don't have to b had to c will have to

MY TURN!

Give advice in these situations using modals.

1 I want to go to a party tonight but I don't have anything nice to wear.
You should stay at home. You mustn't worry about clothes.
....

2 I don't have any friends. Nobody likes me.
....
....

3 There's nothing on TV and I'm bored.
....
....

4 I don't know what to buy my mum for her birthday.
....
....

5 I am always late.
....
....

MY TEST!

Circle the correct option.

1 An astronaut .... be strong. a has to b have to c is able to
2 .... astronauts watch TV on space stations? a Are able b Need c Can
3 Astronauts .... do some exercise every day. a should b need c ought
4 You .... study hard if you want to be an astronaut. a can b could c must
5 Astronauts .... be tall but they should be healthy. a have to b don't have to c must

My Test! answers: 1a 2c 3a 4c 5b

11 Modals of ability and obligation 2

He should have given the dog a biscuit.

Yesterday the police **had to** help a robber who **couldn't** get down from a tree. Jim Sly went into the house of 80-year-old Emily Bishop while she was asleep. Her dog, Rover, woke up and ran after Sly. The dog **could** run fast but Sly **was able to** get into the garden and up the tree. Emily said, 'The man **needn't have** run away. Rover is a very nice dog. He **should have** said Hello and given him a biscuit.'

The multi-millionaire Kelly Rogers has sold both her houses and gone to live in a small village in Scotland. 'I **should have** done this years ago,' she said. 'I **needed to** change my life and do something new. This simple life is so exciting. This morning my chef **had to** walk to the shops! (He **couldn't drive** the Rolls Royce there because my gardener was using it.) I feel like a normal person again.'

Tom Brown has finished his university course – after 24 years. He started his course in 1985 but he **wasn't able to** finish it until this June. 'It's been a long time,' said Tom. 'I **should have** finished in 1988 but I **had to** get a job to pay for the course. I **didn't have to** do this course but it was interesting. Maybe I'll study something new now.'

? Match each person to the correct action:

1 Emily	**a** finished university
2 Sly	**b** bought a new house
3 Kelly	**c** ran away from a dog
4 Tom	**d** phoned the police

Answers: 1d 2c 3b 4a

Modals of ability and obligation 2

Could and *be able to*

1 **Use *could* (*not*) or *was* / *were* (*not*) *able to* for ability in the past. *Could* is more common than *was* / *were* *able to*.**

*The dog **could** run fast.*
*He **wasn't able to** finish it.*

2 **Use *was* / *were able to* (NOT ~~*could*~~) when talking about one event in the past. In the negative, both forms are possible.**

*He **was able to** get into the garden.* NOT ~~*He could ...*~~
*Luckily, I **was able to** open the door in time.*
NOT ~~*... I could ...*~~
*I **wasn't able to** / **couldn't** open the door in time.*

Had to

3 **There is no past form of *must*. Use *had to* for statements and questions about obligation in the past. Use *couldn't* or *wasn't allowed to* for negatives.**

*I **had to** get a job.*
*I was on a diet so I **couldn't** eat chocolate.*

Needed to and *didn't have to*

4 **Use *needed to* and *had to* for what was necessary in the past.**

*I **needed to** / **had to** change my life.*

Use *didn't need to* and *didn't have to* for what was not necessary in the past.

*I **didn't need to** / **didn't have to** do this course but it was interesting.*

Should have

5 **Use *should have* + past participle for something that was necessary in the past but that you didn't do. Use *should not have* + past participle for something that was unnecessary in the past but that you did anyway.**

*I **should have** finished in 1989.* (I didn't finish then, unfortunately.)
*We **shouldn't have** broken it.* (We did break it, unfortunately.)

Ought to have and *need to have*

6 **We sometimes use *ought* (*not*) *to have*, *need to have* and *need not have* for obligation in the past but these forms are not very common.**

*You **ought to have** listened to me.*
*The man **needn't have** run away.*

Practice

A Match the famous people to the correct sentence endings. (Look on the Internet if you're not sure about the answers.)

1 Elvis
2 Napoleon
3 Pandora
4 Houdini
5 Juliet
6 Nelson Mandela
7 Jane Austen
8 Princess Diana

a shouldn't have opened the box.
b wasn't allowed to marry Romeo.
c didn't need to die so young. It was tragic.
d could sing very well.
e should have written more books.
f was able to get out of strange places.
g had to go to prison for many years.
h didn't need to fight at Waterloo.

1 d ...... 2 ...... 3 ...... 4 ......
5 ...... 6 ...... 7 ...... 8 ......

B Rewrite these sentences in the past.

1 I need to see her.
I needed to see her.
2 We must go.
....
3 We mustn't go.
....
4 You should buy it.
....
5 She doesn't need to come.
....
6 They can speak French.
....
7 He has to sleep.
....
8 He's not able to be here.
....

C Underline the correct option.

1 I could / had to read when I was three years old.
2 It was very cold and we *could / had to* put on warm coats.
3 Mike *should have spoken / needed to speak* to Mel, so he phoned her.
4 We *couldn't / didn't have to* do it if we didn't want to.
5 I *was able to / could* speak to her before the lesson began.
6 That's a secret. You *shouldn't have / couldn't have* told her.
7 Sharon loved food and she *could / needed to* cook very well.
8 We *needn't have / didn't need to* spend so much money.
9 *Were you able / could you* to open the box?
10 The children *didn't have to / weren't allowed to* watch TV late.

D Yesterday, Alice's boss left her a list of things to do. Change the notes into sentences using past modals.

Hi, Alice.

1. Phone James!!!
2. Don't eat all the chocolates.
3. Use my computer (if you want).
4. Buy some more paper – very important!
5. Not necessary to finish the report.
6. Check my emails (please).
7. Don't worry about going to the meeting.
8. Don't forget Maggie's birthday.

See you tomorrow,

Brian

1 She had to phone James.
2 ....
3 ....
4 ....
5 ....
6 ....
7 ....
8 ....

E What were the consequences of these facts? Answer using past modals.

1 25 years ago, there were no mobile phones.
People had to phone from home.
They couldn't phone their friends on the train.

2 50 years ago, there were no home computers.

3 75 years ago, not many people had cars.

4 100 years ago, not many children went to school.

5 150 years ago, there were no fridges.

6 500 years ago, there were very few hospitals.

F Circle the correct option.

Student Helen Jones spent the night in Lincoln History Museum. She [1]... get out after the museum closed and [2]... stay there until the morning. Helen [3]... get some information for a history project, so she went to the museum on Saturday afternoon. Her friends [4]... go, they [5]... do a project, so she was alone.

Helen [6]... take photos (you are not allowed to use a camera in the museum) but she [7]... get a lot of information. She was so interested in the museum that she didn't notice the time. There [8]... two museum workers on Saturday, Ted and Bill, but Ted was ill and Bill [9]... close the museum himself. Bill closed the museum while Helen was still inside. Helen [10]... call anyone because she didn't have her mobile phone with her.

The next morning, Bill opened the museum and found Helen. Helen was very tired after such a long night but she [11]... get up and answer our phone call this morning. 'I don't feel well,' she said, 'I was hungry, so I ate some sweets I found in the museum. I [12]... eaten those sweets. They were 500 years old!'

1 a could b should c couldn't d shouldn't
2 a must b must have c had to d has to
3 a needed to b needed c needed have d need
4 a had to b have to must not d didn't have to
5 a didn't need b hadn't to c didn't need to d need not
6 a was able to b couldn't c mustn't d needed to
7 a should have b ought to c need d was able to
8 a should have been b could be c was able to be d were able to be
9 a have to b must c needed d had to
10 a didn't have to b couldn't c didn't need to d needn't have
11 a could b was able to c had to d should have
12 a was able to have b wasn't able to have c shouldn't have d should have

MY TURN!

Give reasons for these situations using modal verbs. They can be funny!

1 You didn't do your homework.
I had to give my pet elephant a bath last night.
My baby brother drew on my book and I couldn't read it.
....
....

2 You are meeting your friend but you are late.
....
....
....
....

3 You forgot your friend's birthday.
....
....
....
....

4 You didn't do the shopping.
....
....
....
....

5 You had an argument with your mum.
....
....
....
....

6 You didn't wash your hair last night.
....
....
....
....

MY TEST!

Circle the correct option.

1 Emily was 80 years old but she .... see very well. a could b had to c didn't have to
2 Rover .... outside because the road was very dangerous. a mustn't go b wasn't allowed to go c needed to go
3 .... Tom .... become a professor? a Had ... to b Needed ... to c Should ... have
4 Emily .... get out of bed and phone the police. a could b was able to c needed
5 Tom was very clever, so he .... hard. a had to study b must study c didn't have to study

My Test! answers: 1a 2b 3c 4b 5c

12 Possibility and certainty in the present and future

It must be 3.

The brain, just like the body, needs exercise. Some scientists say that doing puzzles **may** help you to think more clearly. Puzzles **could** also improve your memory, especially as you get older. One puzzle a year **may not** make much difference – but doing one every day **might** even prevent mental illness.

Sudoku are number puzzles which are very popular in Japan, the UK and the USA. In this example, each row, column and box should contain each of the numbers 1 to 6.

This number **can't** be 1.
It **must** be 3.

This number **must** be 1.

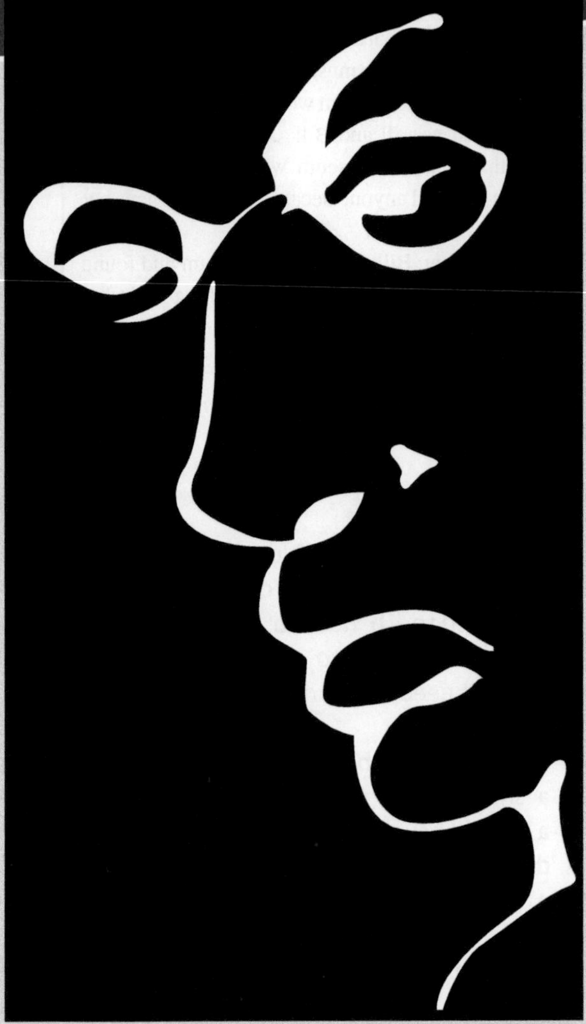

Now look at this puzzle picture. What do you see? It **might** be a woman's face. She **might** be looking down. It **could** be a man's face. He **could** be looking over his shoulder. Turn the picture on its side and you **may not** see a picture any more – you **may** see a word instead.

?

1 Why is it good to do puzzles?
2 What are the different things people may see in the puzzle picture?

Answers: 1 Puzzles may help you think more clearly. They could improve your memory and might prevent mental illness when you are older.
2 A woman's face or a man looking over his shoulder; the hidden word is 'liar'.

Possibility and certainty in the present and future

1 ***Must, may, might, could*** **and *can't* are modal verbs. After modal verbs we use the infinitive without *to*. The modal verb does not change.**

*He **could be** looking over his shoulder.*
*They **may not know** the answer.*

2 **Use *must* to say that you think something is certain or very probable. The negative of *must* is *can't*.**

*It **must** be 3.* (= I am certain the answer is 3.)
*It **can't** be 1.* (= I am certain the answer is not 1. OR 1 is not possible.)

> TIP
>
> **In this context, the negative of *must* is *can't*, not *mustn't*.**
>
> *It can't be 1.* NOT ~~*It mustn't be 1*~~.

3 **Use *may, might* or *could* to mean *'It is possible that …'*. We often use *might* when something is less likely.**

*You **may** see a word.* (= It's possible that you can see a word.)
*He **could** be looking over his shoulder.* (= It's possible that he's looking over his shoulder.)
*It **might** be a woman's face.* (= It's possible that it's a woman's face.)

> **We don't use *can* to mean *'It is possible that …'*.**
>
> *It could be a man's face.*
> NOT ~~*It can be a man's face*~~.

4 **Use *may not* and *might not* to mean *'It is possible that … not …'*. We don't often use *could not* in this context.**

*The story **may not** / **might not** be true.* (= It's possible that the story is not true.)

5 **We use *may, might* or *could* to talk about something which will possibly happen in the future. Negatives are *may not* and *might not*. We don't often use *could not* in this context.**

*It **could** improve your memory as you get older.*
*It **may not** make any difference to you in the future.*

> **Note the difference:**
>
> ✓ *I **will** see you later.*
> **?** *I **may** see you later.*
>
> ✗ *They **won't** be at the party tomorrow.*
> **?** *They **might not** be at the party tomorrow.*

Practice

A **In this sudoku puzzle, each of the four shapes (♦, ★, ● and ☾) appears in every row, column and box. Write sentences using *must* and *can't*, then complete the puzzle.**

1 The blue square ....*can't be a*........ ●.
2 The green square .... ☾.
3 The yellow square .... ★.
4 The pink square .... ☾.
5 The grey square .... ●.
6 The white square .... ★.

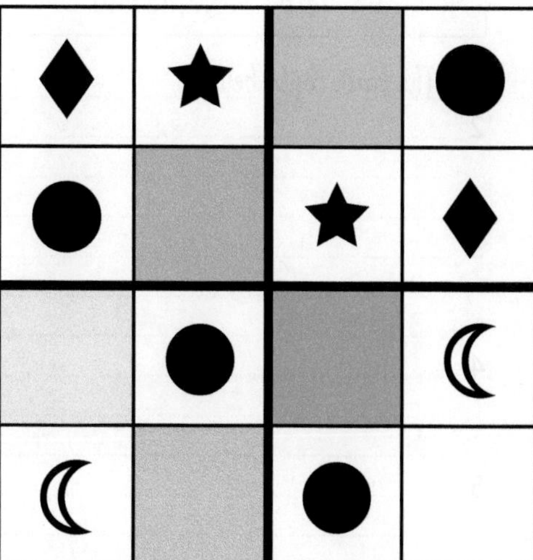

B Complete the dialogues using *must* and an adjective from the box.

angry bored disappointed ~~excited~~ fit rich tired

1 A: We're going on holiday tomorrow.
B: You must be excited!.

2 A: He bought his wife a new car for her birthday.
B: He ....

3 A: She goes to the gym every day.
B: She ....

4 A: We were working until midnight last night.
B: You ....

5 A: I didn't pass the exam.
B: You ....

6 A: They studied this Science lesson last week, and now they're doing it again.
B: They ....

7 A: My friend borrowed my mobile and now she's lost it.
B: You ....

C You are having a party and you are worried about one of your friends who has not arrived. What do you think the problem is? Write sentences using the words in the box and *could, may* or *might*.

buying a present not / coming not / have the address have / problem with her phone ill ~~train / late~~ working late

1 The train could be late.
2 ....
3 ....
4 ....
5 ....
6 ....
7 ....

D Rewrite each sentence so that it has a similar meaning, using the word in brackets.

1 It's possible that vitamin tablets are not the best thing for your health. (may)
Vitamin tablets may not be the best thing for your health.

2 The scientist said it is possible that life exists on other planets. (might)
....

3 Maybe he will go to prison. (could)
....

4 Perhaps he doesn't know much about cars. (might)
....

5 It's possible we won't see her again. (may)
....

6 Perhaps wearing glasses will make your eyesight worse. (might)
....

7 Maybe he's wrong. (could)
....

8 It's possible we won't go on holiday this summer. (might)
....

9 Perhaps I will phone her later. (may)
....

10 He doesn't say much – perhaps he's shy. (may)
....

E Complete the dialogues using *must, may, could, might* or *can't*.

1 A: I phoned my parents but there was no reply.
B: They *might not be at home.*
2 A: Is dinner ready? I haven't had anything to eat all day.
B: You ……………………………………………………… !
3 A: Look! What's the name of that actor on the TV?
B: Ask your brother. He ……………………………………………… .
He sometimes watches this show.
4 A: Hi, Lewis, have you seen Olivia? I've been waiting for her for half an hour!
B: There's another entrance at the back. She
……………………………………………………… .
5 A: I ……………………………………………………… –
I found my first grey hair this morning.
B: Well, you'll be 70 next month!
6 A: Jamie is coming to see the film tonight.
B: He ……………………………………………………… !
He's on holiday!
7 A: I found this jacket. Is it yours or Maria's?
B: It's not mine. It ……………………………………………… .
I'll ask her.
8 A: Look! Is that Amy driving the car?
B: It ……………………………………………………… .
She's too young to drive.

F Write at least one reason for these situations, using *may* (*not*), *might* (*not*) or *could*.

1 A train comes into a station, but none of the waiting passengers move.
The passengers could be going the other way.
It might be a model train.
………………………………………………………
………………………………………………………

2 Georgina only eats leaves.
………………………………………………………
………………………………………………………
………………………………………………………
………………………………………………………

3 Jack gets into his car and sits there for five minutes. Then he gets out again.
………………………………………………………
………………………………………………………
………………………………………………………
………………………………………………………

4 The cat is running away from the mouse.
………………………………………………………
………………………………………………………
………………………………………………………
………………………………………………………

MY TURN!

Complete these sentences about your plans for the future using *will, won't, could, may* (*not*) or *might* (*not*).

When I'm 18, ...

1 I …………*may*………… leave home.
2 I …………………… continue studying.
3 I …………………… have a job.
4 I …………………… have a bank account.
5 I …………………… be married.
6 I …………………… still live with my parents.
7 I …………………… have my own car.
8 I …………………… travel.

Now write sentences about two more plans you have.

9 I ………………………………………………
10 I ………………………………………………

MY TEST!

Circle the correct option.

1 It ………… months before the building is finished. **a** could **b** can be **c** could be
2 I'll ask Ted. He ………… the answer. **a** may not **b** may **c** may know
3 I don't know if I'm going shopping next weekend. I ………… enough money.
a might not have **b** not might have **c** could not have
4 A: Who's that in the house? B: It ………… Gemma, she's still in the States. **a** must be **b** mustn't be **c** can't be
5 She's worked for the company for years. She ………… nearly old enough to retire.
a must **b** mustn't **c** must be

My Test! answers: 1c 2c 3a 4c 5c

Possibility and certainty in the past

It must already have been there.

The Great Sphinx

Who built the Great Sphinx, and when?

The Great Sphinx is at Giza in Egypt next to the Great Pyramids. The Pyramids were built by pharaohs in approximately 2500 BC. The Great Sphinx has the body of a lion and the face of a man. Many scientists think the man **may have been** Khafre, a pharaoh at that time.

However, scientists do not all agree on this. John West and Robert Schoch have discovered water erosion on the Sphinx. But, in the middle of the Egyptian desert, where **could** the water **have come from**? Heavy rain was only common in Egypt around 5000 BC. So West and Schoch believe that Khafre **can't have built** the Sphinx. The Sphinx **must** already **have existed** at Giza when the pyramids were built. But we have no idea who **might have built** it.

?

1 Whose face does the Sphinx possibly have?
2 Why do some scientists think the Sphinx is from 5000 BC?

Answers: 1 Khafre, a pharaoh in approximately 2500 BC
2 Because of water erosion on the Sphinx.

Possibility and certainty in the past

1 **Use *must have* + past participle to say that you think something in the past was certain or very probable.**
The Sphinx ***must have existed*** *at Giza when the pyramids were built.* (= The scientists are certain it existed at Giza.)
There's a message from Lily. She ***must have called*** *when we were out.*

2 **The negative of *must have* is *can't have* or *couldn't have*. Use *can't have* or *couldn't have* + past participle to say that you think something in the past was not possible or did not happen.**
Khafre ***can't have built*** *the Sphinx.* NOT ~~*Khafre mustn't have built ...*~~ (= The scientists are certain Khafre did not build the Sphinx or it is not possible that Khafre built the Sphinx.)
The driver didn't stop. He ***couldn't have seen*** *the red light.*

3 **Use *may have* or *might have* + past participle to say that you think something in the past was possible.**
The man ***may have been*** *Khafre.* (= It's possible that the man was Khafre.)
The man ***might not have been*** *Khafre.* (= It's possible that the man was not Khafre.)
She didn't do the homework. She ***might have found*** *it too difficult.*

4 **Use *might have* or *could have* + past participle (but not usually *may have*) to say that something in the past was possible, but did not happen.**
He ***could / might have become*** *a great ruler, but he died young.*
You didn't tell me you had no money. I ***could have lent*** *you some.*

▶ **See Units 10, 11 and 12 for the form of modal verbs and for the use of modal verbs to express possibility in the present and future.**

Practice

A Match phrases a–g to the correct spaces in the text.

Easter Island, 3,600 km off the coast of Chile in the Pacific Ocean, is very far from land. Now it is a small island with few people or trees, but at one time a lot of people lived there. Scientists believe the original inhabitants [1] ....c.... by accident. Around 100 people [2] .... But then the number of inhabitants increased too quickly. Scientists are all agreed that the inhabitants [3] .... on the island and finally all died.
The Easter Island statues are famous but nobody knows why they are there or why there are so many. The statues [4] ...., or Easter Island [5] .... The statues are very large and very heavy, so they [6] .... Scientists still do not know how the inhabitants [7] ....

a must have used up all the food
b could have been part of a much bigger island
c may have discovered the island
d might have done this
e might have been gods
f may have landed there
g can't have been easy to move

B Match sentences 1–8 with what *could* or *might* have happened but didn't (a–h).

1 The weather was terrible at the beach.
2 I missed the goal.
3 I didn't study for my exam.
4 We didn't leave home until midday.
5 She gave up tennis when she was 12.
6 She's been talking on the phone all morning.
7 She didn't take her medicine.
8 I didn't go to drama school.

a She might have been a good player.
b I could have been an actor.
c We could have gone swimming.
d We might have won the match.
e She could have done her homework by now.
f I could have passed it.
g She might have got better more quickly.
h We could have got there earlier.

C Complete the dialogues using *must have* + past participle and the verb phrases from the box.

~~be difficult~~ be very frightening go out look silly make a mistake pass his test sleep very well

1 A: My parents got divorced last year.
B: That must have been difficult for you.
2 A: He's driving the car alone.
B: ....
3 A: I put my shirt on the wrong way.
B: ....
4 A: The man in the shop gave me the wrong money.
B: ....
5 A: I was out in the boat when it started to fill with water.
B: ....
6 A: My parents are not at home.
B: ....
7 A: I didn't hear the thunder last night.
B: ....

D Look at the marriage certificate and check if statements 1–7 are possible or not. Write sentences using *must have, can't have, couldn't have, may have* or *might have* + past participle.

MARRIAGE CERTIFICATE

Date	Name	Age	Profession
14th August 1920	Henry Ellis	25	servant
	Sarah MacDonald		servant
	H E J Ellis S. E. MacDonald London, 1920		

1 Henry Ellis was born in London.
He might have been born in London – we don't know.
2 He was a teacher all his life.
He can't have been a teacher all his life – he was a servant in 1920.
3 He got married in London.
....
....
4 He was born in 1900.
....
....
5 He didn't have any children.
....
....
6 His wife was older than him.
....
....
7 Henry and Sarah met when they were working.
....
....

E **Complete the sentences about the pictures, using the verbs in brackets and *must have, can't have, might have* or *may have*.**

1

2

3

4

5

6

1 It ....*must have come*........ from the farm. (come)
2 He .... a ghost. (see)
3 They .... an accident. (have)
4 You .... it very well. (look after)
5 She .... her arm. (break)
6 She .... it by herself. (make)

F **Rewrite each sentence so that it has a similar meaning, using a modal verb from this unit.**

1 It certainly wasn't an easy decision.
It can't / couldn't have been an easy decision.
2 I'm sure you were a good friend of John's.
....
3 It is possible she did not understand.
....
4 They were lucky the accident wasn't a lot worse.
....
5 She didn't play very well – perhaps she was nervous.
....
6 I certainly didn't imagine it.
....
7 Maybe you didn't hear what he said.
....
8 Something definitely went wrong.
....

MY TURN!

You get home and your teacher is sitting in the kitchen talking to your mum. Write sentences using the modals in brackets.

1 (can't have) ....*My mum can't have invited her / him.*....
2 (may have) ....
3 (may not have) ....
4 (might have) ....
5 (might not have) ....
6 (must have) ....

MY TEST!

Circle the correct option.

1 She may have .... all about it. **a** forget **b** forgot **c** forgotten
2 Her car is not there. She .... have come home last night. **a** may **b** might **c** can't
3 She drank a whole bottle of water. She .... have been thirsty. **a** might **b** must **c** couldn't
4 The scientists .... have found a cure, but they need to do more tests. **a** may **b** must **c** can't
5 The man may not have .... the truth. **a** know **b** knowing **c** known

My Test! answers: 1c 2c 3b 4a 5c

Requests, permission, offers, suggestions, promises

Could you take your hat off, please?

?

1 In cartoon B, where are the snails' homes?
2 In cartoon D, why does the man want to come in?

Answers: 1 The snails' homes are on their backs! 2 The man wants to steal the woman's things!

Requests, permission, offers, suggestions, promises

Requests

> **TIP**
>
> To make a polite request, it is not sufficient to just add *please*. You should use a modal verb to be polite.
>
> ***Could*** *you take off your hat, please?*
> NOT ~~*Take off your hat, please.*~~

1 Use the modal verbs ***can*** / ***could*** / ***may*** to ask for something politely. ***May*** is more formal.
A: ***Can*** / ***Could*** / ***May*** *I have your name and address, please?*
B: Sure / No problem.

2 Use ***can*** / ***could*** / ***will*** / ***would*** to ask someone politely to do something.
A: ***Can*** / ***Could*** / ***Will*** / ***Would*** *you take off your hat, please?*
B: Of course.

3 If we want to be very polite, we can make requests with ***Do you think you could …?, Could you possibly …?*** or ***Do / Would you mind*** + verb + ***-ing …?***
A: ***Do you think you could*** / ***Could you possibly*** *take off your hat?*
B: Of course.
A: ***Do*** / ***Would you mind opening*** *the window?*
B: No, not at all. OR *Of course not.*

> **TIP**
>
> ***Could*** and ***would*** are more polite than ***can*** and ***will***.
>
> ***Would*** *you take a photo of us, please?*
> *I'm taking these boxes to the car.* ***Could*** *you help?*

Permission

4 We can use the modal verbs ***can, could*** and ***may*** with the first person to ask for permission. ***Could*** is more polite than ***can***. ***May*** is formal.
We usually give permission with ***can*** or ***may***, or we can just say ***Of course, Sure*** or ***Sorry***.
A: ***Can I*** *come in?* *B: Yes, you* ***can***. / ***Sure***.
A: ***Could we*** *come in?* *B: No, you* ***can't***! / *No,* ***sorry***.
A: ***May I*** *come in?* *B: Yes, you* ***may***. / ***Of course***.

5 Other ways of asking for permission without using a modal are ***Do you mind if …?*** or ***Is it all right if …?***
A: ***Do you mind*** / ***Is it all right if*** *I come in?*
B: Yes, of course / Sorry, no.

▶ See Unit 20 for *let* and *allow*.

Offers

6 Use ***I'll*** / ***We'll*** to offer to do something for someone (NOT ~~***shall / will***~~).
I'll *do that for you!*
We use ***Shall I / we …?*** or ***Can I / we …?*** for a more polite offer.
Shall / ***Can*** *I help you cross the road?*

Suggestions

7 Use the modal verbs ***could, might*** or ***Shall we …?*** to suggest an idea for you or other people to do.
Shall *we go out?*
We ***could*** / ***might*** *go to the cinema.*

8 Other ways of making suggestions are: ***Let's …, Why don't we …?, How about*** + verb + ***-ing?***
Let's *go home.*
Why don't we *go home?*
How about going *home?*

Promises

9 Use ***I / We will*** or ***I'll / We'll*** to make promises.
I ***will*** *always love you.*
In British English, ***shall*** is sometimes used after ***we*** and ***I***.
I ***shall*** *always love you.*

▶ See Unit 10 for the form of modal verbs.

Practice

A **Underline the correct option.**

1 *Is it / Would it* all right if I give Alex my ticket?
2 *Could / May* you open this for me?
3 *Will / Shall* you talk to him for me?
4 *Might / Would* you pass me the salt?
5 Would you mind *not to make / not making* so much noise?
6 What *shall / let's* we do today?
7 Why don't we *sit / sitting* down?
8 I *might / will* definitely see you there.

B **Complete the sentences using verbs from the box. Sometimes more than one verb is possible.**

could 'll mind shall will

1 What ....shall / could.... we give him for his birthday?
2 .... you possibly come back later?
3 Would you .... giving me your email address?
4 I .... be careful, I promise.
5 .... you come with me to the hospital?
6 Do you think you .... bring the book in the morning, please?
7 .... I put the boxes over here?

C **Molly and her friend Yasmin are bored. Make Molly's suggestions for things to do based on the web page below, using different wording each time.**

WHAT'S ON this weekend!
Saturday 25th May
SUMMER'S HERE. ENJOY EVERY MINUTE OF IT!
Go camping at Sandy Beach this weekend. Ring 40288 NOW!
The Fantastic Phone Company
Get a new phone and save money too! Too good to be true? Ring us today and find out for yourself! 0888 214365
Transporters 3
The film of the summer! Don't miss it! At your local cinema from Saturday.
This is what you have been waiting for! Bexham's wonderful new swimming pool opens on Saturday 25th. Come and see us!
20% off all summer clothes at Turner's. This week only.
2 for 1 at Pizza Country. Saturday lunchtimes only.

1 ....We could go swimming at Bexham....
2 ....
3 ....
4 ....
5 ....
6 ....

D **Molly asks her dad for permission to do the things in Exercise C. Write what Molly says, using as many different ways of asking for permission as you can.**

1 ....Can we go swimming?....
2 ....
3 ....
4 ....
5 ....
6 ....

E **Look at the scenes at the station. What do the people say? Write requests and offers of help.**

1 Can I sit here, please?
2 ....
3 ....
4 ....
5 ....
6 ....

F **Complete each sentence b so that it means the same as sentence a. Use two to five words, including the word in brackets.**

1 a How about having a party? (let's)
  b Let's have .... a party.
2 a Is it a good idea for me to tell you a story? (shall)
  b .... a story?
3 a Is it a good idea to talk tomorrow? (why)
  b .... tomorrow?
4 a I'll make dinner tonight. (shall)
  b .... tonight?
5 a Can I leave early? (right)
  b .... I leave early?
6 a May I ask you some questions? (do)
  b .... if I ask you some questions?
7 a Do you think you could pick me up later? (possibly)
  b .... pick me up later?
8 a I'd like to see the doctor, please. (may)
  b ...., please?

MY TURN!

Complete these dialogues with a request, offer, suggestion or promise.

1 A: I'll pay you back! — B: I know you will.
2 A: .... — B: Yes, please. It's going to rain!
3 A: .... — B: Yes, of course. But only for an hour.
4 A: .... — B: That's a great idea!
5 A: .... — B: No, you can't!
6 A: .... — B: Thanks! I don't understand it.
7 A: .... — B: Cool! I'll see you there.
8 A: .... — B: I hope not!

MY TEST!

Circle the correct option. Sometimes more than one option is possible.

1 .... you speak more slowly? a Can b Might c Could
2 Would you mind .... us alone? a if I leave b leaving c to leave
3 .... I go outside? a Do you mind b May c Can
4 .... I wait for you? a Will b Could c Shall
5 A: What would you like to do tonight? B: We .... go to the cinema. a might b shall c could

My Test answers: 1a and c 2b 3b and c 4c 5c

R2 Review: modals

A Cross out ONE sentence with a different meaning.

1 a I don't know how to drive but I'm going to learn.
  b ~~I'm planning to learn to drive though I don't have to.~~
  c I'm going to have driving lessons; I can't drive yet though.

2 a I must do a bit of shopping.
  b I could get a few things in the shops.
  c There are a few things I've got to buy.

3 a You should get more sleep, then you wouldn't be so tired.
  b If you're very tired, you ought to sleep more.
  c You must get up earlier so you don't get so tired.

4 a You don't have to take your mobile phone to school.
  b You can't take your mobile phone to school.
  c You mustn't have your mobile phone with you in school.

5 a You'd better check your homework for mistakes.
  b You ought to make sure there aren't any mistakes in your homework.
  c You could check that your homework doesn't have mistakes in it.

6 a You mustn't wear smart clothes to this party.
  b At this party we don't have to wear smart clothes.
  c There's no need to wear smart clothes for this party.

7 a Are we able to buy tickets for the show from the website?
  b Have we got to use the website to buy tickets for the show?
  c To buy tickets for the show, do we have to use the website?

B Match the pairs.

1 Zina was on holiday,
2 Karen was very ill,
3 Amy felt much better,

a so she had to go to school.
b so she didn't have to go to school.
c so she wasn't able to go to school.

4 My plane was leaving at 6.30 am,
5 I had a nice, long sleep,
6 My friend came later than I expected,

a so I needn't have got up so early.
b so I was able to get up early.
c so I needed to get up early.

7 I should have worn a coat
8 I couldn't wear my T-shirt
9 I needn't have taken my warm boots

a because it was dirty.
b because it was really cold.
c because it wasn't cold.

10 Rob shouldn't have bought that mobile phone
11 Steve ought to have bought a new phone
12 Terry didn't have to buy the phone himself

a because his old one is broken.
b because his mum was with him.
c because it was very expensive.

C <u>Underline</u> the correct option.

1 I'm sure the traffic is really bad today. That <u>*must*</u> / *can't* be the reason why Eva is so late.
2 I don't really know where Wayne is at the moment. He *must* / *might* be in his bedroom.
3 Newspapers sometimes invent things, so this story *might not* / *mustn't* be true.
4 Lots of my friends have passed that test, so it *can't* / *could* be all that difficult.
5 Fashions change very quickly these days, so you *can* / *may* not like this style next year.
6 I'm thinking of going to the cinema with some friends this evening, so I *must not* / *might not* be here when you come back.
7 We don't yet know if we're leaving next Tuesday or next Wednesday. It *could* / *can* be either of the two.
8 Mrs Mallet doesn't drive, so that *can't* / *mustn't* be her car.
9 Sometimes computers are difficult to repair, so yours *can't* / *may not* be ready for a few more days.
10 This is the first time that Andrea's ever run 10 kilometres, so she *must* / *can't* be very tired.

D Complete each sentence b so that it has a similar meaning to sentence a. Use a modal verb from the box and the correct form of the verb in brackets.

can't may might not must

1 a I'm sure schools 50 years ago weren't the same as they are nowadays. (be)
b Schools 50 years ago ......must have been...... very different from nowadays.

2 a It's possible that Josef went to school by bus. (take)
b Josef .... the bus to school.

3 a I'm sure their holiday wasn't very nice because the weather was terrible. (have)
b With that terrible weather, they .... a very nice holiday.

4 a I wonder if Jayne remembers how to get here. (forget)
b Jayne .... how to get here.

5 a I'm sure Chloe isn't still looking for her watch. (find)
b Chloe .... her watch by now.

6 a We are going in the wrong direction. (miss)
b Yes, we .... a turning.

7 a Shakespeare and Voltaire weren't alive at the same time, so they definitely never met. (know)
b Shakespeare and Voltaire weren't alive at the same time, so they .... each other.

8 a Alison looks happy about her exam results, so she's certainly done well. (do)
b Alison looks happy about her exam results, so she .... well.

9 a I'm not sure it's right to blame Ray for that mistake. (make)
b Ray .... that mistake.

10 a Joe can't open the door. Maybe he can't remember where he put the key. (lose)
b Joe can't open the door. He .... the key.

E Cross out ONE incorrect option.

1 ... have something to eat?
a Shall we b ~~How about~~ c Why don't we

2 ... if my brother comes with us?
a Is it all right b Do you think c Do you mind

3 ... you give a message to Claudia for me please?
a Shall b Would c Could

4 ... waiting for a few minutes?
a Could you b Would you mind c How about

5 ... help me with this homework please?
a Do you think you could b Could you possibly
c Would you mind

6 That bag looks heavy. ... help you with it?
a Shall I b Would I c Can I

7 ... I borrow your dictionary?
a Do you mind if b May c Would you mind

8 ... we meet at about 5 o'clock tomorrow?
a Why don't b Could c Let's

F Complete the dialogue with one or two words in each space. Sometimes more than one answer is possible.

Leo: Hi, Laura. Is everything OK?

Laura: Not really. I'm on the train and it keeps stopping. There [1] ......must...... be a problem. [2] .... you ring the hospital and tell them I'm going to be late? I don't have the number with me. I [3] .... left it at home.

Leo: Oh no! I'll [4] .... try and find it. You [5] .... caught the earlier train.

Laura: I know – I [6] .... left at 7.00 but I didn't want to get up so early!

Leo: What time are you seeing the doctor?

Laura: 9.00, but you [7] .... to arrive 20 minutes before to give them your details.

Leo: Oh dear. You'd [8] .... get a taxi from the station or you're going to be really late. Well, I'll ring them, but you [9] .... have to go again another day. Why [10] .... go and get a coffee? I'll ring you back.

Laura: Thanks, Leo! I [11] .... imagine what I'd do without you!

15 Question forms

What is language?

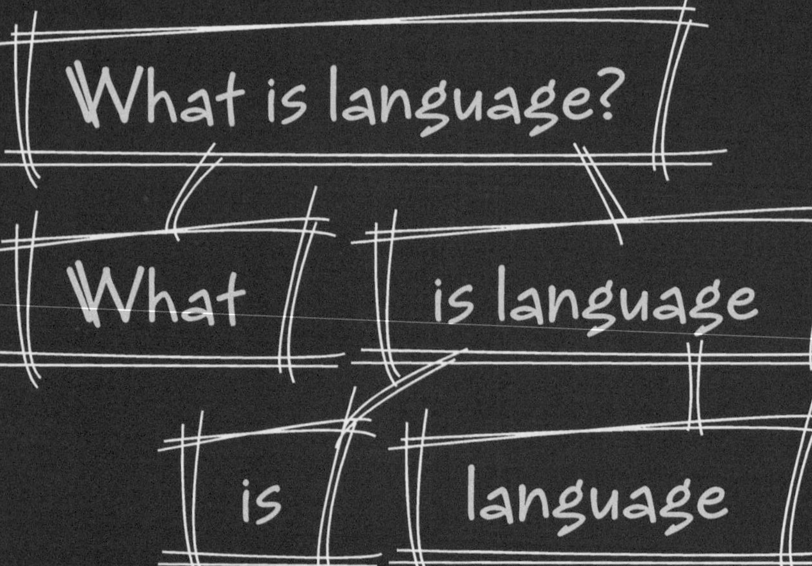

What is language?
A system where signs (words) are put into patterns (grammar) for people to use and understand.

Do animals have languages?
A difficult question. Some animals can communicate well but they usually have different systems of communication; for example, bees dance. Scientists have trained monkeys to learn and repeat words, but monkeys can't really use grammar.

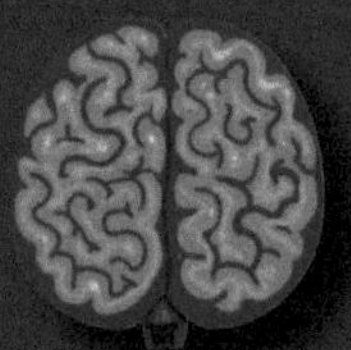
human brain

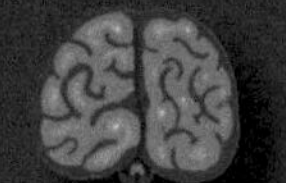
monkey brain

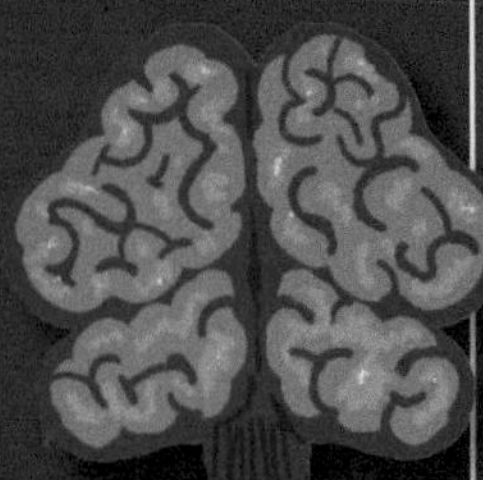
elephant brain

Why do we have language, then?
We have big brains and we can make a lot of different sounds. Some people think we are born with a special language-learning program in our brains.

How many languages are there in the world?
About 6,000. Sadly, that number is going down because many small languages are dying.

Which language has the most words?
English. There are over 500,000 words in the English language. English speakers only know a small number of these words. Shakespeare used about 30,000 different words.

What is the longest word in English?
Many scientific words are very long. For example, there is a disease pneumonoultramicroscopicsilicovolcanoconiosis which has 45 letters. **Can you say it?!**

? True or False?
1 Animals can learn grammar.
2 Shakespeare knew 500,000 words.

Answers: 1 False 2 False

Question forms

Yes / no questions

1 **To make a yes / no question, put the auxiliary verb (e.g. *am, were, have, should*) before the subject.**
Is it an English word?
Have you studied French?
Can you pronounce it?

2 **If there is no auxiliary verb, use *do, does* or *did*.**
Do you speak English?
Did she understand?

3 **Make a yes / no answer with just the subject pronoun and the auxiliary verb.**
*A: Is it true? B: Yes, **it is**. / No, **it isn't**.*
*A: Was she speaking? B: Yes, **she was**. / No, **she wasn't**.*

Wh-questions

4 **With *where, when, why, how* and *whose,* the word order is question word + auxiliary + subject + main verb.**
***Where** are you going?*
***Why** do we have language, then?*

5 **If *who, what* or *which* are the subject, we don't use *do*.**
***Who** knows French?*
***Which** language has the most words?*

6 **If *who, what* or *which* are the object, we use *do*.**
***Who** did you see?*
***What** has she done?*

7 **Use *what* + noun for general questions when there are many possibilities, and *which* + noun when there is a small or limited number of possibilities.**
***What** time is it?*
***Which** language is more difficult – Chinese or Japanese?*

8 **Ask questions about size, age, time, etc. using *How* + an adjective or an adverb.**
***How big** is the Cambridge Advanced Dictionary?*
***How long** did you learn Italian?*
***How old** is the English language?*
***How tall** is your father?*

Short questions

9 **Make a short question with an auxiliary verb and pronoun.**
*A: Children in Ireland all learn Irish. B: **Do they**?*
*A: Jane hasn't passed her French test. B: **Hasn't she**?*

TIP

If a yes / no question is negative, the answer we want or expect is *yes*.
Don't they speak Spanish in Argentina? (Of course they do!).
Wasn't Columbus an Italian?

Practice

A Make the questions by putting the words in the correct order.

1 born / you / where / were
Where were you born?

2 Clare / washing / her / is / hair
.... ?

3 did / when / you / her / see
.... ?

4 of / was / the / first / America / who / president
.... ?

5 on / a / ever / horse / been / have / you
.... ?

6 apples / buy / how / did / many / you
.... ?

7 the / time / start / what / game / does
.... ?

8 in / standing / are / rain / why / the / you
.... ?

B Read the text and write questions about the missing information (?).

It was [1]**?** at night in the small village and Simon was at home. He couldn't sleep because [2]**?**. Simon went to the kitchen to get some water. Then he heard [3]**?** . Simon went [4]**?** and looked outside. He couldn't see anything but he still felt [5]**?**.
[6]**?** was happening that night. Simon was right because [7]**?** was near the house. The animal was very dangerous and it wanted [8]**?**...

1 *What time was it?*
2 .... ?
3 .... ?
4 .... ?
5 .... ?
6 .... ?
7 .... ?
8 .... ?

If you want to know the answers, see below.

C Reply to each statement with a short question.

1 I came at six o'clock. *Did you?*
2 It finished very late. .... ?
3 We haven't decided yet. .... ?
4 Tom is still working there. .... ?
5 I was going to ask Sam. .... ?
6 Stacy hasn't been feeling well. .... ?

D Complete the questions in the speech bubbles.

1 *Which bag do you* like?
2 .... the chocolates .... ?
A3-T4 GATES 20-50
ARRIVALS
DUTY FREE
INFORMATION
3 .... a nice holiday?
4 .... our plane?
5 .... Spanish?
6 .... my dog?
7 .... my mum and dad?
8 .... phone me?

Exercise B: 1 It was 2 o'clock. 2 It was very hot. 3 An animal sound. 4 To the window. 5 Worried. 6 Something strange. 7 A wolf. 8 Food.

E Complete each quiz question using two words, then circle the correct option.

1 ......How many...... languages are there in the world?
(a) thousands b hundreds c millions d twenty-six

2 .... the word 'tea' come from?
a Latin b Greek c Chinese d German

3 .... you call sounds like the 'a' in cat and the 'e' in 'better'.
a letters b vowels c consonants d diphthongs

4 .... these words is an adverb?
a she b nice c here d and

5 .... Americans call 'taxis'?
a buses b trams c trains d cabs

6 .... the most common letter in English words?
a e b a c p d u

7 .... people speak Dutch?
a the Netherlands b Denmark c the Philippines d Germany

8 .... do children usually say their first words?
a At the age of 6 months. b At the age of 1.
c At the age of 2. d At the age of 3.

F Write three questions to match each short answer.

1 Yes, I did.
Did you tell Martin?
Did you remember the flowers?
Did you read it?

2 No, she didn't.
..........................?
..........................?
..........................?

3 Yes, we have.
..........................?
..........................?
..........................?

4 No, they weren't.
..........................?
..........................?
..........................?

5 Yes, you did.
..........................?
..........................?
..........................?

MY TURN!

Write your own quiz and swap with a friend.

1 Who ...wrote the song 'Yesterday'...?
2 What ....?
3 Who ....?
4 How ....?
5 When ....?
6 Why ....?

MY TEST!

Circle the correct option.

1 .... there a lot of people who know Latin? a Is b Are c Does
2 .... small children learn a second language? a Do b Does c Can
3 Why .... English become an international language? a did b was c were
4 Who .... you see there? a was b did c has
5 A: Did she translate it? B: Yes, she .... a was b does c did

My Test! answers: 1b 2c 3a 4b 5c

16 Question tags

Babies don't have teeth, do they?

TEETH

New babies don't have teeth, **do they**?

Yes, they do, but their teeth don't show until they are about six months old.

A baby doesn't have the same number of teeth as an adult, **does it**?

No, it doesn't. We have two sets of teeth in our lives. The first set has 20 teeth, the second set has 32. Children start getting their second teeth when they are about six years old.

There are different types of teeth, **aren't there**?

Yes, there are. We have incisors and molars. The incisors cut food and the molars make food easier to eat.

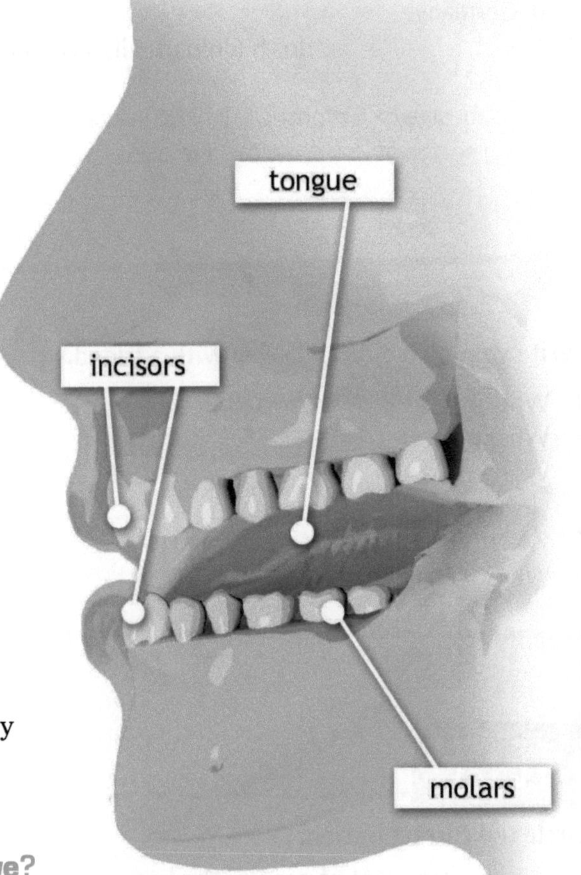

We should clean our teeth every day, **shouldn't we**?

Twice a day is better. Our molars have the most problems because we use them a lot in eating.

But people's teeth are healthier today, **aren't they**?

Yes and no. We have dentists and technology, but we eat, and drink, a lot of sweet things. Food today is often cooked and easy to eat, so we don't use our teeth so much and, like people, teeth get lazy!

So we won't need so many teeth in the future, **will we**?

Maybe not! That's bad news for dentists, isn't it?

?

1 Very small children have .... teeth.
 a no b 20 c 32

2 When you bite into an apple you use your ....
 a incisors b molars c tongue

Answers: 1b 2a

Question tags

1 A sentence with a question tag has a main clause (*You know Simon ...*) and a question tag (*... don't you?*). The question tag has an auxiliary (e.g. *is, do, have*) or a modal (e.g. *will, can*) + a subject pronoun.

main clause	question tag
He's coming,	***isn't he?***
They won't go,	***will they?***

If there is no auxiliary or modal, use a form of *do* in the correct tense.

*You know Dr Jones, **don't you**?*

I'm in the main clause → ***aren't I*** in the question tag.

I'm** right, **aren't I?

2 Usually, if the main clause is affirmative, the question tag is negative.

*She's a dentist, **isn't she?***
*It could help, **couldn't it?***

If the main clause is negative, the question tag is affirmative.

*You don't feel well, **do you?***
*We won't need so many teeth, **will we**?*

However, ***I'll*** in the main clause → ***shall I*** in the question tag.

I'll** buy some toothpaste, **shall I?

▶ See point 5 for more exceptions to this.

3 If there is a negative word like *never, no* and *nobody* in the main clause, the question tag is affirmative.

*There is nothing wrong with my teeth, **is there**?*

> **TIP**
> After *somebody, nobody* and *everybody*, the verb in the main clause is singular but the tag is plural.
> *Nobody knows, **do they?***

4 Use question tags in speaking to check information or to check that the listener agrees with you.

*Chocolate isn't good for your teeth, **is it?***
*We should clean our teeth every day, **shouldn't we**?*

5 We sometimes tell people to do things using the question tags *will / would / can / could you*? In these situations, the question tag is in the affirmative, not the negative.

*Be quiet, **could you?***
*Stop it, **will you?***

6 We use a rising intonation (our voice goes up ↗) if we aren't sure of the answer. We use a falling intonation (our voice goes down ↘) if we are fairly sure of the answer.

*You're American, **aren't you?*** ↘ (*You have an American accent.*)
*You're American, **aren't you?*** ↗ (*Or are you Canadian?*)

7 Make a short answer with a subject pronoun and an auxiliary verb.

A: You're OK, aren't you? *B: **Yes, I am.***
A: Did you see the dentist? *B: **No, I didn't.***

8 We can agree to affirmative statements with *so* + auxiliary verb + subject, or subject + auxiliary verb + *too*.

A: I'm a dentist. *B: **So am I.** / **I am too.***
A: Boys like science. *B: **So do girls.** / **Girls do too.***

> **TIP**
> In conversation, we can use *Me too.* This is informal.
> *A: I'm hungry.* *B: **Me too!***

9 We can agree to negative statements with *neither* + auxiliary verb + subject, or subject + auxiliary verb + *not* + *either*.

A: I don't like Biology. *B: **Neither do I.** / **I don't either.***
A: Jack hasn't finished. *B: **Neither have we.** / **We haven't either.***

> **TIP**
> In conversation, we can use *Me neither.* This is informal.
> *A: I'm not happy about it.* *B: **Me neither.***

Practice

A Match the main clauses to the correct question tags.

1 It's six o'clock,
2 Paula speaks Spanish,
3 It wasn't raining hard,
4 I'm the winner,
5 You won't tell Sam,
6 They've been to New York,
7 Everybody likes music,
8 There is no news yet,
9 You've got a cat,
10 That can't be right,

a aren't I?
b haven't you?
c doesn't she?
d was it?
e haven't they?
f is there?
g can it?
h isn't it?
i don't they?
j will you?

B <u>Underline</u> the correct option, then complete the answers.

1 A: New York is the capital of America, *is it* / <u>*isn't it*</u>?
B: No, it isn't. It's Washington .

2 A: Napoleon wasn't Italian, *was he* / *wasn't he*?
B: No, he wasn't. He was ....

3 A: The 2008 Olympics were in Greece, *wasn't they* / *weren't they*?
B: No, they weren't. They were in ....

4 A: Martina Navratilova didn't play football, *did she* / *didn't she*?
B: No, she didn't. She played ....

5 A: There are 31 days in June, *are there* / *aren't there*?
B: No, there aren't. There are .... days.

6 A: We should sleep four hours a night, *should we* / *shouldn't we*?
B: No, we shouldn't. .... hours is better.

7 A: A 'dozen' isn't eleven, *is it* / *isn't it*?
B: No, it isn't. A dozen is ....

8 A: In Germany you must drive on the left, *must you* / *mustn't you*?
B: No, on the ....

C Complete the questions with the correct question tags.

1 You don't know the way to planet Zog, do you ?

2 Dad has been making dinner, ... ?

3 We started a bit early this year, ... ?

4 They're real, ... ?

D Complete the sentences.

1 It's a nice day, isn't it? I think I'll go for a walk.
2 .... *Terminator V*, haven't you? It's a great film.
3 .... true, is it? I just can't believe it.
4 .... chocolate, don't you? Everyone does!
5 .... the right place, aren't we? I hope we're not lost!
6 .... to the party, can't they? Their mum and dad said it was OK.
7 .... difficult, was it? I got 100%!
8 .... some milk in the fridge, isn't there? Or do we need to buy some more?

E Rewrite the underlined replies to make them shorter and more natural.

Shelly: Oliver, look – I've got green hair!
Oliver: [1]<u>I also have green hair</u>. I just don't know what went wrong.
Shelly: [2]<u>I too don't know what went wrong</u>. Dad will be angry when he finds out.
Oliver: Yes and [3]<u>Mum will be angry</u>. She said it would be a mistake.
Shelly: [4]<u>Dad also said it would be a mistake</u>. He hasn't seen our hair yet.
Oliver. And [5]<u>Mum hasn't seen it</u>. I don't want to show them!
Shelly: [6]<u>And I don't want to show them either</u>. Oh, I thought it was such a good idea at the time.
Oliver: [7]<u>I also thought it was a good idea</u>. Our neighbours will laugh at us.
Shelly: [8]<u>Our friends will also laugh at us</u>. Well, I've learned my lesson.
Oliver: Yes, [9]<u>I too have learned my lesson</u>.
Shelly: I will never buy that green grass shampoo again.
Oliver: [10]<u>And I will never do this again</u>.

1 So have I. / Me too.
2 ....
3 ....
4 ....
5 ....
6 ....
7 ....
8 ....
9 ....
10 ....

F Circle the correct option.

Dentist: You're John, [1]... . Nice to meet you. This is your first time here, [2]...

John: Yes, I've just moved to this area. I really like it here.

Dentist: [3]... . It's a lovely place. Now, your front tooth has been bad, [4]...

John: [5]... . It hurts most when I drink hot or cold things.

Dentist: Please sit down in the chair. Open your mouth, [6]... Hmm. I see.

John: There isn't a big problem, [7]... I'm not going to need an operation, [8]...

Dentist: Don't worry! It's not so bad. You don't go to the dentist very often, [9]...

John: No, [10]... . I never have time.

Dentist: [11]... but our health is important! You should go to the dentist twice a year. Now, this won't take long

John: All right ... It won't hurt, [12]...

1 ⓐ aren't you? b are you? c do you? d don't you?
2 a does it? b doesn't it? c is it? d isn't it?
3 a Neither do I. b So do I. c I do so. d I don't either.
4 a was it? b hasn't it? c doesn't it? d has been it?
5 a Yes, it has. b Yes, it did. c Yes, it is. d Yes, it had.
6 a do you? b may you? c might you? d will you?
7 a is there? b isn't there? c is it? d isn't it?
8 a need I? b do I? c am I? d will I?
9 a do you? b are you? c don't you? d aren't you?
10 a I didn't. b I don't. c I am not. d I haven't.
11 a So am I b I neither c So do I d Neither do I
12 a does it? b is it? c will it? d won't it?

G Write questions with question tags and short answers for each situation.

1 You find 100 euros in the street.
Someone has lost it, haven't they? Yes, they have.
I'm very lucky, aren't I? Yes, you are.

2 You wake up and your head feels very hot.

3 You go to school but everything is closed.

4 Your best friend phones you at 2.00 in the morning.

5 Your father says he needs a serious talk with you.

6 You win a holiday to Cuba.

MY TURN!

Write questions for things you know about your friend but are not sure about.

1 Where he / she lives.
You've always lived in Milan, haven't you?

2 His / her birthday.

3 What he / she likes.

4 His / her favourite food.

Now use your own ideas.

5

6

MY TEST!

Circle the correct option.

1 You're a dentist, ... a is he? b are you? c aren't you?
2 We've got 32 teeth, ... a do we? b aren't we? c haven't we?
3 Jack didn't forget his toothbrush, ... a did he? b didn't he? c does he?
4 I'm next, doctor, ... a am not I? b I am? c aren't I?
5 Some animals .... teeth, do they? a don't have b have got c haven't got

My Test! answers: 1c 2c 3a 4c 5a

Multi-word verbs 1: prepositional verbs

What are you looking for?

Imagine the scene. It's the end of a long day. The teacher is still talking but you're not listening any more. You start drawing pictures – or doodles – in the back of your notebook. But are they just doodles? Graphologists say that your doodles tell us a lot about you …
So what are you **thinking about**? What are you **worrying about**? And what are you **looking for**? Let's take a look.

Lots of lines
This means: Don't **put up with** things any more. You need to make some changes to your life.

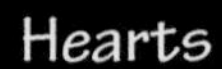

Hearts
This means: Your happiness **depends on** others.

Dark shapes
This means: You **are worrying about** something in your life.

Flowers
This means: You like people and **get on with** them well.

1 What are doodles?
2 Why might doodles be important?

Answers: 1 Pictures you draw – often when you are bored.
2 They tell graphologists a lot about people.

Multi-word verbs 1: prepositional verbs

1 **Prepositional verbs have two or three words: verb + preposition (+ preposition).**

*Your happiness **depends on** others.*
*You **get on with** people well.*

2 **The meanings of some prepositional verbs are clear but you need to know which preposition to use.**

Your happiness depends on others. NOT ~~*... of others.*~~

Some two-word verbs like this are:

(dis)agree with	*learn about*
believe in	*listen to*
belong to	*look at*
come from	*pay for*
complain about	*run into*
consist of	*smile at*
depend on	*speak to*
get in (to)	*suffer from*
get off	*talk about*
get on	*talk to*
get out (of)	*think about*
happen to	*think of*
hear of	*wait for*
know about	*work on*
laugh at	*worry about*

> **TIP**
>
> ***get in(to)*** **and *get out (of)* + a car, taxi**
> *Quick – **get in** the car!*
>
> ***get on*** **and *get off* + bike, bus, train, ship, horse**
> ***Get on** the train – it's just leaving!*

3 **Sometimes the meaning of the verb + preposition is very different from the meaning of the verb on its own.**

Note the difference:

***Look!** Eve's got a new bike.*
*We **looked after** my neighbour's dog last weekend.*
(= took care of)

Some two-word verbs like this are:

ask for	*go with*
come across	*look after*
deal with	*look for*
go for	*look like*
go through	

Some three-word verbs are:

come up with	*look forward to*
get on with	*put up with*
go up to	

> **TIP**
>
> **Sometimes the same verb can have more than one meaning:**
>
> *She's **going for** gold at the next Olympics.* (= trying to win or get something)
> *I don't know which to **go for**.* (= choose)

4 **Usually the noun or pronoun comes immediately after the preposition.**

*I'm **worrying about my exams**.*
*You **get on with him** well.*

5 **Questions that begin with *What* or *Who* may end with the preposition.**

*What are you **worrying about**?*
*Who are you **looking for**?*

6 **Some prepositional verbs take two objects.**

*She **asked me for some money.***

Some prepositional verbs like this are:

accuse (someone) *of* (something)
ask (someone) *for* (something)
blame (something) *on* (someone)
blame (someone) *for* (something)
congratulate (someone) *on* (something)
discuss (something) *with* (someone)
divide (something) *into* (something)
pay (someone) *for* (something)
remind (someone) *of* (somebody)

▶ **See Unit 18 for phrasal verbs.**

> **TIP**
>
> **There is often a one-word verb equivalent for prepositional verbs. The one-word verb is usually more formal than the prepositional verb.**
>
> *look for = search*
> *go for = choose*
> *talk about = discuss*

Practice

A Complete the sentences with the nouns in the box.

~~boat~~ bus dad exams football job taxi yellow

1. The old man got into the ......boat...... with difficulty.
2. You can't get on the .... without a ticket.
3. He congratulated her on passing her ....
4. Alice is bored at work. She's decided to go for a .... on the farm.
5. Look! That's somebody famous getting out of the .... !
6. My sister knows everything about ....
7. I talk to my .... about my problems.
8. I don't think purple goes with ....

B Match the sentence beginnings to the correct endings.

1. I'm looking forward
2. I didn't agree
3. Always believe
4. It depends
5. Nobody laughs
6. I need to learn more
7. I'm not waiting
8. They come

a in yourself.
b from a small village.
c about computers.
d for the bus.
e with everything she said.
f at my jokes.
g to the holidays.
h on your opinion.

1 ...g... 2 ...... 3 ...... 4 ......
5 ...... 6 ...... 7 ...... 8 ......

C Underline the correct option. Try to do it without looking at the list of verbs on page 75, then check.

1. He doesn't eat very well. His lunch seems to consist *of / with* cakes and crisps!
2. I won't put up *for / with* this behaviour any more.
3. I don't want to go to the museum – I don't like looking *at / for* paintings.
4. I don't want you to worry *for / about* anything.
5. I went to the hotel desk and asked *for / to* my key.
6. She blamed her sister *on / for* the trouble.
7. I'm thinking *in / of* going on holiday.
8. When I was in Angola, I learnt a lot *about / of* the country's history.
9. Have you heard *of / to* this actor?
10. She smiled *to / at* her new friend.
11. She's always complaining *about / of* the weather.
12. When he laughs, he reminds me *to / of* my uncle.

D Complete the sentences using the correct forms of the verbs in the box.

deal with get off go through ~~go up to~~ know about look after look like run into suffer from work on

1. When the president entered the room, the prince immediately ......went up to...... her and shook her hand.
2. At last, the government is .... the transport problems.
3. The man .... the bus at the last stop.
4. We .... their young son on Saturday.
5. I don't .... anything .... golf.
6. They both .... bad headaches.
7. He's .... a really bad time at the moment.
8. Everyone thinks my sister .... me. We've both got green eyes.
9. My dad .... the new kitchen all weekend.
10. She wasn't looking where she was going and .... a streetlight.

E Make questions by putting the words in the correct order.

1. marriage / in / believe / you / Do
   Do you believe in marriage?
2. What / were / music / listening / to / you
   .... ?
3. What / thinking / you / about / are
   .... ?
4. about / What / you / to / want / do / talk
   .... ?
5. ever / to / famous / Have / spoken / you / person / a
   ....
   .... ?
6. smiling / you / are / Who / at
   .... ?
7. you / happened / What / to
   .... ?
8. Who / meal / for / the / paid
   .... ?

F Rewrite each sentence so that it has a similar meaning, using the word in brackets in a prepositional verb.

1 Can anyone think of a better idea? (come)
Can anyone come up with a better idea?

2 Whose bag is this? (does)
....
....

3 Do you have the same opinion as her? (with)
....
....

4 Did you find my passport when you were tidying my room? (across)
....
....

5 I don't know whether to choose the black boots or the brown ones. (go)
....
....

6 That shirt doesn't match your jacket. (with)
....
....

7 I'll buy the tickets from him. (pay)
....
....

8 We discussed films for hours. (about)
....
....

MY TURN!

Complete the sentences using prepositional verbs so that they are true for you.

1 I never agree .... *with my brother.*
....

2 I often think ....
....

3 I get on well ....
....

4 I like talking ....
....

5 I always worry ....
....

6 I don't know much ....
....

7 I love learning ....
....

8 I'm looking forward ....
....

MY TEST!

Circle the correct option.

1 She's looking .... a job at the moment. **a** for **b** at **c** after
2 He got .... his bike and rode away. **a** off **b** on **c** into
3 Nobody could .... up with a better solution to the problem. **a** put **b** come **c** get
4 I stayed with a family in London last summer but I didn't get .... very well with them. **a** on **b** in **c** off
5 Who are you ....? **a** talking **b** talking of **c** talking to

My Test! answers: 1a 2b 3b 4a 5c

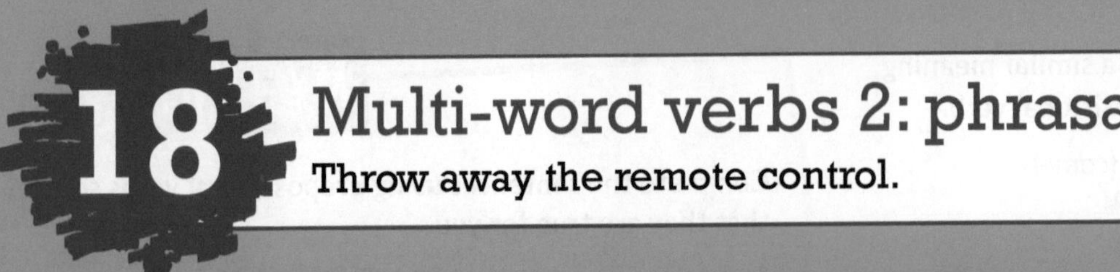

18 Multi-word verbs 2: phrasal verbs

Throw away the remote control.

Are these the 6 best ways to get fit?

1 Surprise your friends and **tidy up**. It uses a lot of energy to **pick up** all those clothes from under the bed.

2 Do you like chocolate? The good news is, you can still have chocolate! But why don't you **put on** your trainers and run to the shop to buy some?

3 Don't ask your parents to **pick** you **up**. Walking home with your friends is fun and gets you fit.

4 Put your alarm clock outside your bedroom door. When it **goes off**, run and **turn** it **off** … before it **wakes** everyone else **up**!

5 You don't have to **take up** a new sport to get fit. Just include sport in your weekend. Is there a swimming pool near you? **Find out** and go with your friends.

6 Are you someone who is always changing the TV programme? Why don't you **throw away** the remote control? And then **get up** to change the TV programme every ten minutes …

?
1 Do you do any of these things?
2 Which do you think is the best way of keeping fit?

Multi-word verbs 2: phrasal verbs

1 **Phrasal verbs have two words: verb + particle (usually an adverb). Some phrasal verbs have an object and some don't.**

__Put on__ your trainers.
Why don't you __find out__?

2 **Some phrasal verbs which we often use without an object are:**

break down	*go off*
come in / go in	*go on*
come on	*hurry up*
come out / go out	*lie down*
come over	*run away*
get away	*run out*
get in	*sit down*
get out	*stand up*
get up	*turn round*

3 **Some phrasal verbs which we usually use with an object are:**

look up	*take back*
make up	*take up*
pick up	*tell off*
put down	*throw away*
put on	*turn off / on*
set up	
take away	

4 **There are some verbs we can use in both ways.**

I __got back__ very late.
I went to the shop and __got__ my money __back__.

Other examples are:

find out	*turn down / up*
give up	*wake up*
take off	*wash up*
tidy up	

5 **If the phrasal verb takes an object, it can go before or after the particle.**

__Put on__ your trainers.
__Put__ your trainers __on__.

This is different from prepositional verbs.

▶ See Unit 17 point 4.

6 **If the object is a personal pronoun, it always comes before the particle.**

Put** them **on. NOT ~~*Put on them.*~~

TIP

There is often a one-word verb equivalent for phrasal verbs. The one-word verb is usually more formal than the prepositional verb.

come in = enter	*hold up = delay*
find out = discover	*run away = escape*

7 **Sometimes one verb can have more than one meaning.**

The alarm clock __goes off__ at 6 am. (= makes a loud noise)
There's a problem with the lights – they often __go off__. (= stop working)

They __turned up__ late. (= arrived)
Can you __turn__ the music __up__? (= make louder)

TIP

There are some nouns which are based on phrasal verbs, e.g.:

break-in	*lie-in*
breakdown	*printout*
check-out	*takeover*
hand-out	*turn-out*

▶ See Unit 17 for prepositional verbs.

Practice

A Complete the sentences using the verbs in the box.

get up   hurry up   stand up   ~~tidy up~~   turn off   wash up

The 6 best ways to annoy your brother:

1 ....Tidy up..... his bedroom.

2 .... every time he sits down.

3 .... really early and sing loudly in the bathroom.

4 Tell him to .... and then walk really slowly.

5 Ring his mobile phone and when he answers, ... it ....

6 Ask him to .... when the football's on TV.

B Match the sentence beginnings to the correct endings.

1 They heard a noise behind them and turned [h]
2 Will was late. He turned [ ]
3 The meeting went [ ]
4 They set the company [ ]
5 The car door was locked. I couldn't get [ ]
6 There's no more petrol – we've run [ ]
7 It was a really old car and it was always breaking [ ]
8 Hello! Can I come [ ]

a out.
b on for hours.
c up at 8.
d out.
e down.
f up last year.
g in?
h round.

C <u>Underline</u> the correct option.

1 I'll go <u>*in*</u> / *to* on Monday and speak to the teacher.
2 It was nice in the pool and Oscar didn't want to come *on* / *out*.
3 I get home quite early – I usually get *in* / *on* around 5.00.
4 Don't stand up if you can sit down. Don't sit down if you can lie *down* / *up*!
5 If the computer doesn't work, try turning the power *up* / *off* for a few minutes.
6 I can't wake *up* / *away* without coffee.
7 If you press this button, the light comes *in* / *on*.
8 I'd like to go *in* / *out* tonight. Is there a good film at the cinema?
9 The cat ran *away* / *over* when it saw the dog.
10 She put the cup *down* / *on*.

D Make sentences by putting the words in the correct order. Write two things that each pronoun could refer to.

1 tidy / up / it / Please
Please tidy it up.
'it' = your bedroom / the kitchen
....

2 make / up / it / I'll
....
....

3 Can / the Internet / it / up / you / look / on?
....
....
....

4 put / your head! / Don't / on / it
....
....
....

5 The / off / told / man / us
....
....

6 please? / Can / pick / you / that / up
....
....
....

7 going / back / them / to / take / I'm
....
....
....

8 up? / Can / it / turn / you
....
....

E **This email has been written in a hurry and seven object pronouns are missing. Write them in the correct places.**

You'll never guess what happened to me today. And I promise I'm not making *it* up! I was in the shop 'Hats and Things' at lunchtime. There was a tall woman in the shop. She was trying on hats. She picked up a blue one and put on. I remember thinking it looked good on her. I had tried on some gloves and was just taking off. The woman came over, picked up some gloves and put on too. Then she started looking at some bags. She dropped one on the floor by my feet. I bent down to pick up and when I turned round she was just going out. And she was still wearing the clothes! I ran out to stop her taking away, but then I felt someone's hand on my shoulder. It was the shop owner. I was still holding the bag! And he started telling off while the woman got away!

F **Complete the dialogues using the verbs in the box with the structure: verb + pronoun + particle.**

find out	get back	give up	pick up
~~take away~~	throw away	turn on	wake up

1 Waiter: How is your food?
Customer: I'm not very hungry. Can you *take it away*, please?

2 A: What's on TV tonight?
B: The Music Show. Quick! ....

3 A: I don't know the answer to this question.
B: No, let's see if we can ....

4 A: Mark has taken my shoes.
B: Come on! We'll go and ....

5 A: You haven't been to football practice for a long time.
B: No, I haven't got time. I'm going to ....

6 A: I don't know how I'm going to get home from the station.
B Don't worry – I'll ....

7 A: I don't like this mobile phone any more.
B: You can recycle that – don't ....

8 A: What time are you leaving in the morning?
B: At 6.30. Can you .... ?

MY TURN!

Write about ways to save the planet. Use a phrasal verb for each idea.

The 6 best ways to save the planet:

1 *Is there an environmental group near you? Find out and join!*

2 ....

3 ....

4 ....

5 ....

6 ....

MY TEST!

Circle the correct option.

1 We got home and turned .... the lights. a on b in c round

2 His alarm clock went .... at 7.00. a on b off c away

3 Can you .... later? a pick up me b pick me up c up me pick

4 The plane .... at 12.00. a took it off b took off it c took off

5 He never .... anything .... a throws ... away b throws ... off c throws ... up

My Test! answers: 1a 2b 3b 4c 5a

Verb + *to*-infinitive or *-ing*

He decided to run without shoes.

Abebe Bikila **began running** to school when he was very young but he couldn't **afford to buy** running shoes. So Bikila always ran without shoes. He **decided to run** without shoes in the 1960 Olympic marathon and **managed to win**. Bikila was first again in 1964 but he **failed to win** in 1968 because he had problems with his shoes!

Oprah Winfrey's parents were very poor and she had to live with her grandmother – she **remembers her grandmother hitting** her if she **didn't remember to do** the housework – but she **enjoyed reading** and soon **learned to write**. While she was still at school, Oprah **started to work** on the radio and today she is one of the most famous, and richest, women on American television.

John Grisham wrote his first book while he was working as a lawyer. He sent the book to many publishers but no one **wanted to take** it. Finally, a small publisher **agreed to buy** the book. The other publishers now **regret saying** no to Grisham because he has sold more than 250 million books.

?

1 How many Olympic marathons did Bikila win?
2 Was Oprah's first job on radio or television?
3 Does Grisham still write books?

Answers: 1 Two 2 Radio 3 Yes

Verb + *to*-infinitive or *-ing*

1 Some verbs take a *to*-infinitive, e.g. *ask to go*. Some verbs take an *-ing* form, e.g. *enjoy doing*. Some take both, e.g. *like to do / like doing*. There are no rules for this; you need to learn which verb takes a *to*-infinitive and which takes *-ing*.

2 These verbs take a *to*-infinitive:

afford	*Bikila couldn't* ***afford to buy*** *running shoes.*
agree	*They* ***agreed not to tell*** *Maggie.*
arrange	*They* ***arranged to meet*** *at 6.*
ask	***Ask to see*** *a doctor.*
decide	*Bikila* ***decided to run*** *without shoes.*
deserve	*Bikila* ***deserved to win*** *in 1960.*
fail	*Grisham* ***failed to find*** *a publisher.*
help	*Who* ***helped to make*** *it?*
learn	*Oprah soon* ***learned to write.***
manage	*Bikila* ***managed to win.***
need	*Do you* ***need to phone*** *Louis?*
promise	*You must* ***promise not to be*** *late.*
refuse	*Jan* ***refused to see*** *him.*
seem	*It* ***seems to be*** *a nice day.*
want	*No one* ***wanted to take*** *the book.*

3 These verbs take *-ing*:

admit	*The children* ***admitted not going*** *to the lesson.*
avoid	*You can't* ***avoid meeting*** *him.*
deny	*She* ***denied doing*** *anything wrong.*
enjoy	*Oprah* ***enjoyed reading.***
keep (on)	*Don't stop,* ***keep running!***
miss	*Do you* ***miss having*** *a dog?*
recommend	*Doctors* ***recommend eating*** *more fruit and vegetables.*
suggest	*I* ***suggest writing*** *her a nice email.*

4 These verbs take *to* or *-ing*, with very little difference in meaning:

begin	*Bikila* ***began to run / running*** *to school.*
continue	*Grisham* ***continues to write / writing*** *books.*
hate	*I* ***hate to get / getting*** *up early.*
like	*Susan* ***likes to wear / wearing*** *black.*
love	*Jack* ***loved to read / reading*** *in bed.*
prefer	*Most people* ***prefer to travel / travelling*** *by plane.*
start	*Oprah* ***started to work / working*** *on the radio.*

5 These verbs take *to* or *-ing*, but there is a difference in meaning:

need

need + ***to*** has an active meaning.

I ***need to go*** *home.*

need + ***-ing*** has a passive meaning.

My car ***needs cleaning.***

try

try + ***to*** = 'try, but you may not succeed'.

We've got a busy day tomorrow. ***Try to sleep.***

try + ***-ing*** means 'see how it works', or 'experience' something.

I ***tried sleeping*** *on the floor but it didn't help my back.*

regret

We use *regret* + *to* to give bad news in formal writing.

We ***regret to inform*** *you that your job application has been unsuccessful.*

We use *regret* + *-ing* for things in the past we are sorry about.

They ***regret saying*** *no to Grisham.*

remember **and** ***forget***

We use *remember* and *forget* + *to* for things we need to do.

I ***forgot to buy*** *some flowers.*

We use *remember* and *forget* + *-ing* for memories of the past.

Oprah ***remembers her grandmother hitting*** *her if she* ***didn't remember to do*** *the housework.*

stop

We use *stop* + *to* when we stop in order to do something.

I ***stopped to buy*** *some eggs.*

We use *stop* + *-ing* when we no longer do something.

Bikila ***stopped running*** *in 1971.*

TIP

Would like (short form: ***'d like***) + ***to*** is one way of saying *want* or *might want*. Use ***Would you like*** + ***to*** for a polite invitation.

I'd like to run *in the Olympics.*

Would you like to have *a coffee?*

Practice

A Write the verbs under the correct headings. Try to remember by yourself; if you can't, look at the lists on page 83.

~~afford~~ admit arrange avoid begin continue deny deserve enjoy fail hate help keep love manage miss prefer promise regret remember refuse seem suggest try would like

+ to	+ -ing	+ to or -ing
afford		

B <u>Underline</u> the correct option(s). Sometimes both options are possible.

1 Mike enjoys *to play* / <u>*playing*</u> golf.
2 Do we need *to bring* / *bringing* anything?
3 I never recommended *to do* / *doing* that.
4 Why didn't you ask Jonny *to come* / *coming*?
5 Start *to cook* / *cooking* the potatoes first.
6 Everything will be all right if you keep on *to work* / *working*.
7 Jane doesn't want *to become* / *becoming* a doctor like her mum.
8 I really miss *to have* / *having* a car.
9 Dogs don't like *to be* / *being* alone.
10 Would you like *to go* / *going* first?
11 I avoided *to see* / *seeing* her for a long time.
12 But we arranged *to meet* / *meeting*!

C Match the pairs.

1 I like — a to have a rich husband one day.
2 I'd like — b listening to the radio in the morning.

3 The mechanic needs — a to repair it.
4 The car needs — b repairing.

5 Dear Mr Jones, I regret — a to tell you that you have not passed.
6 Well, I regret — b not studying harder at school.

7 I don't remember — a to give the keys to Simon.
8 Please remember — b giving the keys to Simon.

9 I sat down and stopped — a thinking about it.
10 It's not important. Stop — b to think for a moment.

11 Don't forget — a to meet her at the station.
12 I will never forget — b meeting her for the first time.

D Circle the correct option.

Greg LeMond was the first American winner of the Tour de France cycle race. He decided [1]... a cyclist when he was still at school and [2]... to win a lot of prizes. LeMond missed [3]... to the Moscow Olympics in 1980 because of political problems between the USA and the USSR. Today he regrets [4]... the chance to win a gold medal.

LeMond won his first Tour de France in 1986 and his future seemed [5]... very good, but the next year LeMond had a terrible accident. He was accidentally shot in the back on a hunting trip and he needed [6]... a very serious operation. LeMond had [7]... to take part in the 1987 Tour de France but his doctors didn't recommend [8]... the hospital.

This was a tragedy but LeMond [9]... to retire from the sport and he kept [10]... he could return to cycling. Two years later he started [11]... again. In 1989 he dramatically won the Tour de France on the last day of the race, and he was the winner again in 1990.

LeMond stopped [12]... in 1994 and opened a sports business with his father.

1 a become b becoming (c) to become d to have become
2 a began b enjoyed c would like d remembered
3 a go b to go c going d having gone
4 a to lose b to have lost c to losing d having lost
5 a to be b to being c being d having been
6 a to have b have c having d had
7 a suggested b liked c denied d arranged
8 a to leave b leaving c not leaving d not to leaving
9 a denied b missed c refused d avoided
10 a believe b to believe c believing d belief
11 a train b trains c training d to training
12 a to cycle b cycle c having cycled d cycling

E Rewrite each sentence so that it has a similar meaning, using the verb in brackets.

1 Susan really likes shopping. (love)
Susan loves shopping.

2 Mick: Why don't you buy some flowers? (suggest)
....

3 Andy won't be able to finish all the work. (manage)
....

4 Steve wants to have a coffee. (would like)
....

5 Kate: I won't do it. (refuse)
....

6 Jo: I didn't steal the money. (deny)
....

7 Kay wanted to meet at 7.00. (arrange)
....

8 Maggie's hair is dirty. (need)
....

F Complete the news story using the words in the box and the correct form of the verbs in brackets.

arrange	continue	~~admit~~	forget	like	manage
prefer	remember	seem	would like		

Seventy-two-year-old Ruth Wilkes was surprised to find a zebra in her garden yesterday morning. The zebra ran away from Chester Zoo on Wednesday and the zoo [1] ....*admits being*........ (be) responsible. No one knows how the zebra got into Mrs Wilkes's garden.

Mrs Wilkes doesn't [2] .... (see) the zebra on Wednesday evening. She often [3] .... (take) a little walk in her garden in the morning and that is when she saw the zebra. Mrs Wilkes was shocked but she did [4] .... (phone) the zoo and they quickly came to help her.

'Well, it didn't [5] .... (be) dangerous,' said Mrs Wilkes, 'but I [6] .... (have) birds in the garden!'

The manager of Chester Zoo said, 'I [7] .... (apologise) to Mrs Wilkes. We will [8] .... (give) her and her grandchildren free tickets to the zoo.' But what about the zebra? 'I'm sure the zebra will never [9] .... (go) on its little holiday!'

Chester police [10] .... (investigate) the incident.

MY TURN!

Complete these sentences so that they are true for you.

1 I enjoy *watching horror films.*
2 I really hate ....
3 One day I would like ....
4 I sometimes forget ....
5 I've never tried ....
6 I can remember .... when I was very young.

MY TEST!

Circle the correct option.

1 Oprah wanted .... to college. a to go b going c either a or b
2 Did she promise her grandmother .... hard? a to study b studying c either a or b
3 I've always enjoyed .... a to run b running c either a or b
4 I suggested .... the Oprah Winfrey show. a to watch b watching c either a or b
5 Oprah wants to continue .... on TV. a to work b working c either a or b

My Test! answers: 1a 2a 3b 4b 5c

20 Verb + object + *to*-infinitive

Greg made the children work 60 hours a week.

Samuel Greg (1758–1834) had a clothes factory near Manchester. The industrial revolution in England **helped him become** very rich. Greg needed workers but he **wanted them to work** for little money, so he **invited children to work** for him. Soon half of his workers were children.

Greg **made the children work** 60 hours a week. There was nothing illegal or strange about this at that time. The law **let him employ** children as young as five years old. Greg **forced them to stay** in a special house for children and **warned them not to leave** without his permission. However, the house was quite comfortable and the children had enough to eat. Meat was expensive then but Greg **allowed the children to eat** meat on Sundays, and his wife, Hannah, **encouraged them to read** and write.

A new law in 1844 **ordered factories to stop** using child workers. Today, Greg's factory is a museum where you can **watch museum workers make** clothes in the traditional way, ask them questions and **hear them talk** about the hard times of the past.

?

1 Who was Samuel Greg?
   a a factory worker **b** a businessman **c** a teacher
2 How often did the children eat meat?
   a once a week **b** once a month **c** never

Answers: 1b 2a

Verb + object + *to*-infinitive

1 These verbs take an object and *to*:

advise	*I* ***advise you to study*** *history.*
allow	*Greg* ***allowed the children to eat*** *meat on Sundays.*
ask	*Don't* ***ask me to work*** *at the weekend!*
encourage	*Hannah* ***encouraged them to read.***
force	*Greg* ***forced them to stay*** *there.*
order	*The new law* ***ordered factories to stop*** *using children.*
persuade	*Please* ***persuade Alice to take*** *the job.*
invite	*He* ***invited children to work*** *for him.*
need	*The boss* ***needs me to do*** *it.*
remind	*Remind* ***Samuel to tell*** *Hannah about the meeting.*
teach	*She* ***taught them to read.***
tell	*Greg* ***told the children to go*** *to bed.*
warn	*He* ***warned them not to leave*** *the house.*
want	*Greg* ***wanted his workers to be*** *cheap.*

TIP

In speaking, *get* + object + *to* = *persuade*.
Get *Jack* ***to*** *help. He's not very busy.*

2 These verbs take an object and the infinitive without *to*:

feel	*I* ***felt his hand touch*** *my shoulder.*
hear	*Did you* ***hear him say*** *it?*
let	*The law* ***let him employ*** *five-year-olds.*
make	*Greg* ***made them work*** *hard.*
notice	*I didn't* ***notice the machine start.***
see	*Did you* ***see it happen****?*
watch	*You can* ***watch people make*** *clothes.*

3 *Help* can take *to* or the infinitive without *to* after the object.

It ***helped him (to) become*** *rich.*

TIP

There are no rules for which verbs take which forms. When you learn a new verb, learn also the form which it takes. A good dictionary will show this information.

remind /rɪˈmaɪnd/
▶ ***verb*** [T] **E** to make someone think of something they have forgotten: *Could you remind Paul* ***about*** *dinner on Saturday?* ○ [+ **to** INFINITIVE] *Please remind me* ***to*** *post this letter.* ○ [+ (**that**)] *I rang Jill and reminded her* ***(that)*** *the conference had been cancelled.*

Practice

A Match sentences 1–10 to sentences a–j which have the same meaning.

1 Sid asked Jo to do it.
2 Sid allowed Jo to do it.
3 Sid encouraged Jo to do it.
4 Sid made Jo do it.
5 Sid warned Jo not to do it.
6 Sid advised Jo to do it.
7 Sid taught Jo to do it.
8 Sid noticed Jo do it.
9 Sid reminded Jo to do it.
10 Sid helped Jo do it.

a Jo, I'll let you do it.
b Jo, you must do it!
c Jo, this is how you do it.
d Jo, I saw you do it!
e Jo, will you do it, please?
f Jo, you know you can do it!
g Jo, let's do it together.
h Jo, you shouldn't do it.
i Jo, it would be a good idea to do it.
j Jo, don't forget to do it!

1 ...e... 2 .... 3 .... 4 .... 5 ....
6 .... 7 .... 8 .... 9 .... 10 ....

B Underline the correct option.

1 My dad taught me <u>*to ride*</u> / *ride* a bike.
2 Lucy persuaded me *to buy* / *buy* the shoes.
3 Mum, please *let* / *make* me stay at Jane's on Friday night.
4 I could feel the car *to go* / *go* faster and faster.
5 Mr Green made Sam *to pay* / *pay* for the broken window.
6 A: Richard is really angry.
B: Get him *to sit* / *sit* down for five minutes.
7 Her grandmother warned her *not to get* / *not get* lost in the forest.
8 The captain ordered the soldiers *to run* / *run* back to the camp.
9 Did you hear John *to say* / *say* that?
10 My parents always encouraged me *to play* / *play* the piano.

C What does each text say? Tick a, b or c.

1

Children are not allowed
to play ball-games

a It tells children not to play football. ✓
b It encourages children to play football.
c It lets children play football.

2

Rob,
Don't forget to
get the flowers!
Sarah

a Sarah promises Rob to buy some flowers.
b Sarah advises Rob to buy some flowers.
c Sarah reminds Rob to buy some flowers.

3

MEMO
Thanks for the message.
It's a lot of money but I'll
make John pay the bill
this week.
Sandra.

a Sandra promises to pay John the money.
b Sandra will pay the money instead of John.
c Sandra will tell John to pay the money.

4

Please let old people
sit here.

a It makes old people sit in this place.
b It gets bus passengers to offer this place to old people.
c It doesn't allow young people to sit in this place.

5

Lesley,
We would love you
and Max to come to
our party on Saturday
at 7pm.
Love, David

a David orders Lesley and Max to go to a party.
b David invites Lesley and Max to go to a party.
c David reminds Lesley and Max to go to a party.

6

DANGER
DO NOT
ENTER

a It warns people not to go inside.
b It encourages people to go inside.
c It forces people to go inside.

D Complete the text using the verbs in the box and the correct form of the verbs in brackets

advise ask force ~~invite~~ help let need see tell warn

The famous biologist Doctor Singh has written a new book called *You Are What You Eat*. We decided to [1] ...*invite*... the doctor ...*to come*... (come) to our studio so that we could [2] .... him .... (answer) a few questions about the book.

Doctor Singh says he wrote the book to [3] .... teenagers not .... (eat) unhealthy food, but does he [4] .... his children .... (go) to fast-food restaurants? 'Sometimes,' he laughs. 'You can't [5] .... children .... (do) everything you want. I [6] .... them .... (be) sensible and not eat there every day!'

The next question: Do vegetables really [7] .... teenagers .... (grow) faster? 'It's not as simple as that,' he says. 'But it's true that teenagers don't eat enough of them. When I do my research in school canteens, I don't often [8] .... teenagers .... (choose) vegetables. Maybe we [9] .... teachers .... (talk) to teenagers about this.

Last question: Does Doctor Singh [10] .... teenagers who eat too much .... (go) on a diet? 'Usually, the problem is not eating too much but eating the wrong food. If teenagers eat sensibly, there is no need for a diet.'

E Samuel Greg wrote some instructions for his wife. Complete the sentences about what Hannah did.

1 Some children play football next to the factory windows. Stop them!
...*Hannah didn't allow the children to play football.*...
2 Charles must clean the machines.
Hannah made ....
3 Nancy can visit her mother on Saturday.
Hannah let ....
4 It would be nice if the workers had a bath on Sunday.
Hannah encouraged ....
5 Robert must remember to do his Latin homework.
Hannah reminded ....
6 Emily still doesn't know how to use the new machine.
Hannah taught ....
7 Jonas has to paint the walls.
Hannah ordered ....
8 Ask Lady Grey to come to tea next Friday.
Hannah invited ....

F Complete sentences 1–8 using information from the text. What do you think is going on?

It was terrible and Graham was in shock. Graham sent a text to Amanda: [1]'Phone me!' [2] His heart was beating very fast as he explained everything to her. [3]'Amanda, come round, please!' he said at the end.

Graham looked out of the window [4]so he could see Amanda as she drove to the house. She came in and [5]took off her coat, with Graham's help. Graham's room was a complete mess with cupboards open, things on the floor and clothes everywhere.

[6]'Don't panic, it will make things worse,' said Amanda. [7]'Sit down and think.' Amanda was looking at the chaos in the room when [8]she saw that Graham had started to cry.

See below for the end of the story.

1 Graham wanted .... Amanda to phone him.
2 He felt ....
3 He asked ....
4 He watched ....
5 He helped ....
6 Amanda warned ....
7 She told ....
8 She noticed ....

MY TURN!

Do you think you will be a good parent? Write sentences about what you will *allow, make, ask,* etc. your own teenage children (to) do.

1 I will let them stay up late sometimes.
2 ....
3 ....
4 ....
5 ....
6 ....

MY TEST!

Circle the correct option.

1 Greg made them .... hard. a work b to work
2 He didn't let the children .... games. a play b to play
3 Greg didn't allow the children .... a leave b to leave
4 Hannah advised Greg .... a new factory. a open b to open
5 Did Greg notice the boy .... the machine? a break b to break

My Test answers: 1a 2a 3b 4b 5a

Exercise F: The end of the story.
'Don't worry,' Amanda said. 'I'll help you choose what to wear to the party.' 'Oh thank you, Amanda!' cried Graham. 'You're a great friend!'

21 Linking verbs: *be*, *get*, *feel*, etc.

It looks a bit yellow but it tastes great.

organic

Most food is grown or made with chemicals so that it **stays fresh** for longer or **looks nicer**. But organic food **is natural** – it has no chemicals. Only about 2% of food **is organic** but it is **getting more popular**. We asked three teenagers to try organic food and see what they think.

'Lovely! It **smells** really nice but it **doesn't keep** fresh so long. I bought some last week but it **went sour** after one day.'

Diego, 13, Italy

'I can't see the difference between this and a normal banana, so why is the organic one more expensive? It **seems strange** to me.'

Bom-i, 15, Korea

'It **looks a bit yellow** but it **tastes great**. It**'s** nice to think these eggs **are not from chickens** that live in factories.'

Kirsten, 14, Scotland

? Match the people to the opinions:

1 Kirsten	a Organic food doesn't last a long time.
2 Diego	b Organic food is a waste of money.
3 Bom-i	c Organic food is kinder for animals.

Answers: 1c 2a 3b

Linking verbs: *be*, *get*, *feel*, etc.

1 A linking verb links a noun or a pronoun with an adjective or noun. The most common linking verb is *be*.

*Organic food **is natural**.*
***Is** it **a banana**?*

2 Some linking verbs describe things that change (*become, get, go, grow, turn*) or stay the same (*keep, remain, stay*).

*The milk **turned** green.*
*Organic food **stays** fresher for longer.*

3 Some verbs of change are used in special ways.

We use *turn* and *go* with colours. *Go* is more informal.

*The sky **turned** / **went** black.*

Go describes bad changes.

*The milk **went** bad.*

We use *get* or *become*, not *go*, with *old, tired* and *ill.*

*She **becomes** / **gets** tired very quickly.* NOT ~~*... goes ...*~~

4 We can often use either *get* or *become*. *Get* is more common and informal.

*Organic food is **getting** / **becoming** more popular.*

Become, not *get*, can be followed by a noun when it is a linking word.

*I **became** a student.* NOT ~~*I got a student.*~~

Use *get*, not *become*, in imperatives, and for shorter processes.

***Get** dressed!* NOT ~~*Become dressed!*~~
*Could you please **get** ready on time?* NOT ~~*... become ready ...*~~

▶ See Units 33 and 34 for *get* in passives and *get* as a causative verb.

5 Some linking verbs describe senses, e.g. *appear, feel, look, seem, smell, sound, taste.*

*This milk **smells** bad.*
*It **tastes** great.*

TIP

Note the difference:

*He **looked** strange.*
(*Look* describes a sense, so it is a linking verb followed by an adjective.)

*He **looked** at me strangely.*
(*Look* is an action, so it is followed by an adverb.)

6 Use *What does it look / feel /* etc. *like ...?* or *What is it like?* to ask questions about the senses. The answer has a linking verb and an adjective, or a linking verb + *like* and a noun.

*A: **What does she look like?** B: She's tall and slim.*
*A: **What does it taste like?** B: It's **like** a lemon.*
*A: **What's your new bike like?** B: It's great!*
*A: **What's Birmingham like?** B: It's **like** Manchester.*

TIP

We often ask about the weather with *What + be + the weather like?*

*A: **What's the weather like?***
B: It's cold and it's raining.

7 Prepositional verbs with *like*, e.g. *look like, smell like* etc. mean *resemble*. They are followed by a noun.

*I **look like** my father.*
*It **feels like** winter.*

8 A few descriptive verbs, e.g. *lie, fall, sit* and *stand*, can sometimes be linking verbs.

*I **lay awake**.*
*Mike **fell** ill.*

9 All linking verbs can be followed by an adjective, but *be, become, feel, look, remain, stay* and *sound* can also be followed by nouns.

*I **felt** foolish / a fool.*
*It **looks** nice / a nice day.*
*We **stayed** friendly / friends.*

TIP

Some adjectives (e.g. some beginning with *a-*, like *afraid, alive, alone, asleep, awake*, and *ill* and *well*) are usually used after linking verbs, especially *be*.

*The baby **is asleep**.*
*I don't **feel well**.*

Practice

A Underline the correct option.

1 This room smells / tastes strange.
2 Wayne *goes* / *keeps* fit by running every morning.
3 Do you think I *feel* / *look* all right in this dress?
4 Jack *went* / *remained* very red when he understood his mistake.
5 The plan *turned* / *went* wrong.
6 Don't eat those tomatoes, they *taste* / *grow* strange.
7 That *seems* / *is* OK, but I'm not sure.
8 The start of the test was easy but it soon *stayed* / *grew* very difficult.
9 What *feels* / *is* summer like in your country?
10 A: What does his new album sound like?
B: It *sounds like* / *sounds* very different.

B Complete the sentence about each picture using one linking verb and one adjective from the box.

difficult	lovely	seem	smell	sound	terrible

1 He ....!

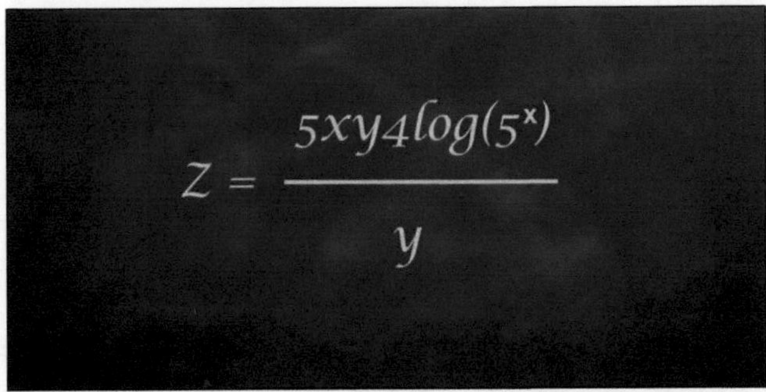

2 It ....

3 They ....

C Complete the sentences with *become* or *get*. Sometimes both are possible.

1 Have you always wanted to ......become...... a pilot?
2 After you .... dressed, brush your teeth.
3 It may .... dirty.
4 Who wants to .... a millionnaire?
5 I want to .... rich.
6 You need to .... changed quickly.
7 It might .... a problem if we do nothing.
8 I started to .... interested in Spanish literature.

D Circle the correct option.

Steve: Welcome everyone! [1]... ready for a very interesting show tonight with our special guest, Sue Timms, an organic farmer.
Sue: Hi, Steve. It feels [2]... to be on the programme.
Steve: Sue, why did you [3]... an organic farmer? To many of our listeners, it might [4]... a strange decision.
Sue: Well, it might appear [5]... to you but it just seemed [6]... to grow more healthy food. It's good for my farm and good for my customers.
Steve: Some people still [7]... unsure about organic food. They say it only gives farmers more profit, and only rich people can afford it.
Sue: Well, prices [8]... lower, slowly. As the market [9]... bigger, prices should fall. I really think the taste of my food is better.
Steve: Just before the programme, I [10]... tasted some of your milk, and, you're right, it tasted [11]... !
Sue: You'll never [12]... ill if you have a glass of my milk every morning!
Steve: Thanks for coming on the show, Sue!

1 a become (b) Get c be d Stay
2 a good b well c nicely d best
3 a get b be c turn d become
4 a become b go c appear d make
5 a stranger b strange c strangely d strangest
6 a a good idea b rightly c well d being right
7 a get b remain c become d be
8 a are getting b are c are turning d are seeming
9 a is b stays c keeps d grows
10 a quicker b quick c quickly d quickest
11 a greater b great c greatly d greatest
12 a seem b go c turn d fall

E Answer the questions using the verbs in brackets.

1 How do I look? (look)
You look great!

2 What do you want to do when you leave school / university? (become)

3 What's wrong with you? (feel)

4 Why don't you eat the salad? (look)

5 Did you hear about the man who bit a dog yesterday?! (sound)

6 Is the weather still cold? (get)

7 What does a cold shower feel like? (feel)

8 Who do you look like? (look)

F Complete the sentences and add explanations.

1 Ruth fell asleep in the concert. It was so boring.

2 John feels .

3 Her new friend seems .

4 The weather is turning .

5 Life in big cities is getting .

6 Not many young people want to become .

MY TURN!

Solve the riddles, then write two of your own using linking words.

1 People like to drink it but it doesn't taste good or bad. It gets hot and cold.

Water

2 **They are green but they turn yellow and brown in autumn.**

3 It stays the same but it looks bigger or smaller every night.

4 .

5 .

MY TEST!

Circle the correct option.

1 That sandwich looks .... a nice b nicely
2 Organic food .... popular. a is seeming b is growing
3 Tracy .... ready to go to the restaurant. a got b became
4 Does it taste .... ? a good b well
5 I .... green when I realised what I had eaten. a got b went

My Test! answers: 1a 2b 3a 4a 5b

Answers: 2 Leaves 3 The Moon

R3 Review: questions; multi-word verbs; verb structures

A Complete the questions.

1 A: How long have you had that jacket?
B: Oh, about six months.
2 A: .... did your jacket cost?
B: I don't know. It was a present.
3 A: .... gave it to you?
B: My aunt.
4 A: .... did you get those shoes?
B: From a shop in London.
5 A: .... size are your shoes?
B: I think they're size 36.
6 A: .... tall are you?
B: 1 metre 65.
7 A: .... do you go shopping?
B: Two or three times a week.
8 A: I've got these two hats. .... one do you think suits me best?
B: Oh, I think the blue one.
9 A: .... bag is this?
B: It's mine.
10 A: .... can't you go out tonight?
B: Because I've got lots of homework.

B Complete each sentence with the correct question tag.

1 It's been a lovely day, hasn't it ?
2 There were about 20 people there, ... ?
3 I'm getting better at this, ... ?
4 I'll ring you later, ... ?
5 Everyone's happy, ... ?
6 I haven't forgotten anything, ... ?
7 He won't come back now, ... ?
8 It's still quite early, ... ?
9 Jessica plays basketball well, ... ?
10 Give me a chance, ... ?
11 We have to be really careful, ... ?
12 He really shouldn't talk like that, ... ?
13 They've got a serious problem, ... ?
14 You'll be going on holiday soon, ... ?
15 He can't be serious about that, ... ?

C Complete the short answers.

1 A: I love chocolate.
B: Mmm, yes. I do too .
2 A: Have you read that book?
B: Yes, I ....
3 A: I can't swim very well.
B: Oh, neither ....
4 A: Should I say sorry to Mrs Porter?
B: Yes, I think ....
5 A: I've never been in a big ship.
B: .... either.
6 A: Will Helen be at home?
B: No, she ....
7 A: You played really well in that game.
B: So ....
8 A: Did you have time to watch that film?
B: No, I ....
9 A: I don't think English is all that difficult.
B: .... I.
10 A: I'm not very happy about what we have to do next week.
B: Me ....
11 A: I should make a telephone call.
B: So ....
12 A: Were you thinking of playing basketball this weekend?
B: No, I ....
13 A: My mobile phone takes great photos.
B: Mine ....
14 A: Would you like to learn another language?
B: Yes, I ....
15 A: I'm never going back to that shop.
B: I'm ....

D Put the word in brackets in the correct place in each sentence. Sometimes more than one answer is possible.

1 Can you wake ^me up at 7 o'clock tomorrow, please? (me)
2 I need to look up in a dictionary. (this word)
3 I love parties and I'm really looking forward to. (it)
4 They were talking too much in class and the teacher told off. (them)

5 I don't believe you. You've just made up. (that)

6 I've decided to give up. (chocolate)

7 The music's quite loud. Maybe we should turn down. (it)

8 Irma is really good at dealing with. (problems)

9 There's no point keeping this old mobile. I'll just throw away. (it)

10 Yan is always coming up with. (strange ideas)

11 Can you turn off when you leave the room? (the light)

12 If the jacket's the wrong size, you can just take back to the shop. (it)

E Complete the questions with the correct prepositions and match the questions to appropriate replies.

1 Where do you come from ?
2 Who does this belong .... ?
3 Who are you waiting .... ?
4 What do you want to talk .... ?
5 What are you looking .... ?
6 What are you listening .... ?
7 Who do you look .... ?
8 Who would you like to speak .... ?
9 Who do you agree .... ?
10 What are you smiling .... ?

a Well, I've got my mum's eyes.
b I'd like to ask you for some advice.
c My keys. I'm sure I left them here.
d It's mine.
e Kathy. But only if she's free.
f Well, I think you're all wrong.
g Well, I was born and grew up in India.
h I just feel happy, that's all.
i My friend. He'll be here soon.
j It's classical music, actually.

F Complete the sentences using the correct form (infinitive with *to* or *-ing*) of the verbs in brackets.

1 I can't afford to go on holiday at the moment. (go)
2 Fatima recommended .... the tomato soup. (try)
3 Alfie promised .... me an email next week. (send)
4 This note is to remind me .... the book to the library tomorrow. (take)
5 I'm sure Rory will deny .... the window. (break)
6 I regret .... to Portugal when I had the chance. (not go)
7 The police are warning people .... because of the extreme weather. (not drive)
8 She seems .... a very nice person. (be)
9 My company allowed me .... a few extra days' holiday. (take)
10 Fiona admitted .... a big mistake. (make)
11 The classroom really needs .... very soon. (tidy)

G Circle the correct option.

I'm Irish and I've always lived in Ireland but a couple of years ago I [1]... very interested in Japanese culture, so when my dad suggested going there on holiday it sounded [2]... a really good idea. So, last April we – that's my parents, my seven-year-old brother Charlie and me – flew to Tokyo. At first, everything [3]...amazing. It all [4]... so different from Ireland – the people, the language, the shops, and the food, which we'd been a bit nervous about, tasted [5]... . But after about three days my dad [6]... ill with a stomach infection and he didn't want to leave the hotel. Also, Charlie [7]... tired of going round Tokyo, so my mum suggested that we should visit a special children's theme park called Kidzania. At first I [8]... afraid it would only be suitable for small children but I was pleased we went in the end. What happens is you choose a job, you [9]... dressed up in the clothes of that job and you act it out, so you can [10]... like you are really doing that job. Charlie, for example, [11]... a pilot – well, he wore a pilot's clothes and pretended to fly a plane, while I chose to be a doctor. I felt a bit [12]... at first, but in the end I had a really good time. It's definitely one of the best things to do in Tokyo.

1 a went b looked (c) became d turned
2 a what b like c as d so
3 a kept b stood c was d went
4 a became b stayed c got d seemed
5 a great b greatly c greater d greatest
6 a appeared b fell c went d stayed
7 a went b got c remained d turned
8 a seemed b stood c came d was
9 a keep b appear c get d become
10 a sound b taste c seem d feel
11 a became b got c went d did
12 a strangely b fool c embarrassed d shame

Articles

A famous code

CREDIT CARD
0977 6965 9005 4597
VALID FROM
10/10
UNTIL END
01/13
MR M E HAYS

People have used codes to send secret messages since Roman times. But codes are not just something used by Julius Caesar or **a** spy. People today use codes every time they pay for something by credit card or send **an** email to **a** friend. Codes protect our personal information.

Before computers, **the** biggest users of codes were governments, who used them particularly in war. **The** ancient Greeks sent and received messages using **a** *scytale*, **a** cylinder made of wood. **An** officer would put cloth around **the** cylinder and write **a** message along it. When he took **the** cloth off, **the** writing appeared to mean nothing. But **the** officer who received **the** cloth had **a** similar cylinder and could easily read **the** message.

Julius Caesar used **a** simple system to communicate with his army. Instead of writing **the** letter A, he would write D (+3 letters). (See **the** key below.)

CODE LETTERS:	D	E	F	G	H	I	J	K	L	M	N	O	P	Q	R	S	T	U	V	W	X	Y	Z	A	B	C
MESSAGE LETTERS:	A	B	C	D	E	F	G	H	I	J	K	L	M	N	O	P	Q	R	S	T	U	V	W	X	Y	Z

Use **the** key to help you understand this message:

Computer security systems today are not so different from **the** one Caesar used. But **the** keys are much bigger and there are billions of possibilities for each letter or number.

?
1 What does the message say?
2 Do you ever use code?

Answers: 1 Caesar was here.
2 Yes, when you send an email to a friend.

Articles

A / an

1 Use ***a / an*** with singular countable nouns.
a friend, an email, a message

2 Use ***a / an*** to talk about something that the listener or the reader doesn't know about yet.
*The Ancient Greeks sent and received messages using **a** scytale.*

3 Use ***a*** before a consonant sound and ***an*** before a vowel sound.
Note: it is the sound not the letter that is important!
We say ***a house*** /ə haʊs/ but ***an hour*** /ən 'aʊə/. (***Hour*** begins with a vowel sound.)
We say ***an umbrella*** /ən ʌm'brelə/ but ***a university*** /ə ˌjuːnɪ'vɜːsəti/. (***University*** begins with a consonant sound.)

4 Use ***a / an*** to talk about professions and to describe what something or someone is.
*She's **a** spy.*
*It's **a** cylinder made of wood.*
*It's **a** secret code.*

5 ***A / an*** can mean ***every*** in expressions of time or quantity.
*once **a** day, 100 miles **an** hour*

6 We can use the expression ***What a ...!*** when we are surprised, angry or excited about something.
*What **a** terrible day!*

We use ***What ...!*** (with no article) for plural or uncountable nouns.
***What** terrible weather! **What** smart shoes!*

The

7 Use ***the*** with singular and plural countable nouns and uncountable nouns.
***the** officer, **the** officers, **the** information*

8 Use ***the*** when the listener or reader knows what the speaker or writer is talking about.
*Give me **the** money.* (The speaker or writer does not explain which money he or she is talking about. The listener or reader already knows.)

9 Use ***the*** when the speaker specifies what or who they are talking about.
***the** key below, **the** woman with the curly hair*

10 Use ***the*** with things that are the only ones around us, or that are unique.
***the** sun, **the** planets, **the** sky*

11 ***The*** is used in a number of expressions referring to the world around us or things that we all know about.
***the** mountains, **the** city, **the** universe, **the** government, **the** Internet*

12 ***The*** comes before superlatives.
***the** most popular film, **the** highest mountain*

13 Use ***the*** when you talk about well-known groups of people.
***the** police, **the** Chinese, **the** young*

No article

> **TIP**
> With seasons, we can use ***the*** or no article.
> *in summer / in the summer*
> ***In the summer*** can also mean ***next summer.***

14 We use no article with plural or uncountable nouns when we are talking about things in general.
Codes** protect our **personal information.
***Life** is difficult sometimes.*

Compare with:
*On this website you can find out about **the** codes used in World War II.*
*She had **a** wonderful life.*

15 Most names of people and places have no article.
Jackie** lives on **King Street.
*The offices are in **Johannesburg** in **South Africa.***

16 We use ***the*** with the names of a few countries.
***the** UK, **the** USA, **the** Netherlands*

We also use ***the*** with island groups, oceans and names of rivers.
***the** Philippines, **the** Atlantic, **the** Thames*

17 Meals, months, days and special times of the year do not usually take an article.
I never eat breakfast.
I visit my family on New Year's Day.

18 There is no article with words like ***these, my, us.***
Your coat is a beautiful colour. NOT ~~*The your coat ...*~~

> **TIP**
> Articles are often omitted in newspaper headlines, mobile phone text messages and Internet chatrooms.
> POLICE CATCH SPY
> c u at park

Practice

A <u>Underline</u> **the correct option.**

1. You need *<u>a hammer</u> / hammer* to fix that.
2. It's *a beautiful country / the beautiful country.*
3. *The Amur leopard / Amur leopard* is one of *the most endangered / most endangered* animals *in the world / in world.*
4. *The Diwali / Diwali* is a Hindu celebration *in October or November / in the October or the November.*
5. Use *water / the water* in the bottle.
6. My aunt and uncle love *a sun / the sun*! They stay *in UK / in the UK* in summer and visit friends *in Australia / in the Australia* in winter.
7. It's *an old car / the old car*, but I love it and it's *only car / the only car* I have!
8. Stephen Hawking wrote *A Brief History of the Time / Time.*

B Complete the sentences with the nouns from the box. Add *a, an* or *the* if necessary.

aunt government hour ~~lunch~~ Mondays safe water Romans Canada

1. I had ......lunch...... before you came.
2. 884 million people in the world do not have enough ....
3. He runs for .... every day.
4. .... were in Britain for over 350 years.
5. She visits on ....
6. My sister's baby was born this morning, so I'm now ....
7. .... has introduced some new laws on factory waste.
8. My friends want to go to a summer school in ....

C Make sentences by putting the words in the correct order. Add *a, an* or *the* if necessary.

1. smile / got / She's / nice
   She's got a nice smile.
2. Dr Hammond / good / me / gave / advice
   ....
3. country / like / you / living / Do / in
   .... ?
4. house / What / untidy
   .... !
5. We / school / planets / about / at / are / learning
   ....
6. moon / Earth / round / Why / go / does
   .... ?
7. This / runs / electricity / car / on
   ....
8. bed / on / your / Put / coat
   ....

D Write full versions of these text messages, including *a* and *the* where necessary.

1
Hi.
Have U got tickets?

Hi. Have you got the tickets?

2
Yes. Got them 4 film at 3.
What time U get here?

....

3
At 2.
Didn't have lunch.
U hungry?

....

4
Yes let's eat b4 film.

....

5
OK.
Where's best café?

....

6
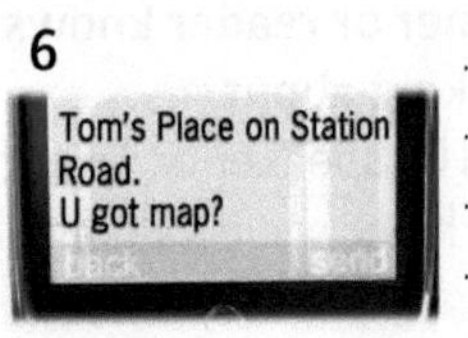

Tom's Place on Station Road.
U got map?

....

7

....

Got one from Internet. C U there.

E Complete this text about famous codes with *a, the* or – (= no article). Sometimes more than one answer is possible.

In 1897, Edward Elgar, [1] ...*a*... British composer, sent [2] .... message in code to [3] .... 23-year-old friend, Miss Dora Penny. [4] .... message is still [5] .... mystery. [6] .... famous author, Edgar Allan Poe, often included [7] .... codes in [8] .... his poems and [9] .... writing. In 1839, [10] .... Poe asked [11] .... readers of [12] .... magazine to send him [13] .... messages in code. [14] .... 150 years later, two of [15] .... codes were still not solved.

The first of [16] .... these codes was finally solved in 1992. Around this time, [17] .... Williams College in [18] .... USA offered $2,500 to [19] .... person who could solve [20] .... final code. [21] .... website was also set up. [22] .... competition attracted [23] .... worldwide interest. [24] .... engineer, Gil Broza, finally solved it in [25] .... October 2000.

F Rewrite each sentence so that it has a similar meaning, using the word in brackets.

1 She studies at university. (a)
She's a university student.
2 That boy has a famous father. (with)
....
3 He's been working with young people for ten years. (the)
....
4 The journey was terrible. (What)
....
5 Her house is lovely – it's by the sea. (lives)
....
6 The potatoes cost £1 for one kilo. (a)
....
7 No one in my class is taller than me. (I'm)
....
8 He speaks very quietly. (voice)
....

In your notebook, write answers to the questions, using *a, an, the* or no article in each answer. Answer five questions truthfully, but write an untrue answer for the other three.

1 What's your favourite food? *My favourite food is salad.*
2 How often do you brush your teeth?
3 What colour and type of car would you like to have?
4 What does your mum do?
5 Where do you live?
6 Which do you prefer: mountains, city or sea?
7 Where would you like to go on holiday next?
8 What's your favourite time of year?

Show your answers to a friend or to your teacher. Can they guess which answers are not true?

MY TEST!

Circle the correct option.

1 Mt Kilimanjaro is .... highest mountain in Africa. a the b a c –
2 I watched .... interesting programme yesterday. a a b the c an
3 We eat in a restaurant once .... month. a a b an c the
4 Have you called .... police? a – b the c a
5 I love .... pasta for .... dinner. a the / the b a / a c – / –

My Test! answers: 1a 2c 3a 4b 5c

23 Quantifiers 1

Anything can happen in the mountains.

You need to be prepared to go mountain climbing. You can't carry **everything** with you but these are **some** things that you may need.

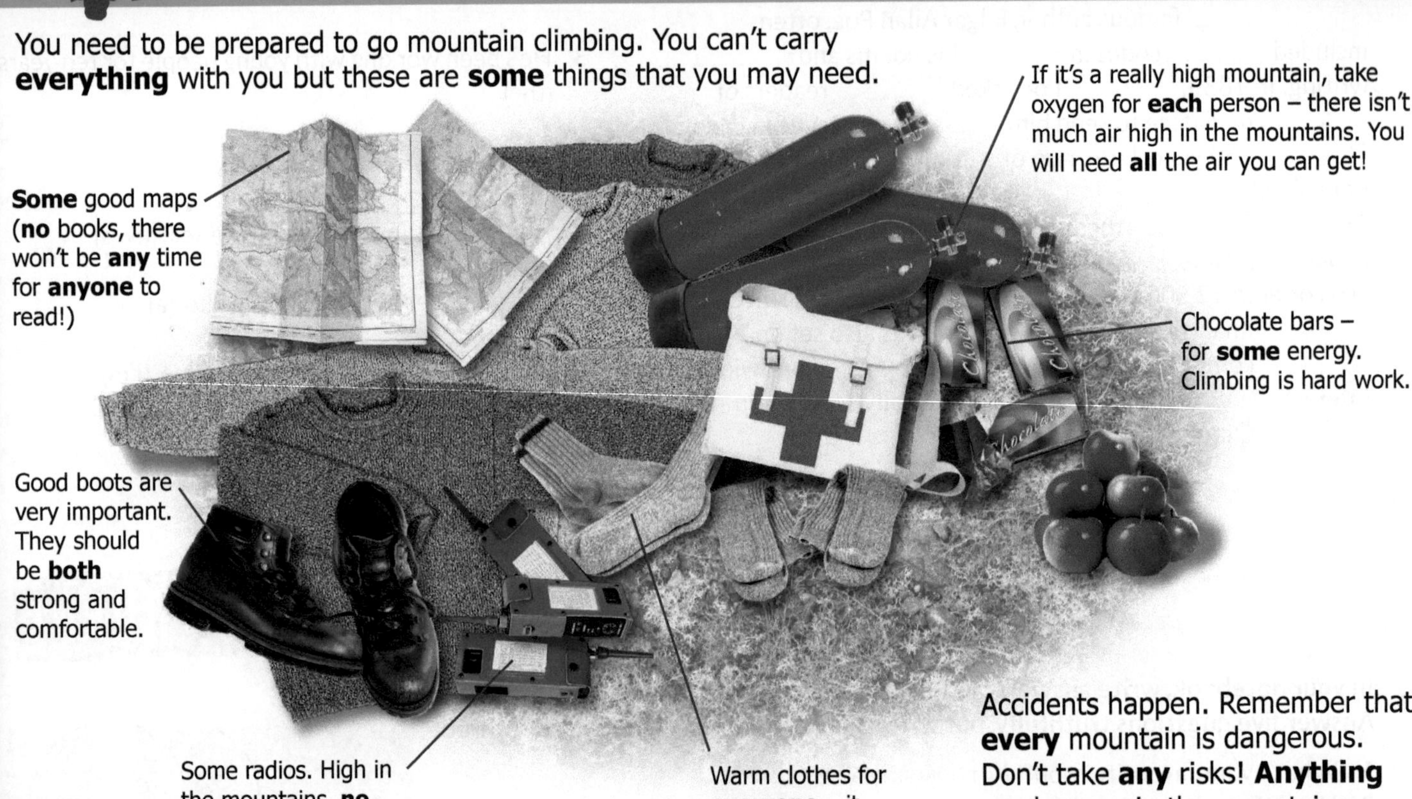

Some good maps (**no** books, there won't be **any** time for **anyone** to read!)
If it's a really high mountain, take oxygen for **each** person – there isn't much air high in the mountains. You will need **all** the air you can get!
Chocolate bars – for **some** energy. Climbing is hard work.
Good boots are very important. They should be **both** strong and comfortable.
Some radios. High in the mountains, **no one** will hear you shout for help ...
Warm clothes for **everyone** – it could be very cold at the top.

Accidents happen. Remember that **every** mountain is dangerous. Don't take **any** risks! **Anything** can happen in the mountains.

? Cover the picture.
Which three things in this list are <u>not</u> in the picture?
jumpers, first aid kit, books, maps, chocolate, rice, oxygen tanks, pens, radios

Answer: books, pens, rice

Quantifiers 1

1 Use quantifiers, e.g. *some, any*, or numbers to say how many or much of something there is.
every night, some mountains, not any books

2 Countable nouns are nouns we can count. They have singular and plural forms. Use *a* or *an* before a singular noun.
a mountain, an apple, a woman

Use quantifiers or nothing before a plural noun.
some mountains, two apples, women

3 Uncountable nouns often refer to materials, liquids, abstract or general concepts. Uncountable nouns are singular – they don't usually have plural forms. Don't use *a* or *an* before uncountable nouns – use quantifiers or nothing.
some metal, no rain, freedom, time

TIP

Some nouns which are uncountable in English may be countable in your own language.
In English, these nouns are uncountable:

accommodation	*knowledge*	*pasta*
advice	*luggage*	*traffic*
homework	*money*	*transport*
information	*music*	*news*

Can I have some information?
NOT ~~*... some informations*~~*?*
The news is bad. NOT ~~*The news are ...*~~

4 **Some nouns can be both countable and uncountable, with a difference in meaning.**

wood (uncountable = the material),
a wood (countable = a small forest)
coffee (uncountable = the substance),
a coffee (countable = a cup of coffee)
hair (uncountable), *a hair* (countable = one hair)

Other examples are:

danger	*paper*	*thought*
experience	*room*	*time*
glass	*tea*	*work*
life		

5 **Use the quantifiers *all, both, each* and *every* to describe everything in a set.**

all *the air,* ***both*** *mountains,* ***every*** *night*

6 ***Both*** **= A + B. Use *both* either before or after nouns, but only after pronouns.**

Lucy and Roger ***both*** *like climbing.*
OR ***Both*** *Lucy and Roger like climbing.*
They ***both*** *like climbing.*

7 ***Each*** **and *every* often have the same meaning but we usually use *every* when we talk about all of a big set, and *each* when we talk about people or things separately. Only *each* is possible when there are two people or things.**

She has been to ***every*** *country in Europe.*
Wash ***each*** *shoe in warm water.*

TIP

All day answers the question 'How long?'.
Every day answers the question 'How often?'.

It rained ***all day*** *on Sunday.*
I run ***every day.***

8 **Use *some* to describe small quantities. We usually use *some* in statements.**

You need ***some*** *warm clothes.*
Some of *us want to climb Everest.*

We can use *some* in questions when we expect the answer 'yes', especially for offers, requests and suggestions.

Fred, do you want ***some*** *cake?*

9 **We usually use *any* instead of *some* in questions and negatives with plural nouns or pronouns, or uncountable nouns.**

Have you got ***any*** *sugar?*
There won't be ***any*** *time to read.*

10 **We can use *any* in statements to mean 'it doesn't matter which one'.**

I'm free all day. Ring me ***any*** *time.*

11 ***Either*** **= A or B.** ***Neither*** **= not A and not B.**

Take ***either*** *bag.*
... ***neither of*** *the maps ...*

Don't use a second negative after *neither, never, no one*, etc.

Neither *phone works.* NOT ~~*Neither phone doesn't work.*~~

12 **We can use *both ... and, either ... or, neither ... nor* to join nouns, other kinds of words, phrases and even sentences.**

They should be ***both*** *strong* ***and*** *comfortable.*
You can ***either*** *come with me* ***or*** *stay at home.*

13 ***No*** **means the same as *not any* but is often more emphatic. *None of* refers to a set.**

There are ***no*** *shops on Everest.*
None *of them.*

14 ***Both, each, some, any, either, neither*** **and *none* can be pronouns. They can be followed by *of*.**

I bought ***some****. Do you want* ***any****?*
Some of *them know.*

15 ***Everyone, everybody, everything, anyone, anybody, anything, someone, somebody, something, no one*** **and *nobody* are also pronouns. They can be followed by adjectives.**

You can't carry ***everything*** *with you.*
There is ***something strange*** *on that mountain.*

16 **We usually use *something, somewhere, somebody* and *someone* in statements. We often use *anything, anywhere, anybody, anyone* in negative sentences and questions.**

Somebody ***phoned*** *for help.*
I can't see ***anything.***

17 **We can also use pronouns beginning with *any-* in statements to mean 'all' when it doesn't matter who, what or where.**

Anyone *can make a mistake.*
I'd do ***anything*** *to be famous.*

18 ***Anywhere, nowhere*** **and *everywhere* are also adverbs.**

I'll go ***anywhere*** *with you.*
I looked ***everywhere.***

Practice

A Write the words from the box under the correct headings.

~~accommodation~~ advice chair computer danger hair information knowledge luggage map money mountain news nose pasta piece street torch traffic wood

countable	uncountable	both
....	accommodation	....
....	....	....
....	....	....
....	....	....
....	....	....
....	....	....
....	....	....
....	....	....

B Underline the correct option.

1 We went to every / both cafe in town.
2 I want *each / every* of you to decide.
3 There isn't *any / some* milk in the fridge.
4 *All / Some* the information is on the website.
5 *Both / Every* of them know.
6 *Everyone / Anyone* should speak a foreign language.
7 I've got *some / any* good news.
8 I'll have *some / any* book, it doesn't matter.
9 In maths, an answer is *either / neither* right or wrong.
10 That's *no / none* problem.

C What colour are the things in the picture on page 100? Use quantifiers in your answers.

1 All the oxygen tanks are red.
2 ....
3 ....
4 ....
5 ....
6 ....
7 ....
8 ....

D Rewrite each sentence so that it has the opposite meaning, using a different quantifier.

1 I've got some friends.
I haven't got any friends.
2 There are lots of museums.
....
3 Either will be OK.
....
4 Use some salt.
....
5 I didn't go to any shops.
....
6 Somebody asked me.
....
7 None of us can.
....
8 There were no questions.
....
9 Neither of her two brothers knew.
....
10 You can swim everywhere here.
....

E Could you survive in the desert? Write the correct quantifier in each option, then circle the best answer.

1 What is the most important thing to take with you? (some, every, all)
a all your money (b) some water
c every computer game you have
2 What will be the biggest problem? (neither, no, some)
a .... dangerous animals b .... free time
c .... a nor b
3 What food should you take? (none, any, some)
a .... b .... , it doesn't matter.
c .... bananas.
4 How will you carry all your things? (anything, all, both)
a I won't need .... !
b On .... of the camels (See the picture!)
c My friend will carry .... our things.
5 If you get sick, what should you do? (nothing, some, all)
a Phone for .... help. b Do .... c Eat .... the ice cream.
6 If you want to prepare properly for the trip, what should you do? (every day, no, all day)
a Train ....
b Stay in bed .... before the trip.
c I have .... idea!

F Complete the dialogue with the quantifiers in the box.

all any anything both either every ~~everything~~ no no one none some

Chris: Is [1] *everything* ready for Peter and Joyce's party?
Pascale: I think so. Wait a minute. How many bottles of cola did you buy?
Chris: [2] .... You know they don't like cola. I bought [3] .... juice instead.
Pascale: OK. We still need the cake. I went shopping yesterday but I couldn't find [4] .... nice. Well, one shop had a nice chocolate cake and a lovely cream cake but they were [5] .... very expensive.
Chris: I saw them too and I didn't like [6] .... of them. Maybe we should forget about the cake?
Pascale: What, [7] .... cake?!
Chris: Look, there's lots of food. [8] .... will be hungry – don't worry. I have an idea for what to do after the party.
Pascale: Oh no, I don't want to listen to [9] .... of your crazy ideas.
Chris: Peter and Joyce go dancing [10] .... Saturday night. We could organise a dancing competition in the club they go to.
Pascale: I'm not sure they'll be able to dance after [11] .... that food.

MY TURN!

What do you need for these things? Use the ideas in brackets and write answers with quantifiers.

1 Happiness (friends, stress, family, money, health)
Some good friends
No stress All of these things!
....
....
....

2 Good health (fun, food, exercise, vitamins)
....
....
....
....
....

3 An interesting film (actors, special effects, marketing, story)
....
....
....
....
....

4 A great holiday (friends, money, rain, sun)
....
....
....
....
....

MY TEST!

Circle the correct option.

1 The news .... about two women who climbed Everest. a be b is c are
2 .... of the two climbers are safe. a Each b All c Both
3 There is .... time left before it gets dark. a all b none c some
4 Oh no, I haven't got .... matches to make a fire. a no b any c some
5 .... started a forest fire. a All b Anyone c Someone

My Test answers: 1b 2c 3c 4b 5c

24 Quantifiers 2

There are plenty of activities.

Are our teenagers doing **enough** exercise?

Being stronger, happier and healthier are just **a few** of the reasons for doing regular exercise. Yet **many** teenagers today still do **little** or no sport.

Do you think you have a good reason *not* to do sport? Think again!

'My friends don't do sport.'

Be the first! **Most** people enjoy some kind of sport. You may soon find that your friends are happy to join you.

'I prefer computer games.'

You must be playing **too many** computer games if you can't find **enough** time for **a bit of** sport, too. We think you can do both!

'It's not cool.'

Oh, really? **How many** footballers do you know who are not cool? Sport can give you **a lot of** confidence. But not being able to run for the bus ... that's really not cool!

'I don't like being in teams.'

Don't worry **too much** about the team. There are **plenty of** activities that you can do by yourself or with a friend.

? True or False?

1 You have to give up computer games if you want to get some exercise.
2 You don't have to be in a team to get some exercise.

Answers: 1 False – you can do both sport and computer games.
2 True – there are plenty of activities that you can do by yourself or with a friend.

Quantifiers 2

Much, many, too much, too many, a lot of, lots of, plenty of, most

1 Use *much* with singular uncountable nouns and *many* with plural countable nouns.
much love, many teenagers

2 We usually use *much* and *many* in negative sentences and *How much ...?* and *How many ...?* in questions.
*We don't have **much** time.*
***How many** footballers do you know?*

3 We can sometimes use *many* in formal statements.
***Many** teenagers today still do not do enough sport.*

But we don't usually use *much* in statements; we use *a lot of* or *lots of* instead.
*Sport can give you **a lot of** confidence.*
NOT ~~*... much confidence.*~~

4 Use *a lot of* or *lots of* with both singular uncountable nouns and plural countable nouns, mainly in statements. These are usually informal.
*Sport can give you **a lot of** / **lots of** confidence.*

5 We use *plenty of* with singular uncountable and plural countable nouns in informal statements to mean 'enough' or 'more than enough'.
*There are **plenty of** activities.*

6 *Too much* and *too many* mean 'more than is reasonable or necessary'.
*You must be playing **too many** computer games.*

7 *Most* (without *the*) can also mean 'the majority of'.
***Most** people enjoy some kind of sport.*
NOT ~~*The most people ...*~~

▶ See Unit 31 for the use of *most* with superlatives.

(A) *little*, (a) *few*, *several*, *a couple of*, *a bit of*, *enough*

8 These describe smaller quantities.
*They do **little** sport.*
*There are **several** new cafés in town.*

9 Use *a little, little* and *a bit of* with singular uncountable nouns.
*Find time for **a bit of** / **a little** exercise.*

> **TIP** *A bit* is more informal than *a little*.

10 Use *a few, few, several* and *a couple of* with plural countable nouns.
***A few** / **A couple of** / **Several** friends may want to join you.*

> **TIP** *A couple of* means 'two or three'.

11 *A few* and *a little* mean 'not very many / much, but enough'.
*There is **a little** money.* (You can just buy it.)
*I have **a few** friends.* (That's fine for me.)

Few and *little* (without *a*) mean 'not enough'.
*There is **little** money.* (You cannot buy it.)
*I have **few** friends.* (I'm lonely.)

12 Use *enough* before a noun, but after an adjective or adverb.
*I haven't got **enough** time.*
*I can't reach – I'm not tall **enough**.*

13 We can use *many of, much of,* (*a*) *little of,* (*a*) *few of, most of* and *several of* in front of words like *the, these, my, us, them.*
*These are just **a few of the** reasons for doing regular exercise.*
*I don't do a lot of sport with my friends, but **some of us** play football in the park on Sundays.*

14 We can use these quantifiers as adverbs or pronouns (without a noun after them): (*too*) *much,* (*too*) *many,* (*a*) *little,* (*a*) *few, several, enough, a lot of, lots of, plenty of, a couple of, a bit of.*
*Don't worry **too much**.*
*It doesn't cost **a lot**.*

▶ See Unit 23 for use of *some* (*of*).

> Use *too* + adjective / adverb to mean more than is reasonable, possible, necessary.
> *I can't do this exercise. It's **too hard**.*

Practice

A Matthew Robson, from London, wrote a famous report about teenagers in 2009, when he was 15. Complete his report by putting the quantifiers in brackets in the correct places.

1 ....Many.......... teenagers between 13 and 14 visit the cinema. 2 .... go once they are 15. This is because they have to pay the adult price. 3 .... buy the DVD instead. (~~many~~ / most / not many)

Teenagers listen to 4 .... music – usually while travelling or using the computer. 5 .... teenagers listen to the radio these days. 6 .... teenagers listen to music online or on a personal music player. (most / a lot of / few)

Every teenager can use the Internet – either at home or at school. Only 7 .... teenagers shop online as 8 .... do not have a credit card. 9 .... teenagers read a newspaper regularly – they prefer to find out the news from the Internet. (most / few / a few)

10 .... of teenagers have mobile phones. 11 .... teenagers have expensive phones – in case they are stolen. 12 .... teenagers only change their phone on their birthday – when their parents buy them a new one. (99% / most / few)

B Complete the sentences with *many, much, too many, too much, How much ...?* or *How many ...?*

1 I've got ....too much.......... soup – I can't eat all this!
2 My brother has a lot of computer games, but I don't have ....
3 .... people have helped me over the years.
4 I didn't like the pasta – there was .... cheese.
5 .... hours did the journey take?
6 There isn't .... space in the apartment.
7 .... does it cost?
8 Teenagers have .... exams.

C Make sentences by putting the words in the correct order.

1 Kirsty / several / has / me / phoned / times / this week.
Kirsty has phoned me several times this week.
2 lot / We / been / a / missing / have / you
....
3 about / We / little / the / given / were / information / war
....
4 Japan / of / like / would / to / few / us / go / A / to
....
5 enough / understand / You're / old / to / not
....
6 are / couple / good / here / restaurants / a / of / There
....
7 has / little / health / a / His / improved
....
8 a / of / news / I've / good / bit / got
....

D Match each question to the best reply.

1 Does your daughter eat sweets?
2 Do you want me to get some milk?
3 Are there any drama courses at the university?
4 Would you like some salad?
5 Can I buy this?
6 Have you been to Morocco?
7 Do you like him?
8 Did you get all the tickets for the match?

a Yes, there are several.
b No, I could only get a couple.
c Yes, a lot. He's very kind.
d No, it costs too much.
e Yes, please, I'll have a bit.
f Yes, a few times.
g Yes, too many!
h No, we've got enough.

1 ....g.... 2 .... 3 .... 4 ....
5 .... 6 .... 7 .... 8 ....

E Rewrite each sentence so that it has a similar meaning, using the word in brackets.

1 There's only a little traffic on the roads at night. (much)
There isn't much traffic on the roads at night.
2 I only remember a bit of the story. (much)
....
3 He often talks to her. (lot)
....
4 I've got too many bags. (luggage)
....
5 How often do you eat chocolate? (much)
....
6 Drink plenty of water. (lot)
....
7 There's too much work and few people to do it. (enough)
....
8 We knew one or two people at the wedding. (couple)
....

F Underline the correct options in this extract from a teen forum.

File Edit View Favorites Tools Help

Haylee15 ***My mum is telling me to get a job and earn*** [1] ***a bit of / a few money – but I don't want to. What do you think?***

Kris01	[2] *Many / Too much* teenagers in my class have a job, but it's not just for the money. Even just working [3] *a few / a little* hours a week will help you grow up!
worriedmum	My teenage son always wants the latest clothes, games and music. It costs [4] *a lot of / much* money. [5] *How much / How many* clothes does one person need? He has a part-time job but he doesn't have [6] *much / plenty of* time to see his friends. I think it's a shame.
sisterT	I work at a restaurant every Saturday. But my boss often asks me to work [7] *a couple of / a bit of* evenings too, perhaps Thursday and Friday. I can't work and study at the same time – it's [8] *much / too much* for me.
2368	Only [9] *a few / a little* teenagers don't work these days, but you're right, Haylee. You need [10] *much / plenty of* time to do your homework and you need to get [11] *enough / too much* sleep. Teenagers who work [12] *a lot of / a lot* will not do well in their exams.

MY TURN!

Look at these opinions about teenagers. Write whether you agree with them or not, and add a sentence or two. Use at least one quantifier in your sentences.

1. They spend too much money on clothes!
   I don't agree. My friends never have enough money to spend on clothes. We only buy a few things when we need them.
2. They eat too much junk food!
   ....
3. Teenagers spend too much time on computers!
   ....
4. They don't read!
   ....
5. They go out too much!
   ....
6. They don't get enough exercise!
   ....
7. They never walk anywhere!
   ....
8. They change their mobile phones all the time!
   ....

MY TEST!

Circle the correct option.

1. Don't worry! You've got .... time. **a** plenty of **b** many **c** several
2. A: I've never had *cous cous* before. B: Why don't you try ....? **a** a little **b** little **c** a lot
3. .... his employees have complained about him. **a** Several **b** Several of **c** Several of the
4. I had .... homework this week. **a** much **b** a lot **c** lots of
5. Parents want teenagers to have mobile phones and .... pay for them. **a** most of **b** most **c** too much

My Test! answers: 1a 2a 3b 4c 5b

Reflexive and reciprocal pronouns

Do it yourself!

She did it herself!

He did it himself!

They did it themselves!

It's fun and easy to do it yourself! For example, see how you can make this beautiful table yourself. Just read our simple instructions.

1
Get **yourself** a friend – you can help **each other.**

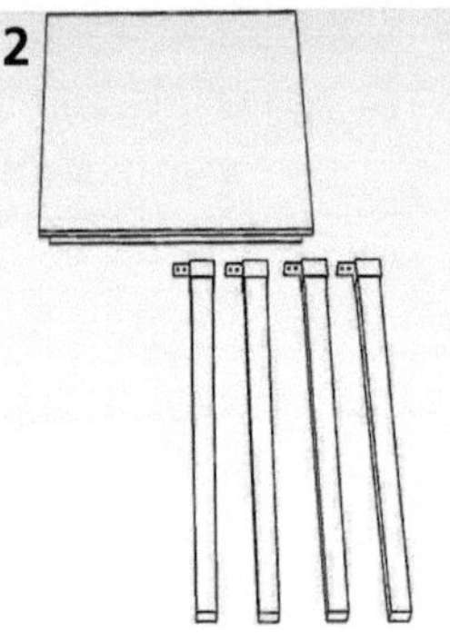

Take everything out of the box.

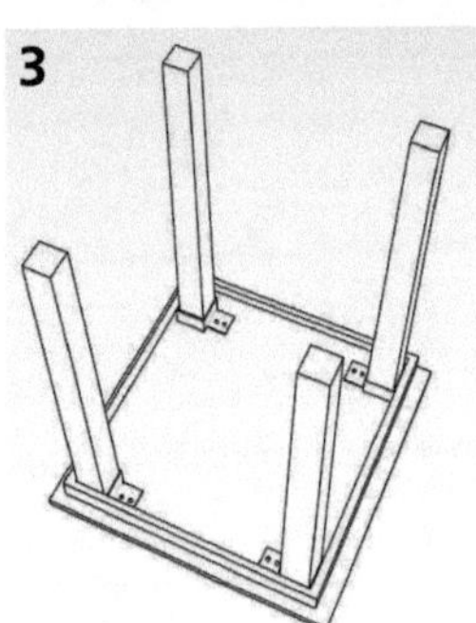

Put the four table legs on the big piece of wood. (The legs should be 50 cm from **one another**.)

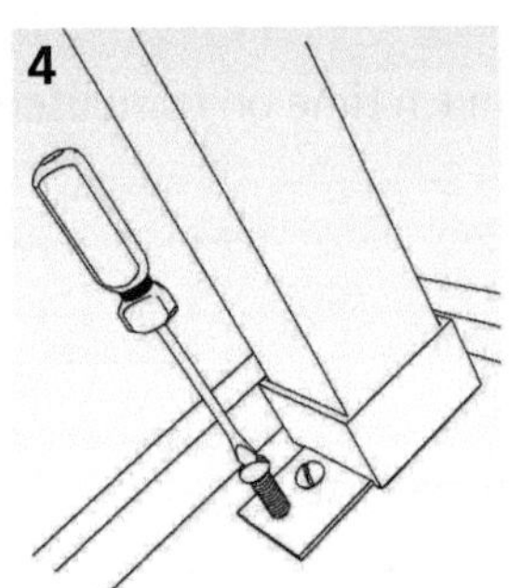

Take the screwdriver (Be careful, don't cut **yourself**!) and fix the legs into the table.

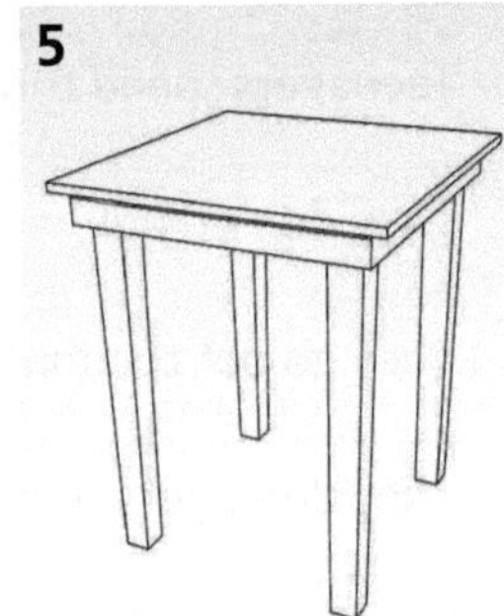

The table should now stand **by itself**. You've finished! Now you can say, 'I did it **myself**!' (or 'We did it **ourselves**!').

See, easy! You get great furniture, you save **yourself** a lot of money, and even have a good time: many people say the activity **itself** is fun.

Any questions, phone 737 5226, and I will be happy to answer any of your questions **myself**.

Michael Morgan

1 Why should people go to this shop?
a It is famous. b The furniture is easy to make. c The furniture is made from special wood.

2 How many pieces does the table have?
a four b five c six

Answers: 1b 2b

Reflexive and reciprocal pronouns

Reflexive pronouns

1 **Reflexive pronouns have the following forms:**

I	myself
You	yourself
He	himself NOT ~~*hisself*~~
She	herself
It	itself
We	ourselves
You	yourselves
They	themselves NOT ~~*theirselves*~~

2 **Use reflexive pronouns when the subject and object are the same person.**

*I work for **myself**.*
*Don't cut **yourself**!*

In English, *dress, feel, shave, wash* are not usually followed by reflexive pronouns.

I feel uncomfortable. NOT ~~*... feel myself ...*~~
I dressed. NOT ~~*... dressed myself.*~~

3 **Use a reflexive pronoun to make it clear who / what the pronoun refers to.**

*Jane bought flowers for **herself**.*
(The flowers are for Jane.)

*Jane bought flowers for **her**.*
(The flowers are not for Jane.)

TIP

If a sentence has a preposition of place, the pronoun after the preposition is usually a personal, not reflexive, pronoun.

*She took the table with **her**.* NOT ~~*... herself.*~~
*I kept the book near **me**.* NOT ~~*... myself.*~~

4 **We can use reflexive pronouns for emphasis.**

*We did it **ourselves**.*
*The activity **itself** is very interesting.*

TIP

We can use *I myself* to give a personal opinion.

***I myself** completely disagree.*

5 **In conversation, we can sometimes use reflexive pronouns instead of personal pronouns. We do this after the prepositions: *but, except, as, like* or *and*.**

*... except **ourselves** ...*
*John and **myself** ...*

Reciprocal pronouns

6 ***By* + reflexive pronoun means 'without help'.**

*The table should now stand **by itself**.*
*We got there **by ourselves**.*

7 **Reciprocal pronouns (*each other* and *one another*) show that people or things act on each other in the same way.**

*You can help **each other**.*
*The legs should be 50 cm from **one another**.*

Note the difference:

*We looked at **ourselves**.* (... in a mirror)
*We looked at **each other**.* (= She looked at him and he looked at her.)

Reciprocal pronouns have possessive forms (*each other's* and *one another's*).

*The sisters often borrow **each other's** clothes.*

Practice

A Write the correct reflexive pronouns in the table. Don't look at page 109!

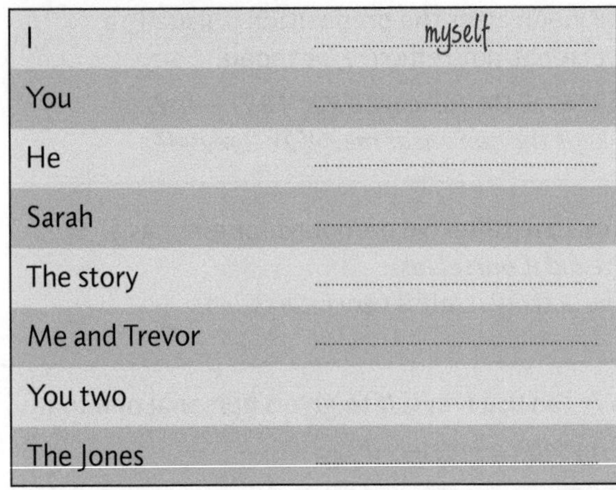

I	myself
You	
He	
Sarah	
The story	
Me and Trevor	
You two	
The Jones	

B Complete the speech bubbles with the correct reflexive pronouns.

1

You ate it all yourself !

2

He put it on his head .

3

I painted it all .

4

Maria needs to buy a new car.

C Match the pairs.

1 Susan is selfish; — a she thinks a lot about her.
2 Susan worries about Mary; — b she thinks a lot about herself.

3 Trevor silently read the story — a to himself.
4 Trevor called his son and read the story — b to him.

5 Graham needed it, so he took it — a for him.
6 Tom needed it, so Graham took it — b for himself.

7 The baby can't — a dress herself.
8 It takes ages to — b dress her.

9 My neighbours organised the party — a each other.
10 My neighbours don't like — b themselves.

11 Remember to try it — a yourselves.
12 Remember to write to — b one another.

D Complete the sentences with the correct pronouns.

1 The children can go to school by themselves .
2 Tom, I'm sure you can finish it .
3 My sister never took lessons in French. She taught .
4 An automatic door opens and closes by .
5 I didn't want to forget my bag, so I put it on the seat next to .
6 The two winners kissed and congratulated .
7 Is this Jennifer's new scarf? Did you buy it for ?
8 I have always believed in it.
9 Get into pairs and ask ten questions in English.
10 We brought enough food with .
11 We ate all the food .
12 Tom and Jo aren't speaking to after their argument last week.

E Answer these questions using reflexive pronouns.

1 Did Liz buy this cake?
No, she made it herself.
2 Why does Jack have blood on his finger?
....
3 Did anyone help the boys to write the card?
....
4 Did you copy this homework?
....
5 Do you like my new dress?
....
6 Who wakes your dog up in the mornings?
....

F Complete the dialogue with the correct pronouns.

Iain: Are you going to help me or do I have to make this cupboard by [1] myself ?
Jo: All right, I'm coming. Where are the instructions?
Iain: Ask [2] .... You had them last.
Jo: Oh, yeah, here they are. Let's see ... . Do you think we can do this [3] .... ?
Iain: Sure. Sue and Steve made their computer table [4] ....
Jo: Yes, and they didn't talk to [5] .... for a week afterwards.
Iain: Well, Sue should blame [6] .... : she dropped a heavy piece of wood on Steve's toes. Steve told me about it [7] ....
Jo: No, that's not true. Steve was carrying the wood with [8] .... and it fell by [9] .... It wasn't Sue's fault that Steve hurt [10] ....
Iain: Why do you always believe what Sue says? Steve did most of the work, not Sue – as usual.
Jo: You should listen to [11] .... You sound just like Steve. You two should go and live with [12] ....

MY TURN!

Complete the sentences using reflexive or reciprocal pronouns.

1 I love to see photos of myself.
2 My best friend hates ....
3 Once I ....
4 People should ....
5 If you want to do something well, you should ....
6 One day I would like to ....

MY TEST!

Circle the correct option.

1 John, paint the chair .... ! a itself b himself c yourself
2 I .... when I saw the finished cupboard. a felt happy b felt me happy c felt
3 Nancy is a bit strange – she talks to .... when she is making something. a her b she c herself
4 Ed, Mum is here, talk to .... about the new furniture. a her b she c hers
5 Mr and Mrs Green helped .... to make it. a them b themselves c each other

My Test! answers: 1c 2a 3c 4a 5c

26 Prepositions of place, movement and time

We waited in front of a petrol station.

'The chase took place **on** 5 September **at** lunchtime. We had a call on the radio from some colleagues. They had seen a black car on CCTV as it went **through** a red light **at** a crossroads. We waited **in front of** a petrol station to see if the car went **past** us. My colleague went to buy a coffee from the shop **at** the station. He was only gone **for** a minute when I saw the black car. "Get in the car!" I called to him.

'The black car drove **through** a housing estate. It was difficult for us to follow it. The police car is good **on** motorways, but not **over** speed bumps! Then the black car drove **out of** the estate and **into** the town centre. It was driving very fast. It was very busy **in** the town centre, and the chase was getting dangerous. We decided to stop. We had to watch the black car disappear **into** the distance, but it was important that nobody was injured. Just **after** 3 pm, we had a call on the radio again. They had found the car **in** a car park. It was a stolen car.'

?
1 Where were the police officers when they saw the car?
2 Did they catch the criminals? Why / Why not?

Answers: 1 In front of a petrol station
2 No, because the chase was too dangerous.

Prepositions of place, movement and time

Prepositions of place

1 ***at, in*** **and** ***on***

Use ***at*** **with a specific point.**

- ***at*** + place, e.g. ***at*** *the crossroads*
- ***at*** *the top / the bottom (of)*
- ***at*** *the end / the beginning (of)*
- ***at*** *the front / back / side of*
- ***at*** + group activity, e.g. ***at*** *the football match*
- ***at*** + somebody's house or shop, e.g. ***at*** *Vince's,* ***at*** *the doctor's*
- ***at*** *school,* ***at*** *college,* ***at*** *work* (without *the*)

Use ***in*** **to talk about somewhere inside a larger space.**

- ***in*** *the box,* ***in*** *a hole,* ***in*** *the building*
- ***in*** city / country, e.g. ***in*** *Los Angeles,* ***in*** *Portugal*
- ***in*** *a taxi / the car*
- ***in*** *the north / the south / the east / the west*
- ***in*** *the corner / the centre*
- ***in*** *a picture / a photo*
- ***in*** *the sky / the country*
- ***in*** *bed,* ***in*** *hospital,* ***in*** *prison* (without *the*)

Use ***on*** **to talk about somewhere on a line or a surface.**

- ***on*** *the river,* ***on*** *the motorway*
- ***on*** *the floor,* ***on*** *the desk,* ***on*** *the shelf*
- ***on*** *the ground / first / second floor*

Or in certain expressions:

- ***on*** *a farm,* ***on*** *an island*
- ***on*** *a bus,* ***on*** *a plane,* ***on*** *a train*
- ***on*** *the (tele)phone,* ***on*** *page ...*
- ***on*** *the left / right*
- ***on*** *the way,* ***on*** *the edge (of)*

2 **Some other common prepositions of place are:**

above	*between*	*opposite*
among	*by / near*	*outside*
around / round	*in front of*	*over*
behind	*inside*	*under*
below		

We can use ***beneath / underneath*** **instead of** ***under.*** ***Under*** **is more common.**

We can use ***around*** **and** ***round*** **to mean 'surrounding' or 'in many different places'.**

He put his arm ***around / round*** *her.*
The film is popular ***around / round*** *the world.*

Note the difference:

between

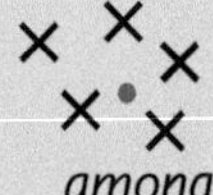

among

Prepositions of movement

3 Some common prepositions of movement are:

across	*between*	*off*	*through*
after	*by*	*onto*	*towards*
along	*down*	*out of*	*to*
around / round	*from ... to*	*over*	*under*
behind	*into*	*past*	*up*

4 We often use *in* and *on* as prepositions of place and *into* and *onto* as prepositions of movement. However, we can sometimes use *in* and *on* as prepositions of movement.

*She threw her bag **on** / **onto** the sofa.*

Other prepositions which we can use for both place and movement are: ***around / round, behind, between, over, under.***

*She ran **between** the cars.*
*In the photo I'm standing **between** Annie and Michelle.*

We don't use *to* after *arrive*. Use *at* (or *in* if it's a very big place).

*When you arrive **at** the hotel ...*
NOT ~~*... arrive to the hotel.*~~
*I arrived **in** Toronto.* NOT ~~*... arrived to Toronto.*~~

Don't use *to* before *home*.

Go home! NOT ~~*Go to home!*~~

5 Use *get on / onto* and *off* with trains, buses, planes, bikes, boats and animals.
Use *get in / into* and *out of* with cars, small boats and small planes.

*Get **off** the boat.*
*He got **into** his Mercedes.*

6 Use *by* (e.g. *car, train, bus*) to show how you travel.

*It is faster **by** plane.*

Prepositions of time

7 *at, in* and *on*
Use *at* with a particular point in time.

***at** six o'clock*
***at** lunch* (*time*)
***at** the wedding, at New Year*
***at** night* (without *the*)
***at** the weekend*
***at** the moment,* (*the*) *time* (*of*)
***at** the end / beginning of*

In British English, use *at **the weekend***.

In American English, use *on **the weekend***.

Use *in* when you are talking about a longer period of time.

***in** July*
***in** the summer*
***in** 2010*
***in** the morning / afternoon / evening*

Use *on* with days and dates.

on + day, e.g. ***on** Thursday, **on** Thursday afternoon*
+ special day, e.g. ***on** New Year's Day*
+ date, e.g. ***on** 1 September*

8 Some other common prepositions of time are:

after	*by*	*from ... to / until*
before	*during*	*until*
between	*for*	*within*

9 We can use *in* to talk about a specific time in the future.

*I'll speak to you **in** an hour.* (= an hour from now)

We can also use *in ... 's time*.

*I'm speaking to her **in** an hour's **time**.*

We use *within* to mean 'inside a period of time'.

*We must finish this **within** a month.* (= before the month has finished)

10 We can use *during* or *in* to talk about something which happens in a particular period of time.

*Why don't you visit **during** / **in** the summer?*

Use *for* to talk about how long something continues.

*I stayed at her house **for** two weeks.* NOT ~~*... during two weeks.*~~

11 Use *by* or *until* to mean 'at this time or before'. Use *by* for a single action and *until* for an activity which is continuing.

*Please complete the form **by** Friday.* (= on or before Friday)
*I'll wait for you **until** 5.00.* (= At 5.00 I'll stop waiting.)

12 We do not normally use a preposition of time before *this, that, some, each, every, last, next* or before the adverb phrases *later, today, tonight, tomorrow, the day after tomorrow, yesterday, the day before yesterday.*

*She left **last** Monday.* NOT ~~*... on last Monday.*~~
*He'll be here **the day after tomorrow**.* NOT ~~*... on the day after tomorrow.*~~

Practice

A Complete the mind maps for *at*, *in* and *on* using the words in the box.

6.20	my birthday	the bus stop	the country	73 Forest Road	~~five o'clock~~	Jo's party	July
New Year	the pocket	Poland	the spring	Sunday evening	the top floor	the wall	the way

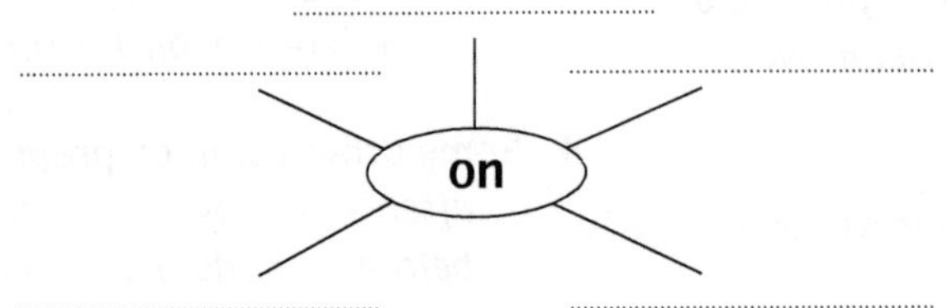

B Match the sentence beginnings to the correct endings.

1 She fell
2 The girl threw a stone
3 Daniel's left without his keys. I'll go
4 I often see Josie hurrying
5 It's time to go
6 The plane can't fly
7 She got off her bike and pushed it
8 He tied the rope

a home.
b up the hill.
c down the stairs.
d over the mountains.
e after him.
f along the road to school.
g around his waist.
h through the window by accident.

1 ...c... 2 ...... 3 ...... 4 ......
5 ...... 6 ...... 7 ...... 8 ......

C Underline the correct prepositions in this police officer's report.

'It's usually quiet [1]*at / on* the motorway [2]*at / in* four [3]*during / in* the morning. But not today. A gang had stolen money from a truck parked [4]*at the side of / at the back of* the motorway. Now they were going north. We waited [5]*in / at* junction 14 [6]*during / for* ten minutes. When we saw the car, we immediately followed it. The gang knew we were [7]*between / behind* them.

'More police cars joined the chase and the gang began to get frightened. They threw the bag of money [8]*off / out of* the window. They were now driving very fast and moving from one side of the motorway [9]*to / until* the other. One of the police cars managed to get [10]*in front of / opposite* the gang, and soon there were police cars all [11]*around / outside* them.

'As the car slowed down, one member of the gang escaped and ran away. He was running [12]*in / into* a small wood [13]*from / on* our left. We ran after him with the police dog and soon caught him. We asked him to lie [14]*on / at* the ground. It was a successful chase. Nobody was hurt and nobody got away. Some other officers found the bag of money [15]*by / at* the motorway. There was about £20,000 [16]*in / into* the bag.'

D Circle the correct option(s). Sometimes more than one option is possible.

1 She walked .... me without saying a word.
a at (b) past (c) by

2 The holidays start .... a week's time.
a in b on c at

3 If you look very carefully, you can see the deer .... the trees.
a across b between c among

4 I met him .... the holidays.
a during b for c within

5 The gardens are open from April .... October.
a in b to c until

6 The bus stop is .... the entrance to the zoo.
a between b opposite c below

7 She threw her coat .... the floor.
a above b in c on

8 I heard a noise coming from the corner of the room. Slowly I walked .... it.
a for b at c towards

9 The dog swam .... the river to the other side.
a across b along c around

10 You must give me your homework .... Monday morning.
a at b on c by

E Complete the sentences.

1 I just need to speak to John. I'll be back in five minutes .
2 Doctors hope to have a cure for this type of cancer within ....
3 I've been waiting to see the doctor for ....
4 Her father lived in Greece until ....
5 Please give me the homework by ....
6 In History we are finding out about life during ....
7 I went to primary school between ....
8 I usually have a meal with all my family at ....

F Answer the questions using prepositions from this unit.

1 Where do oranges grow? in Spain / on a tree
2 Where can you see a goat? ....
3 Where do we usually put adjectives in English? ....
4 When do you blow out candles on a cake? ....
5 Where does the sun rise? ....
6 Where can you find buttons? ....
7 Where can you watch an actor? ....
8 When do you have your Maths class? ....
9 Where can you see clouds? ....
10 Where can you look up a word? ....

MY TURN!

Imagine that something unusual happened on your journey to school this morning. Write at least eight sentences and include as many prepositions as you can. Use the beginning given below.

In the morning, I always walk the same way to school and I always see the same people. But not today. Today was different. . . .

MY TEST!

Circle the correct option.

1 The street is very noisy .... night. a at b at the c in the
2 Let's .... ! a run to home b run at home c run home
3 He arrived .... the party .... a taxi. a at, in b in, by c at, onto
4 Were you at Gary's party .... last night? a on b in c – (no preposition)
5 I've only known him .... a short time. a for b during c at

My Test! answers: 1a 2c 3a 4c 5a

27 Verbs with two objects

Throw her to the dogs!

King Lear Act I, Scene 1 by William Shakespeare (adapted)

King Lear wants to see his three daughters, Regan, Goneril and Cordelia.

King Lear: **Bring me my daughters**! I will **give my country to the daughter** who loves me most. First, Regan.

Regan: I love you very much. You always **buy wonderful presents for me**. You **gave me this ring** – it **cost 500 gold pieces**! You are a perfect father.

King Lear: Thank you, Regan! Now, you, Goneril.

Goneril: I love you more. You **found a rich husband for me** and **built us a palace**. You have **taught me everything** in life.

King Lear: Thank you, Goneril! Now you, Cordelia. **Show me your love**.

Cordelia : I love you, father. I can say no more.

King Lear: What! I will **give you another chance**. **Speak to me**, daughter.

Cordelia: I love you as I should, but I will not **tell you** more than this.

King Lear: Servants, **send Cordelia to another country**! She is not my daughter now. **Throw her to the dogs** if she ever returns.

?

Which daughter, Regan, Goneril or Cordelia ...

1 ... is married?
2 ... makes King Lear angry?
3 ... has an expensive ring?

Answers: 1 Goneril 2 Cordelia 3 Regan

Verbs with two objects

1 **Here are two different types of objects:**

direct object

Goneril married ***a millionaire.***

indirect object

The king gave ***her*** *a beautiful ring.*

2 **Many verbs take an indirect object and a direct object. We can use some of these verbs without *to* or *for* before the indirect object. But then the indirect object comes first.**

The king ***told Cordelia a story.***

OR *The king* ***told a story to Cordelia.***

King Lear ***bought presents for her.***

OR *King Lear* ***bought her presents.***

3 **Some verbs take a direct object and an indirect object with *to*.**

Bring me my daughters!

King Lear ***gave nothing to Cordelia.***

Other verbs like this are: *lend, offer, pass, promise, read, sell, send, show, teach, tell, throw* and *write*.

> **TIP**
>
> **Some verbs, e.g. *deliver, describe, explain* and *suggest*, only take a direct object and an indirect object with *to*.**
>
> ***I explained the problem to Simon.***
>
> NOT ~~*... I explained Simon ...*~~
>
> ***Describe your picture to me.*** NOT ~~*Describe me ...*~~

4 **Some verbs, e.g. *build, buy, find, leave* and *make*, take a direct object and an indirect object with *for*.**

The king ***built a palace for them.***

Who ***bought the ring for Regan?***

5 **If the direct object is a pronoun, the indirect object comes second, and includes *to* or *for*.**

I gave them to Bruce. NOT ~~*I gave Bruce them.*~~

She ***made it for her mother.*** NOT ~~*She made her mother it.*~~

If both objects are pronouns, the direct object usually comes first, then *to* or *for* before the indirect object.

Bring them to me. NOT ~~*Bring them me.*~~

6 **A few verbs, e.g. *allow, charge, cost, fine* and *wish*, never have *to* or *for* with the indirect object.**

They didn't ***allow the prisoner any food.***

NOT ~~*... didn't allow to him ...*~~

The ring ***cost the king 500 gold pieces.***

NOT ~~*... cost for the king ...*~~

7 ***Say, tell, speak* and *talk* are used differently.**

***Say* is the most common reporting verb. We use *to* with an indirect object.**

He ***said*** *'Hello'* ***to*** *him.* NOT ~~*... said him 'Hello' ...*~~

We use *tell* to give instructions or information. *Tell* always has an indirect object without to.

'Go to the king,' they ***told*** *him.* NOT ~~*... they told.*~~

OR ~~*... they told to him.*~~

She ***tells*** *me a lot of funny stories.* NOT ~~*... says me ...*~~

***Speak* can take *to*. We only use *speak* about languages and the ability to speak.**

She ***speaks*** *English.* NOT ~~*... talks ...*~~

***Talk* can take *to*. We use *talk* to mean 'have a conversation'.**

Stop ***talking****, please.* NOT ~~*... speaking ...*~~

Practice

A This is the rest of the story of King Lear. Find the ten verbs which take two objects and <u>underline</u> them.

King Lear <u>gives</u> his country to Regan and Goneril and sends Cordelia to France. Regan and Goneril build their father a small house and wish him luck but they don't allow him any power. They rule England now.

Regan and Goneril soon control everything and they leave nothing for Lear. The King is so angry and disappointed that he goes mad. He walks around the countryside in the wind and rain, telling everyone his story. Lear now understands how poor people live. This teaches Lear the truth about life.

Cordelia has not forgotten her father and brings an army to England to fight her sisters. There is a terrible battle but Regan and Goneril win. Cordelia is killed and Lear dies over her body. Regan and Goneril also die. Lear's terrible mistake costs him his life and his daughters.

B Mattie can't decide what presents to get for her family. Write suggestions using *give* and *buy*.

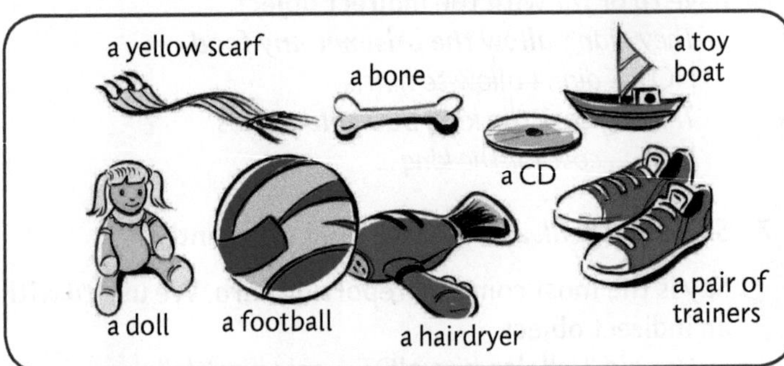

1 Give the bone to Spot. / Give Spot the bone.
2 Buy the boat for Simon. / Buy Simon the boat.
3 ....
4 ....
5 ....
6 ....
7 ....
8 ....

C Make sentences by putting the words in the correct order.

1 gave / he / her / flowers
He gave her flowers.
2 keys / threw / I / the / him
3 his / to / Mike / photos / showed / me
4 sold / Fiona / a / she / bike
5 it / to / promised / me / she
6 him / send / it
7 some / they / advice / us / offered
8 children / Maths / to / she / teaches

D Write prepositions (if necessary) in these sentences. If there is no preposition, write –.

1 Give the pen ....to.... me.
2 Give me ....–.... it now!
3 I wish .... you all the best in your new job.
4 Bring a present .... John.
5 Bring John .... a present.
6 She's never spoken .... me.
7 Tell .... me a story.
8 I passed it .... Sue.
9 Did he explain everything .... you?
10 Lend .... her your bike.

E Complete each sentence b so that it means the same as sentence a. Use two to five words, including the word in brackets.

1 a Trevor said he could give Jane ten euros for it. (offered)
b Trevor ....offered Jane ten euros.... for it.
2 a The mechanic made me pay 150 euros for the repairs. (charged)
b The mechanic ....
150 euros for the repairs.
3 a Denis bought a computer from Natasha. (sold)
b Natasha ....
.... Denis.
4 a Amy said I could have her old printer. (promised)
b Amy ....
....
5 a I want to say something to you. (tell)
b I want ....
....
6 a Philip gave me an explanation of the problem. (explained)
b Philip ....
....
7 a My doctor says I can eat red meat once a week. (allows)
b My doctor ....
a week.
8 a I borrowed my sister's skirt. (lent)
b My ....
....
9 a It is impossible to give you a clear picture of Venice. (describe)
b I cannot ....
....
10 a 'Be careful,' she told me. (said)
b ....
....

F Circle the correct option.

Janek was a poor boy from a small village. He had promised his mother [1]..., so he went into the forest. There was one beautiful flower and, as he went to take it, Janek heard it [2]... him. The flower [3]...: 'Take me! I can offer [4]... . But you must not [5]... anyone about this. You will be rich but you must not give [6]... . If you do this, you will be poor again.'

Janek took the flower and suddenly he was in beautiful clothes in a big house. He built a castle [7]... himself. It cost [8]... a lot of money, and he lived like a king. He didn't see his family or friends again but he thought he didn't need them. He was rich, but he was not completely happy.

One day, many years later, Janek saw an old woman near his garden. She was crying. 'Why are you crying? It must be because you're poor,' Janek [9]... her. 'No,' she said. 'I'm crying because many years ago I lost my son. He is more important to me than any money.'

The woman was Janek's mother. Janek realised he could never be happy without his family. He gave his mother [10]... some money and once again he was a poor man in a small house. But Janek was happy at last.

1 a to some flowers (b) some flowers
c for some flowers d flowers to her
2 a tell b tell to
c speak to d say to
3 a said b told c told to him d said him
4 a you anything b anything you
c you for anything d anything for you
5 a talk of b talk to c talk for d talk at
6 a anything to anyone b anything
c anything anyone d anyone
7 a to b on c for d –
8 a to b of c – d for
9 a talked to her b asked to her
c told to her d said to
10 a to b for c at d –

MY TURN!

Are you happy? Underline the correct options in the questionnaire, then tick your answers and find out! Check your score at the bottom of the page.

1 If you get a bad mark in a test, how do you feel?
a Not too bad, but I will *talk to* / *tell to* a teacher about it.
b Sad. I will cry.
c Embarrassed. I will *write* / *say* my teacher an apology.

2 When do you feel happiest?
a When I'm giving things *to* / *for* people.
b When I'm eating hamburgers.
c When I'm *saying* / *telling* everyone how great I am.

3 What would you *say* / *say to* a friend who won a new bike in a competition?
a I would *wish* / *wish to* my friend all the best.
b Nothing. I would feel too jealous.
c 'Can you lend it *to me* / *for me*?'

4 What do you do when you feel sad?
a I promise *myself* / *to myself* something nice.
b I buy a big cake *for* / *to* me and my friends.
c I buy a big cake and eat it all myself.

5 It's your mum's birthday but you don't have money for a present. What do you do?
a I make a nice card *to* / *for* her.
b I just *say* / *tell* 'Happy Birthday' to her.
c I never give *my mum* / *to my mum* presents.

6 Do you agree that money does not bring *you* / *to you* happiness?
a Of course.
b Find a million euros *to me* / *for me* and then I'll tell *you* / *to you* the answer.
c No.

MY TEST!

Circle the correct option.

1 Tell this story .... all your friends. a for b of c to
2 King Lear promised .... a present. a her b to c for
3 Many people wrote letters and sent .... a Cordelia them b them to Cordelia c them Cordelia
4 Goneril wasn't at home, so Regan left a message .... her. a about b at c for
5 A ticket to the theatre will cost .... a ten euros to you b you c you ten euros

My Test! answers: 1c 2a 3b 4c 5c

My Turn! scores:
Mostly a's. You are a happy person!
Mostly b's. Try to smile and laugh more.
Mostly c's. Don't be so unhappy! Life is not so bad.

28 Prepositions

He was terrible at spelling.

Roald Dahl, who died in 1990, is still one of the world's best-selling authors. His short stories **for** adults are **known for** their unexpected endings. Alfred Hitchcock's movie *Man **from** the South* was **based on** a **story by** Dahl. But Roald Dahl is probably most **famous for** the dark humour in his very popular children's stories, **such as** *Charlie and the Chocolate Factory*, *Fantastic Mr Fox* and *James and the Giant Peach*.

Roald was very organised. He always worked for two hours: from 10 until 12 in the morning and from 4 to 6 in the afternoon. He always wrote **in pencil** and when he started writing for the day, he **insisted on** having six sharp pencils in a jar **by his side**.

Roald Dahl enjoyed writing **for** children. He said that children's jokes still made him laugh – and this was the **reason for** his success.

In 1925, when Roald was 9, he went away to boarding school. He was very homesick and quite often **in trouble**. The world now knows that Roald was very **clever at** making up stories. But **instead of** seeing a future author, English teachers at his school were very **disappointed with** his work. Throughout his school life, teachers complained that he was **terrible at** spelling and that he could not get his thoughts **on paper**.

?

1 What habits did Roald Dahl have when he was writing?
2 What did Roald Dahl's teachers say about him?

Answers: 1 He worked from 10 until 12 in the morning and from 4 to 6 in the afternoon. He always wrote in pencil and insisted on having six sharp pencils by his side.
2 They said he was terrible at spelling and that he could not get his thoughts on paper.

Prepositions

Adjective + preposition

1 **We use prepositions after some adjectives.**
*I'm **afraid of** spiders.*

Other examples:

about	*happy / sad / sorry **about**, right / wrong **about**, sure **about**, worried **about***
as	*known **as***
at	*good / bad **at**, clever **at**, surprised **at**, shocked **at***
for	*famous / known **for**, ready **for**, responsible **for**, sorry **for***
from	*different **from** (US different than), made **from***
in	*interested **in***
of	*aware **of**, full **of**, made **of**, proud **of**, tired **of**, typical **of***
on	*keen **on**, based **on***
to	*kind **to**, married **to**, similar **to**, nice **to***
with	*angry **with** (someone) / about (something), bored **with**, crowded **with**, disappointed **with**, pleased **with**, wrong **with***

2 **In questions that begin with *what* or *who* there is no verb or noun after the preposition.**

*What are you **afraid of**?*

*Who are you **angry with**?*

After a preposition we can use a noun or a verb ending in *-ing*.

*This was the reason **for his success**.*

*He was clever **at making up** stories.*

Verb + preposition

3 **Some verbs take particular prepositions.**

*He **insisted on** having six sharp pencils in a jar.*

Other examples:

die of / from	*spend* (money / time) *on*
prepare for	*translate* (something) *into*

▶ **See Unit 17 for more information on and more examples of prepositional verbs.**

We often leave out the preposition when *spend time* is followed by a verb + *-ing*.

*He **spends** too much **time looking out** of the classroom window.*

NOT ~~*... too much time on looking out ...*~~

Noun + preposition

4 **Some nouns take particular prepositions after them.**

*This was the **reason for** his success.*

Other examples:

details of	*lack of*
example of	*reason for*
idea of	*responsibility for*
information about / on	*sign(s) of*

We use no preposition after the verb *lack*.

He** lacks **confidence. NOT ~~*He lacks of confidence.*~~

5 **We often use the preposition *about* after nouns that refer to written or spoken text.**

*It's **a story about** a fantastic chocolate factory.*

Other examples:

a book about	*a poem about*
a discussion about	*a report about*
a film about	

To talk about the author (e.g. of a book or song) use *by*.

*'Imagine' is a **song by** John Lennon.*

Other prepositions

6 **Other common prepositions in English are:**

about	*from*
against	*of*
concerning	*regarding*
despite	*with*
for	*without*

*Roald Dahl enjoyed writing **for** children.*

7 **Some prepositions, e.g. *in front of* and *such as*, are more than one word.**

*He wrote many popular children's stories, **such as*** James and the Giant Peach.

Other examples:

in addition to	*by means of*
because of	*in place of*
in case of	*in / with regard to*
in charge of	*in spite of*
due to	*thanks to*
except for	*up to*
far from	*as well as*
instead of	

Common prepositional phrases

8 **A number of common expressions and phrases are based on prepositions.**

*He always wrote **in pencil**.*

Other examples:

by accident	*on holiday*
above / below average	*in my opinion*
on average	*on my own*
in cash / by credit card	*on page ...*
by chance	*on the phone*
in danger	*on purpose*
out of date	*on the radio*
in fact	*by your side*
on fire	*in time*
in a hurry	*on time*
in love	*in trouble*
in the newspaper	*on TV*
by mistake	*on the way*
by myself	

We can use *in* to describe what someone is wearing.

*The man **in** the dark glasses.*

▶ **See Unit 26 for prepositional phrases of place, movement and time.**

Practice

A Fill in the crossword with the words that complete the sentences.

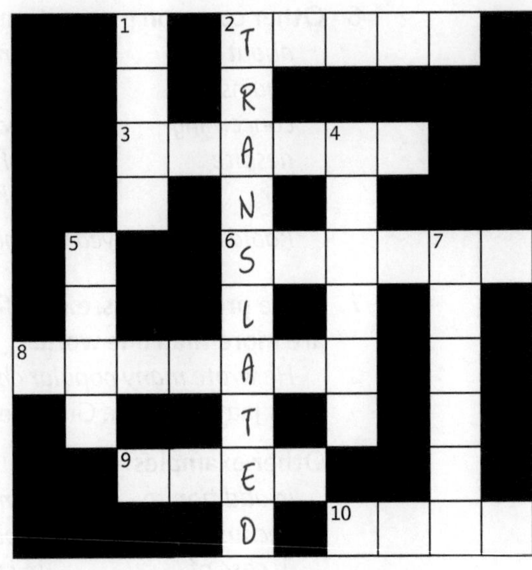

Across

2 I need a holiday. I'm .... of getting up early. (5)
3 I didn't expect to meet her at the airport – I met her by .... (6)
6 She never has any money. She .... all her money on books. (6)
8 On ...., women live five to ten years longer than men. (7)
9 The actor .... from cancer when he was 73. (4)
10 We could see a lot of smoke in the sky. We were surprised to see a building was on .... (4)

Down

1 Mark said the new teacher was friendly, but she wasn't very .... to me. (4)
2 *One Hundred Years of Solitude* by Gabriel García Márquez has been .... into over 27 languages. (10)
4 Colin showed me a chair he had made himself. He's very .... at making things. (6)
5 My grandparents were married for 60 years. They were very much in .... (4)
7 Jenny's son is a soldier. She finds it very hard, because she knows his life is always in .... (6)

B <u>Underline</u> the correct option.

1 The students never arrive <u>on</u> / *in* time – they are always five or ten minutes late.
2 He's always very kind *with* / *to* me.
3 The baby couldn't use a spoon *to* / *for* eating.
4 I had a phone call *of* / *from* Caroline.
5 I am writing *thanks to* / *concerning* your article in the paper.
6 Why did you go out *without* / *despite* telling me?
7 I got to the airport just *in* / *on* time to see my parents before they left.
8 Dr Lauder is not here this week. She's *in* / *on* holiday.
9 They have already started preparing *to* / *for* the wedding.
10 She does not eat meat. It's *against* / *about* her beliefs.

C Complete the sentences with the correct prepositions.

1 J K Rowling is famous ....for.......... creating the character of Harry Potter.
2 Books .... Rowling include *Harry Potter and the Philosopher's Stone* and *Harry Potter and the Goblet of Fire*. The stories are .... a young boy with magical powers.
3 The author originally wrote under the name Joanne Rowling. Her publisher thought that boys would not be keen .... reading a book by a female author. So she called herself J K Rowling.
4 She has said that the character Hermione from the Harry Potter stories is similar .... herself at the age of 11.
5 She says writing is the perfect job for her as she is happy .... herself in a room 'making things up'.
6 The idea for Harry Potter came to her when she was .... the way home on a train, but she did not complete the first book for several years.
7 She was at first disappointed .... the reaction from publishers – twelve publishers were not interested .... the first Harry Potter book.
8 When she wrote the first book, she had little money. She was a single mother, bringing up her child .... her own, but the Harry Potter books turned her into a multi-millionaire.
9 Many parents say that thanks .... the Harry Potter books, their children now enjoy reading again.

D Complete the sentences using the prepositional phrases from the box.

above average except for in case of in fact far from by means of in place of ~~with regard to~~ in spite of up to

1 I am writing *with regard to* your advertisement in *The Yorkshire Times.*
2 The summer school is only for young people .... the age of 16.
3 .... fire, break the glass.
4 We had a good time at the car racing .... the weather.
5 .... helping us, you've actually made things worse.
6 Cows are kept out of the field .... an electric fence.
7 The temperatures this week are .... for this time of year.
8 Maurice appeared to have plenty of money, but .... he owed money to a lot of people.
9 The room was empty .... an old shoe lying in the corner.
10 Rayner is playing in the football match .... the injured Cole.

E Rewrite each sentence so that it has a similar meaning, using the word in brackets.

1 I threw away the letter but I didn't mean to. (mistake)
I threw away the letter by mistake.
2 There was a lack of confidence among the players. (lacked)
....
3 She didn't fall over by accident. (purpose)
....
4 There was a problem with the train. That's why there was a delay. (reason)
....
5 My grandmother's life was not at all similar to mine. (from)
....
6 He writes books for adults and children too. (as well as)
....
7 The trains were delayed because of the snow. (to)
....
8 She's always doing things too quickly. (hurry)
....
9 He is in charge of advertising. (for)
....

F Complete the questions with the correct prepositions. Then answer the questions using a full sentence with a noun or an *-ing* form.

1 What are you afraid *of* ?
I'm afraid of deep water. /
I'm afraid of swimming in deep water.
2 What are you worried .... at the moment?
....
3 What school subject are you not interested .... ?
....
4 When you were younger, what books were you keen .... ?
....
5 What are you proud .... ?
....
6 What's the best thing .... being on holiday?
....
7 Do you prefer to study with friends or .... your own?
....
8 What was the last thing you watched .... TV?
....

MY TURN!

When you are famous, what will your teachers say about you? In your notebook, write six sentences using prepositions from this unit.

Example: *She was terrible at spelling.*

MY TEST!

Circle the correct option.

1 .... my opinion, Roald Dahl was one of the world's best writers. **a** On **b** From **c** In
2 Why don't you go to bed instead of .... on the sofa? **a** lie **b** to lie **c** lying
3 *James and the Giant Peach* is a story .... a boy who makes friends with some insects. **a** by **b** about **c** of
4 Their new car is very similar .... their old one – it's even the same colour! **a** of **b** as **c** to
5 She is very good .... swimming. **a** at **b** for **c** in

My Test! answers: 1c 2c 3b 4c 5a

R4 Review: articles; quantifiers; pronouns; prepositions

A Complete the text with *a*, *an* or *the*.

Stevie Wonder is one of 1 ......*the*...... most famous pop musicians in 2 .... world today. He was born in 1950 in Saginaw, 3 .... small city in 4 .... North American state of Michigan, but, at 5 .... age of four, he moved to Detroit. He has been blind his whole life, but began singing and playing instruments, especially the piano, at 6 .... early age. When he was only 13, he had 7 .... number one record with 8 .... song 'Fingertips'. This was followed by many hit records over 9 .... next 40 years.

B Complete the text with *a*, *an*, *the* or – (= no article)

Stevie Wonder started as 1 ......*a*...... soul singer, but as he got older, he tried 2 .... many different musical styles including 3 .... jazz and electronic music. He has written songs for many other musicians and has made soundtracks for 4 .... films. He has also been involved in 5 .... politics. In 6 .... 1980s, he worked hard with other people to persuade 7 .... American government to make 8 .... birthday of 9 .... Civil Rights leader, 10 .... Dr Martin Luther King, 11 .... national holiday in 12 .... USA. Stevie Wonder is still writing and performing today, and many young musicians all over 13 .... world say that he has been 14 .... great influence on their own musical careers.

C <u>Underline</u> the correct option.

1. We've got <u>*plenty*</u> / *several* of things to do tomorrow.
2. My brother watches *every* / *all* football match he can.
3. Jerry only has a *few* / *little* time before he has to go to the airport.
4. Unfortunately, I've got *a* / *some* homework to do this evening.
5. I still make too *many* / *much* mistakes when I speak English.
6. Can I ask you for *an* / *some* advice?
7. Olivia's not *too* / *enough* young to watch this film.
8. There are *no* / *any* cycle paths in the city centre, unfortunately.
9. Just give me a *couple* / *few* minutes to get ready, will you?
10. I think *most* / *lot of* students in the college speak at least two languages.
11. I didn't know *no one* / *anyone* at the party.
12. You need *a lot of* / *much* patience to play chess well.
13. We can *either* / *neither* have rice or pasta.
14. *None* / *Nobody* of Angela's friends know where she is.
15. Put *both* / *each* hands on the handle and pull as hard as you can.

D Complete each sentence b so that it means the same as sentence a, using three words including the word in brackets.

1. a Joe doesn't care about anyone else. (himself)
   b Joe just ......*cares about himself*...... .
2. a I couldn't do it on my own. (myself)
   b I couldn't do ....
3. a The computer will turn off automatically. (itself)
   b The computer .... off.
4. a Terry and Sandra sent emails to each other. (another)
   b Terry and Sandra .... emails.
5. a We didn't pay for ourselves. (paid)
   b Someone ....
6. a She makes me laugh and I make her laugh. (other)
   b We make ....
7. a No one helped them to work out the answer. (by)
   b They worked out the ....
8. a Farah thinks that what happened was her own fault. (blames)
   b Farah .... what happened.
9. a Nancy borrows Linda's DVDs and Linda borrows Nancy's DVDs. (one)
   b Nancy and Linda .... DVDs.
10. a The children's behaviour was very good. (themselves)
    b The .... very well.

E Circle TWO correct options. Then decide if the two correct options have similar (S) or different (D) meanings.

1 My mum lived in Australia ... the 1990s.
 ⓐ in b on ⓒ during ......S......
2 We had a great time ... school today.
 a at b in c on ....
3 They drove ... a petrol station.
 a over b into c past ....
4 Let's get ... the bus now, shall we?
 a on b up c off ....
5 I saw Jane walking ... the exit.
 a off b to c towards ....
6 They've built a new bridge ... the railway line.
 a along b across c over ....
7 Henry was at work ... twelve o'clock.
 a within b until c before ....
8 It was a beautiful night and we slept ... the stars.
 a under b in c beneath ....
9 You need to get there ... 8.30.
 a by b on c at ....
10 I saw two of my oldest friends ... the weekend.
 a on b within c at ....
11 I'd love to travel ... India.
 a across b among c in ....
12 My aunt lives ... a farm.
 a on b round c near ....
13 They have to complete the construction of the building ... six months.
 a during b within c in ....

F Complete each sentence using the words in brackets. Add *to* or *for* if necessary. Sometimes more than one answer is possible.

1 Can you describe ......*it to me*...... ? (it /me)
2 They promised ......*John a job / a job to John*...... . (a job / John)
3 He's always telling .... (us / stories)
4 Could you pass .... please? (the water / me)
5 These shoes only cost .... (15 euros / me)
6 She just speaks .... (Hindi / her mum)
7 Can you say .... more slowly please? (me / that)
8 Who gave .... ? (you / it)
9 It was John who suggested .... (me / the idea)
10 I need to buy .... for her birthday. (my sister / a present)
11 I want to explain .... (you / something)
12 She'd like you to teach .... you were singing .... (that song / her)

G Complete the text with the most suitable prepositions.

[1] ......*In*...... the opinion of many people, William Shakespeare is the greatest writer in the English language. He wrote 154 love poems known [2] .... sonnets, but he is most famous [3] .... his 38 plays which have been translated [4] .... hundreds of languages and performed worldwide. We can divide the plays [5] .... four main types: 'histories' based [6] .... real historical events; 'comedies' like *A Midsummer Night's Dream* and *As You Like It*, 'tragedies' such [7] .... *Hamlet* and *Romeo and Juliet*, and 'tragicomedies' like *The Tempest*. The plays are known [8] .... their exciting stories and interesting characters, but they are also full [9] .... interesting ideas and some of the most beautiful poetry ever written in English. People all [10] .... the world know Shakespeare's plays, but the funny thing is, [11] .... spite of his fame, we have very little information [12] .... the man himself. We know that he probably lived [13] .... 1564 to 1616, that he got married [14] .... Anne Hathaway [15] .... the age of 18 and that he had three children. But we don't know much more than that. [16] .... fact, we don't even know if Shakespeare wrote all the plays [17] .... his own or whether other people helped him.

29 Adjectives
Totally amazing!

Skateboarding and inline skating are two of the most popular extreme sports in the world. But how easy are they? We gave three beginners a skateboard, a pair of inline skates and some **teaching** DVDs. Here's what they told us.

SPORT: skateboarding

TASK: do an 'ollie' (An 'ollie' is the most **basic** skateboarding trick.)

Louie says: 'This is **not very easy** when you're moving, but it's OK when you are standing. I was really **shocked** the first time I did it! **Totally amazing**!'

Arushi says: 'I couldn't do this. It **looks fun** on the DVD but it's **exhausting**! And **a bit boring** because you have to try it again and again.'

SKATEBOARDING FACT

Skateboarding started in the 1940s or 1950s. Surfers in California, USA used **old, wooden boards** with wheels on the bottom.

SPORT: inline skating

TASK: Skate in a straight line!

Louie says: 'I was **quite afraid** when I started and I'm **surprised** I don't have any **broken** bones! I fell over so many times! But now I'm **quite good**.'

Erin says: 'I ride a **mountain bike**, so my balance is **very good**. I think the DVD was **easy to follow** and I soon got the idea. It's **great**! Can I keep the skates?!'

?
1 Who enjoys skateboarding?
2 Who manages to inline skate?

Answers: 1 Louie 2 Louie and Erin.

Adjectives

1 We usually put the adjective before a noun or pronoun, but after the verb *be*.

wooden boards
*My balance is very **good**.*

2 There are a few adjectives which we only use after the verb *be* or after linking verbs, e.g. *afraid, alive, alone, asleep, awake, glad.* We usually use *ill* and *well* (= *healthy*) in this way, too.

*The boy **was afraid**.* NOT ~~*... the afraid boy ...*~~
*The man did not **look well**.* NOT ~~*... a well man ...*~~

▶ See Unit 21 for use of adjectives after linking verbs, e.g. *It looks fun.*

-ing and *-ed* adjectives

3 We can sometimes use the *-ing* form of the verb (e.g. *breaking*) or the past participle of the verb (e.g. *broken*) as adjectives.

*Surfers ride on the **breaking** waves.* (= the waves that break)
*I'm surprised I have no **broken** bones.* (= bones that are broken)

Other examples:

advanced	*educated*	*retired*	*working*
ashamed	*following*	*sleeping*	
delighted	*lost*	*unemployed*	
disabled	*promising*	*unexpected*	

4 **Some adjectives can end in either *-ing* or *-ed*. Many adjectives with *-ed* endings describe how we feel about something or somebody. Many adjectives with *-ing* endings describe what or who causes the feeling. They show the effect that something or somebody has on us.**

*I was **exhausted** (from skateboarding).*
*Skateboarding is **exhausting**.*

Other examples:

amazing / amazed	*frightening / frightened*
annoying / annoyed	*increasing / increased*
boring / bored	*interesting / interested*
breaking / broken	*pleasing / pleased*
confusing / confused	*shocking / shocked*
depressing / depressed	*surprising / surprised*
disappointing / disappointed	*tiring / tired*
exciting / excited	*worrying / worried*

Gradable and ungradable adjectives

5 **We can use *very* and *quite* with most adjectives which are 'gradable'.**

***very** good*
***quite** afraid*

6 **We can't use *very* with adjectives which mean something absolute or extreme (ungradable). We can, however, use words like *absolutely, completely* or *totally* with these adjectives.**

The 'ollie' was absolutely impossible!
NOT ~~*... very impossible.*~~

Other examples of ungradable adjectives:

amazing, brilliant, fantastic, great, perfect, wonderful
awful, horrible, terrible
enormous, huge, tiny
boiling, freezing, frozen
delicious
exhausted
starving
unique

We can use *a bit* and *a little* before a gradable or comparative adjective on its own.

*He's **a bit** shy.* NOT ~~*He's a bit shy man.*~~
*It feels **a little** colder outside.*

7 **We can use *quite* with a gradable adjective and it usually means 'fairly'. *Quite* with an ungradable adjective means 'completely'.**

*Now I'm **quite good**.* (but not very good)
*It's **quite amazing**!* (= totally amazing)

TIP

We use *quite* + *a* + adjective + noun.

*She's **quite a clever girl**.* NOT ~~*She's a quite clever girl.*~~

▶ **See Unit 32 for more information on adverbs of degree (*very, absolutely*).**

Nouns used as adjectives

8 **We can sometimes use nouns like adjectives. They are usually singular in form.**

an apple tree NOT ~~*... apples tree*~~
a mountain bike NOT ~~*... mountains bike*~~

9 **We can write noun + noun as two words, one word or one word with a hyphen (-). (Hyphens are now not so common.) Check the spelling in a dictionary.**

mountain bike
skateboard
(in the) *north-east*

Order of adjectives

10 **When there is more than one adjective before a noun, the adjectives usually go in a specific order.**

opinion	*lovely, strange*
size	*big, long*
quality	*clever, happy*
age	*old, recent*
shape	*round, square*
colour	*red, black*
origin	*Italian, African*
material	*paper, stone*
purpose	*climbing, football*

an old wooden board
some lovely white Japanese lights

Adjective + infinitive

11 **We can use an infinitive after some adjectives with the verb *be*.**

*The DVD was **easy to** follow.*

Other examples:

able	*difficult*	*happy*	*quick*	*slow*
afraid	*easy*	*keen*	*ready*	*sorry*
anxious	*exciting*	*lucky*	*right*	*surprised*
careful	*frightened*	*pleased*	*shocked*	*wrong*
certain	*fun*	*possible*		

Note the difference:

*The party was **fun**! I really enjoyed it.*
*He's very **funny**. I laughed a lot at his jokes.*

Practice

A **Underline all the adjectives or words used as adjectives in the statements below. Write S next to all the sentences which are about skateboarding (in your opinion).**

1. You stand on a <u>wooden</u> board. S
2. It's quite difficult to learn. ....
3. I'm keen to try it. ....
4. The boots have four small plastic wheels in a line. ....
5. It's absolutely brilliant! ....
6. Old people usually do this sport. ....
7. You need to wear knee pads and a helmet. ....
8. Increasing numbers of teenagers are taking up this sport. ....
9. It's a bit frightening. ....

B **Match words 1–8 to words a–h to make noun + noun combinations. Check in a dictionary to see if the nouns are written as one or two words, then write them below.**

1	tennis	a	keeper
2	racing	b	player
3	wind	c	board
4	table	d	surfing
5	snow	e	pool
6	swimming	f	tennis
7	rock	g	driver
8	goal	h	climbing

1 b tennis player 2 ....
3 .... 4 ....
5 .... 6 ....
7 .... 8 ....

C **Underline the correct option.**

1. The teacher was <u>*disappointed*</u> / *disappointing* with the behaviour of her class.
2. The old woman had fallen over and seemed quite *confused* / *confusing*.
3. The weather is rainy and grey – how *depressed* / *depressing*!
4. Did you hear the news? It's *shocked* / *shocking*!
5. The dog was *frightened* / *frightening* by the noise.
6. I'm having a *bored* / *boring* day.
7. I was absolutely *amazed* / *amazing* by the special effects in the film.
8. He swims every day – it's not *surprised* / *surprising* he's so good at it!
9. I was very *pleased* / *pleasing* to see them.

D **Make sentences by putting the words in the correct order.**

1. voice / She / in / spoke / a / high / strange
   She spoke in a strange high voice.
2. alone / the / in / The / was / woman / building
   ....
3. lovely / They / children / have / happy / three
   ....
4. thing / blue / It's / square / small / a / plastic
   ....
5. tiring / It / quite / was / meeting / a
   ....
6. I / like / black / football / leather / new / boots / some / would
   ....
7. Italian / a / He's / car / red / bought
   ....
8. time / a / quite / They're / worrying / having
   ....

E **Rewrite each sentence so that it has a similar meaning, using the adjective in brackets + infinitive.**

1. She'll definitely succeed. (certain)
   She's certain to succeed.
2. You shouldn't have said that. (wrong)
   ....
3. There were no buses – we couldn't get home. (not possible)
   ....
4. Children are usually fast learners. (quick)
   ....
5. He thinks going out alone at night is frightening. (afraid)
   ....
6. Excuse me for interrupting – but have you seen Mr Lee? (sorry)
   ....
7. I was worried about getting home in time. (anxious)
   ....
8. You did the right thing. (right)
   ....

F Write a sentence to follow each statement below, using an adjective from the box with *very* or *absolutely*.

awful big exhausted freezing hot impossible tasty ~~tiny~~

1 The baby was born at only 25 weeks.
She was absolutely tiny!

2 It was snowing and we didn't have our coats with us.
....

3 We were out all day in the sun.
....

4 She hadn't slept all night.
....

5 The train was very crowded and we couldn't get a seat.
....

6 The new house has got four bedrooms.
....

7 This is a good place to eat burgers.
....

8 I didn't have any instructions, so I couldn't make the model.
....

MY TURN!

Write one or two sentences (each containing an adjective) about the activities below. You can describe each activity, say whether you would like to try it, how it makes you feel or talk about how difficult or easy it is to do.

1 Tennis
....
....

2 Mountain biking
....
....

3 Scuba diving
....
....

4 Cooking a meal
....
....

5 Running a marathon
....
....

6 Playing computer games
....
....

7 Playing the guitar
....
....

8 Painting
....
....

Example: *Tennis is an exciting sport. It is difficult to learn but I am keen to try.*

MY TEST!

Circle the correct option.

1 My new iPod is very easy .... a for use b using c to use
2 They're not .... kind people. a completely b very c a bit
3 This ice cream is .... delicious. a absolutely b a bit c very
4 Eddie felt a bit .... with her. a annoying b annoy c annoyed
5 I'm going to wear my .... coat. a old red nice b nice old red c nice red old

My Test answers: 1c 2b 3a 4c 5b

30 Comparatives

A three-year-old speaks much more fluently.

The development of the early language of children is **similar** all over the world. In a child's third year, **more** development is noticeable in his or her language **than** at any other time.

The obvious difference is that the sentences of a child of three are **much longer** and **more complicated than** those of a two-year-old. The sentences of the **younger** child are mostly limited to two main parts, e.g. *got car.* A three-year-old might say: *Me got lotsa cars like Jimmy* (= *I've got lots of cars like Jimmy*). The two-year-old does not use 'little words' like *is, and, in* and *the.* A three-year-old speaks **much more fluently**, forming sentences such as *Mum went in the house with me and Paul.*

A child's vocabulary increases suddenly towards the end of the third year. An average child of two and a half might use 500 words, but may use **as many as** 1,000 words by the age of three.

Children with an **elder** brother or sister may develop language **faster than** other children. However, bilingual children and twins may **not** develop language **as quickly**. Learning language **faster** does not mean learning **better**. There are many cases of children who are almost silent for the first two or three years before becoming confident speakers.

?

1 When does a child's vocabulary often suddenly increase?
2 What may help children develop language faster?

Answers: 1 Towards the end of their third year 2 An elder brother or sister

Comparatives

Comparative adjectives

1 **To make the comparative of one-syllable adjectives, add *-er* to the adjective.**

slow → slower, long → longer, hot → hotter, nice → nicer, old → older

*The sentences of a child of three are **longer**.*

> **TIP**
>
> **We can say *elder* or *older sister / brother / daughter / son.***
>
> *This is my **elder** / **older** sister.*

2 **To make the comparative of long adjectives (at least two syllables) put *more* before the adjective.**

intelligent → more intelligent

hard-working → more hard-working

*A three-year-old produces **more complicated** sentences.*

Exceptions:

Two-syllable adjectives ending in *-y* have *-er* endings. Change the *-y* to *-i* and add *-er*.

*She seems **happier** now.*

The following two-syllable adjectives usually form comparatives with *-er*: *clever, gentle, narrow, quiet, simple.*

*He's **quieter** than his sister.*

A few comparative adjectives have irregular forms.

good → better

bad → worse

far → farther / further

*Her English is **better** than mine.*

> **TIP**
>
> **We can use *further* (not *farther*) to mean 'extra'.**
>
> *Here's a **further** example.*

3 **We can use *than* after comparative adjectives.**

The sentences of a child of three are ***more complicated than*** *those of a two-year-old.*

We can leave this out if the meaning is clear.

The obvious difference is that the sentences of a child of three are ***much longer****.*

4 **We usually use an object pronoun after *than*.**

He's ***quieter than*** *her.*

But in formal language we can use the subject pronoun.

He's ***quieter than*** *she is / she.*

5 **Use two comparative words with *and* to show that something is changing all the time.**

His language is getting ***better and better****.*
She is getting ***more and more fluent****.*

Comparative adverbs

6 **Add *more* to make the comparative form of most adverbs.**

A three-year-old speaks ***more fluently****.*

Exceptions:
Many short adverbs, such as *early, fast, hard, high, late, long* and *soon* have comparative forms with *-er*.

She is learning ***faster****.*

Some common adverbs have irregular comparative forms.

well → better
badly → worse
far → farther / further
You speak Italian ***better*** *than me.*

Other points

7 **Use *as* + adjective / adverb (+ *as*) to mean 'equal' or 'equally'.**

He is just ***as good-looking as*** *his elder brother.*
I'm sure he works ***as hard as*** *I do /* ***as*** *me.*

The second *as* often comes before *possible*.

He finished ***as quickly as possible****.*

TIP

As soon as possible **is an expression people often use, particularly in emails. It is sometimes written *asap*.**

Please reply ***as soon as possible / asap****.*

8 **The opposite of *more* is *less*. We can use *less* (*than*) before long adjectives and adverbs, but *not as* ... (*as*) is more common in informal language and with short words.**

Twins may ***not*** *develop language* ***as quickly*** *(****as*** *other children). / Twins may develop language* ***less quickly*** *(****than*** *other children).*
She's ***not as tall*** *(****as*** *her husband).*
NOT ~~*She's less tall (than her husband)*~~.

9 **Use (*not*) *as many / much* (+ noun) *as* to talk about quantity.**

You can have ***as many*** *(sweets)* ***as*** *you like.*

Use *as many / much as* + number to add emphasis.

A child may use ***as many as*** *1,000 words by the age of three.*

10 **Don't use *very* on its own before a comparative adjective or adverb. Use *much, far* or *a lot*. *A lot* is more informal.**

The sentences are ***much longer****.* NOT ~~*... very longer.*~~

If you want to say that the difference is small, use *a little* or *a bit*. *A bit* is more informal.

He is ***a little taller****.*

11 ***Little, few, much* and *many* also have comparative forms.**

little → less
few → fewer / less (*less* is more common, especially in informal language)
much / many → more
More *development is noticeable in a child's language (****than*** *at any other time).*

12 **Use *like* or *as* to say that things are similar. Use *like* before a noun or pronoun.**

She's ***like*** *her sister.*
I've got lots of cars ***like*** *Jimmy.*

Use *as* before a clause or a prepositional phrase. We often use *like* instead of *as* in very informal language.

We've been here before, ***as*** *I'm sure you remember.*
OR ... ***like*** *I'm sure you remember.*
Everything happened very slowly, ***as*** *in a dream.*
OR ... ***like*** *in a dream.*

13 **Use *the same* (*as*) or *the same* + noun (+ *as*).**

A: I'll have a burger and chips, please.
B: And I'll have ***the same****.*
Twins are born to ***the same*** *mother at* ***the same*** *time.*

We use *similar* (*to*) to mean 'like, but not exactly the same'.

Her son looks very ***similar to*** *her at the same age.*

Practice

A Read these sentences from advertisements. Match the beginnings to the correct endings.

1 Make counting more
2 Better books for less
3 Fish Oils Plus – for healthier
4 Lunchtimes are more
5 Learn to read more
6 Kids are growing up
7 It's not as
8 These fun cards will encourage your kids to spell

a faster than ever. Remember each special day with this photo book.
b fun with this family card game.
c money!
d better and better.
e interesting with this cool lunchbox!
f and happier kids.
g easily with this bright and happy book.
h simple as it looks! Can you finish the game in just one minute?

1 ...b... 2 ...... 3 ...... 4 ......
5 ...... 6 ...... 7 ...... 8 ......

B Compare the two items using an adjective from the box. Use a different adjective each time.

clean clever far ~~heavy~~ pale rich relaxing valuable

1 salt water / fresh water
Salt water is heavier than fresh water.
2 mile / kilometre
......
3 sky blue / navy blue
......
4 a dolphin / a snake
......
5 gold / silver
......
6 yoga / football
......
7 wind energy / nuclear energy
......
8 a billionaire / a millionaire
......

C Underline the correct option.

1 He's taller *as* / *than* his brother.
2 There were as many *as* / *than* 10,000 people there.
3 Your bag is the same colour *as* / *than* mine.
4 We are here to help people *as* / *like* you.
5 You need to take your studies *far* / *very* more seriously.
6 It's not as cold *as* / *than* it was yesterday.
7 The flower of this plant is similar *of* / *to* a rose.
8 My best friend is better-looking *than* / *then* I am.

D Complete each sentence using the structure *as ... as possible* and a word from the box.

clearly comfortable early far away little ~~much~~ often soon

1 I had not been well and the doctor told me to rest as much as possible.
2 I was very frightened and I ran ....
3 I've got a long journey tomorrow, so I'm going to get up ....
4 The sofa was a bit hard for sleeping on but I made myself ....
5 You had a message from your mum. Can you ring her ...... ?
6 You will pass your driving test more easily if you practise. Go out driving with someone ....
7 She could not hear very well, so I spoke ....
8 I'm saving for a new computer, so I try to spend money ....

E Everybody learns in different ways. Complete the text about different learning styles using the comparative forms of the words in the box.

aware carefully confident easily far fast hard interested logical ~~well~~

Visual

You learn [1] ....better........ if you use pictures and colour to organise information. You communicate [2] .... with people if you use pictures to get your message across.

Aural

You listen [3] .... to the music in a film or TV show than other people do. The right kind of music can help you become [4] .... if you are feeling nervous.

Verbal

You are very good with words, both in speaking and in writing. Remembering things is a lot [5] .... if you don't write them down.

Physical

You are [6] .... of your environment than many people. Reading slows you down, you learn [7] .... if you can touch things. Learning to drive should not be a problem!

$\sqrt{3}$ Mathematical

You may get frustrated with people who are not [8] .... you. You are [9] .... in learning facts than in finding out how something works.

Social

You prefer working with others to working on your own. You like to get [10] .... information about something by telling someone your opinion and listening to what they say.

F Complete the sentences using the comparative forms of appropriate adjectives or adverbs.

1 A: This city is getting very dangerous.
B: You should move to a ....safer........ place.

2 The waiter was very rude to me.
I asked him to be ....

3 I stopped at a hotel for the night. I had been driving all day and it was late.
I couldn't drive any ....

4 I've seen the film and read the book.
The book is a bit .... the film.

5 My leg started hurting in the morning.
It got .... in the evening.

6 There are not many white tigers in the world.
Orange tigers are ....

7 A: I have three books to read by the end of this week.
B: You need to read ....

8 A: What happens when the cost of oil goes up?
B: Petrol prices will get ....

MY TURN!

Think of what you were like when you were at primary school. What has changed between then and now? Write sentences using these verbs and comparative adjectives or adverbs.

1 eat
I don't eat as healthily now. / I eat more healthy food.
I eat more sweets now. / I don't eat as many sweets.

2 wear
....

3 learn
....

4 play
....

5 am
....

6 have
....

MY TEST!

Circle the correct option.

1 I'd like it if you lived a bit .... to us. **a** closer **b** closier **c** more close

2 I am more confident .... I was when I was younger. **a** as **b** than **c** that

3 She's not as .... as her sister. **a** quieter **b** quietly **c** quiet

4 Her vocabulary is .... better. **a** very **b** much **c** more

5 I remember a new word .... when I have a picture of it. **a** more easily **b** much easily **c** a bit easily

My Test! answers: 1a 2b 3c 4b 5a

31 Superlatives

The most dangerous fish is …

The **smallest** fish in the world is the Philippine goby. It is about 1 centimetre long. The **biggest** fish is the Great White shark, which is 6 metres long. The Great White also weighs the **heaviest** (over 2,000 kilograms). This is the **most well-known** shark but there are more than 300 types of sharks.

Probably the **most dangerous** fish is the stonefish. They swim very close to the bottom of the sea. It is a very bad idea to put your foot on a stonefish! It will be very painful.

The sailfish is the **fastest** fish with a maximum speed of 110 km an hour. (The **quickest** that an Olympic swimmer can swim is only about 10 km an hour.) Sailfish are strong but light so they can swim at great speeds.

Fish are great pets. By far the **most popular** pet is the goldfish. This is the **easiest** fish to keep at home. Goldfish do not need a lot of space but you should make sure their water is always clean.

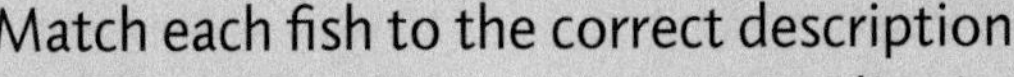

? Match each fish to the correct description:

1 Philippine goby
2 Stonefish
3 Sailfish
4 Goldfish

a It can live in your house.
b It is very small.
c It can hurt you.
d It swims very quickly.

Answers: 1b 2c 3d 4a

Superlatives

Superlative adjectives

1 **To make the superlative of short adjectives, add *-est* to the adjective.**
*The sailfish is the **fastest** fish.*
*The Marina Trench is the **deepest** part of the Pacific Ocean.*

2 **To make the superlative of longer adjectives, put *most* before the adjective.**
*The **most dangerous** fish is the stonefish.*
*What is the **most beautiful** fish?*

3 **We can use *-est* with some two-syllable adjectives, e.g. adjectives ending in *-y* (change the *y* to an *i*).**
*heavy → the **heaviest** fish*
*happy → the **happiest** day of my life*

4 **We usually use *the* or a possessive pronoun before superlative adjectives.**
***The most common** type of shark.*
*That was **my biggest** mistake.*

5 **You can add extra information to superlative adjectives with a *to*-infinitive clause.**
*... the **easiest** fish **to keep** at home.*
*The **best** thing **to do**.*

> **TIP**
> **We can use superlatives + *in* with group words like *team* and *world*. Only use superlatives + *of* before plurals and quantifiers.**
> *... the **biggest** aquarium **in** the world ...*
> NOT ~~*... of the world ...*~~
> *... the **hardest** of many difficult days ...*

Superlative adverbs

6 **Add *most* or *least* to make the superlative form of most adverbs. We usually do not put *the* before *most* and *least* in informal language.**
*Which swims (the) **most quickly**?*
*Which swims (the) **least quickly**?*

7 **Many short adverbs, e.g. *early, fast, hard, high, late, long, quick* and *soon* have superlative forms with *-est*: *early → earliest, fast → fastest*. We usually put *the* before these superlatives, as with adjectives.**
*Which fish lives **the longest**?*
*Jane gets up **the earliest**.*

8 **Some superlatives have irregular forms.**
bad / badly → worst
far → furthest / farthest
few → fewest, least (*least* is more common, especially in informal language)
good → best
little / few → least
much / many → most
well → best

*Australia has the **best** beaches.*
*What is the **furthest** you have swum?*
*The Pacific is the ocean with the **most** fish.*

> **TIP**
> ***Old* has two superlatives: *oldest* and *eldest*. We sometimes use *eldest* instead of *oldest* to talk about people in a family.**
> *Her **oldest** / **eldest** daughter is a biologist.*
> *Albert is the **oldest** man in the village.*
> NOT ~~*... the eldest ...*~~

9 **We can put adverbs like *by far, easily* and *almost* before superlatives. These adverbs come before *the* or a possessive.**
*... **by far** the **most popular** pet ...*
NOT ~~*... the by far most popular ...*~~
*... **easily** their **fastest** runner ...*
NOT ~~*... their easily fastest ...*~~

> **TIP**
> **We can use *very* to emphasise short superlatives and *first, next* and *last*. The word *very* goes after *the* or a possessive.**
> *the **very next** day*
> *her **very best** dress*

Practice

A Complete the sentences with the superlative forms of the words in brackets.

1 Simon is ......the tallest...... in our class. (tall)
2 I think milk is .... drink. (healthy)
3 Marilyn Monroe was .... actress in Hollywood. (beautiful)
4 Bolt finished the race .... (strong)
5 That's not .... idea I've heard. (bad)
6 Michelle stayed up ...., so she was really tired the next day. (late)
7 The last game was .... (exciting)
8 .... teenagers like reading. (many)

B Complete the sentences with the superlative forms of the words in the box. Then find the name of a famous city.

~~clever~~ difficult dry expensive far high less small well

1 Ellen always gets good marks. She is the [C] l e v e r e s t in our class.
2 It's not big. In fact it's the _ _ [ ] _ _ _ _ _.
3 They all cost a lot but which is the [ ] _ _ _ _ _ _ _ _ _ _ _ _ _?
4 It tastes [ ] _ _ _ when it is fresh.
5 Charlotte threw the ball the _ _ [ ] _ _ _ _ _ _.
6 Chinese is maybe the _ _ _ _ _ _ [ ] _ _ _ _ _ _ _ _ language to learn.
7 This has been the [ ] _ _ _ _ _ summer since 1976.
8 Who can jump the _ _ [ ] _ _ _ _ _?
9 You have the most; I have the _ [ ] _ _ _ _.

C Read the survey of teenagers' opinions about places in Clarkesville. Write sentences using superlatives.

1 **Popular shops:** Games Galore 25%; Street Wear 30%; The Beat 28%; Nico's 17%
2 **Interesting places for tourists:** Clarkesville Park 40%; The zoo 38%; The aquarium 22%
3 **Famous people:** The singer, Woka 31%; The footballer, Ray Wooney 30%; The writer, Art Jones 39%
4 **Good ways to get around:** Bus 33%; Walking 25%; Car 25%; Tram 17%
5 **Nice things to do:** Sightseeing 35%; Walking by the river 40%; Shopping in the mall 25%
6 **Cool places to go:** Woka's cafe 20%; The cinema 18%; The river 29%; Route 66 disco 33%

1 The most popular shop is Street Wear.
2 ....
3 ....
4 ....
5 ....
6 ....

D Describe the pictures using superlatives.

1 The basketball player is the tallest.
2 ....

3 ....
4 ....

5 ....
6 ....

E Complete the text using superlative forms of the words in the box.

~~big~~ dangerous deep easy far good large rare tasty unusual

Swordfish are one of [1] ......the biggest...... types of fish. Some swordfish are almost five metres long. [2] .... part of the swordfish is of course its 'sword', the strange long thing coming out of its face! This sword is for catching its food, other fish. Swordfish are fast and their sword can be dangerous. Only the very [3] .... sharks and whales try to catch them.

Swordfish don't usually go very far down in the water. [4] .... they swim is about 150 m below the sea, which is [5] .... place to get food. Swordfish also like to be near the coast and [6] .... they are from the coast is about 60 km.

Swordfish are not [7] .... fish but their numbers have gone down because of fishing. We are [8] .... enemy of swordfish. Swordfish are still a popular food in restaurants and some people think they are [9] .... type of fish. If we want to help swordfish, [10] .... thing to do is not to eat them!

F What do you think? Which of these is the best and why?

1 A Great White shark, a swordfish, a Philippine goby, a goldfish
The goldfish: it is the least expensive.
2 Coffee, tea, water, cola
....
3 History, English, Maths, Biology
....
4 Winter, spring, summer, autumn
....
5 Football, tennis, chess, running
....
6 Dogs, cats, fish, birds
....

MY TURN!

Write sentences about these things using superlatives.

1 Films: By far the most exciting movie is Spider-Man 6.
2 River: The longest river in my country is the Volga.
3 Music: ....
4 Sport: ....
5 Food: ....
6 Holidays: ....
7 Books: ....
8 City: ....
9 Mountains: ....
10 Famous person: ....

MY TEST!

Circle the correct option.

1 Summer is the .... time to go fishing. a best b better c most best
2 It is the .... fish .... the world! a biggest ... of b most big ... of c biggest ... in
3 Sharks are the .... fish. a less interesting b most interesting c interesting
4 Standing on a stonefish will hurt you the .... a bad b most bad c worst
5 Terry swam .... a the furthest b the most far c the most furthest

My Test! answers: 1a 2c 3b 4c 5a

32 Adverbs and adverb phrases

He climbs the monument regularly.

What do people do all day?

Here are some jobs you've maybe not thought about ...

Video Game Tester

Some of Arthur Devine's friends would **really** like his job. **Every week** Arthur is paid to play video games in an office **in New York**. He plays video games five days a week. And yes, he can play **pretty well**!

Dinosaur Duster

Jamie Waters gets up **early**. He needs to be at the Smithsonian Museum of Natural History in Washington before the visitors get **there**. Jamie's job is to clean the dinosaurs **very carefully.** He **never** touches the bones. He uses a feather duster. Jamie likes the Allosaurus **best.**

Crack Filler

At Mount Rushmore in South Dakota, the heads of four American presidents have been made from the rock. The four **very** large heads attract around two million visitors **yearly**. Roger Prince is **definitely** not frightened of heights. He climbs the monument **regularly**; his job is to fill any cracks in the rock.

?

1 Why would Arthur's friends like to have his job?
2 Why does Jamie get up early?

Answers: 1 Because he plays video games five days a week. 2 He has to work before the visitors get to the museum.

Adverbs and adverb phrases

1 **We can use adverbs and adverb phrases with verbs, adjectives, other adverbs and whole sentences.**
*He gets up **early**.*
*The four heads are **very** large.*
*He can play **pretty** well!*
***Maybe** you've not thought about these.*

2 **Adverbs can be a single word or a phrase.**
*He climbs the monument **regularly**.*
***Every week** Arthur is paid to play video games.*

Adverbs of manner

3 **Adverbs of manner describe how something happens; we usually form them by adding *-ly* to the adjective.**
*Jamie works **quickly** and **carefully**.*

4 **Some adjectives already end in *-ly*, e.g. *friendly, lonely*. We don't add *-ly*, but say *in a ... way*.**
*He held out his hand **in a friendly way**.* NOT ~~*... friendlily.*~~

5 **Some adverbs of manner are the same as adjectives, e.g. *early, far, fast, hard, high, late, straight*.**
*He gets up **early**. He likes the **early** morning light.*

TIP

***Hard* means 'difficult' or 'with effort'.**
*It's a **hard** life. She has to work **hard**.*
***Hardly* means 'almost not' or 'not at all'.**
*I could **hardly** see anything.*
*It's **hardly** surprising.*

TIP

We can use the adverb *well* with certain past participles to form an adjective.
*She's a **well-known** actor.*
*a **well-educated** person*

6 **Adverbs of manner usually go at the end of the sentence, but can sometimes come in the middle or (for emphasis) at the beginning.**
*Jamie cleaned the dinosaur bones very **carefully**.*
*He **carefully** cleaned the dinosaur bones.*
***Carefully** he cleaned the dinosaur bones.*

Adverbs of time and place

7 **Use these adverbs to describe where or when something happens.**

... before the visitors get ***there****.*
He gets up ***early****.*

8 **Adverbs of time and place usually come at the end of a sentence, but sometimes come at the beginning for emphasis.**

I visited Mount Rushmore ***yesterday****.* OR ***Yesterday*** *I visited Mount Rushmore.*

9 **Some common time adverbs, e.g. *already, eventually, finally, last* and *soon,* can go before the main verb of the sentence, but after *be* or an auxiliary or modal verb.**

She ***finally*** *told me. He'll* ***soon*** *finish.*

10 **Time expressions such as *every day* or *every week* can go at the beginning or the end of the sentence. Adverbs such as *daily, weekly* or *yearly* usually go at the end.**

Every week *Arthur is paid to play video games.*
It attracts around two million visitors ***yearly****.*

11 **Many prepositional phrases of time and place (e.g. *at night, in China*) function as adverbs and usually go at the end of the sentence. We can put them at the beginning for emphasis.**

Arthur is paid to play video games ***in an office in New York****.*
At Mount Rushmore in Dakota*, the heads have been made from rock.*

> **TIP**
> **If there is more than one adverb or adverb phrase of time, place or manner at the end of a sentence, the order is usually: manner, place, time.**
> *He works hard in the office in the mornings.*
> (manner + place + time)

Adverbs of frequency

12 **Adverbs of frequency describe how often we do things, e.g. *always, frequently, hardly ever, never, normally, occasionally, often, rarely, regularly, seldom, sometimes, usually.***

He can ***usually*** *be found in the museum.*

***Frequently, normally, occasionally, often, sometimes* and *usually* can also go at the beginning or at the end of a sentence.**

Usually *he can be found in the museum.*

***Sometimes* and *occasionally* can go before *be*, auxiliaries and modals in negative sentences.**

They ***sometimes*** *don't arrive until late.*

Focusing adverbs

13 **Some adverbs, e.g. *even, just, only, mainly, mostly, either* (*... or*), *neither* (*... nor*), can be used to put emphasis on a particular part or word of the sentence.**

We ***only*** *want to stay for one night.*
We're ***only*** *here for one night,*
We're here for ***only*** *one night.*

Adverbs of certainty and degree

14 **Adverbs of certainty are *obviously, certainly, clearly, definitely, probably, maybe, perhaps.***

Maybe *you've heard of him.*

15 **We can use adverbs to talk about how much something happens (degree), e.g. *a bit, absolutely, almost, completely, extremely, fairly, hardly, highly, more or less, nearly, practically, pretty, quite, rather, really, slightly, somewhat, terribly, totally, very.***

He can play video games ***pretty*** *well.*

***A bit, pretty* and *somewhat* are more common in informal language.**

16 **We do not use *very* to describe a verb.**

Arthur Devine's friends would really like his job.
NOT ~~*... very like ...*~~

17 **Adverbs of certainty and adverbs of degree usually go before the main verb of the sentence, but after *be* or an auxiliary or modal verb.**

I ***completely*** *agree.*
I'll ***definitely*** *think about it.*

We often use *maybe* and *perhaps* at the beginning of a sentence.

Maybe *I'll see you then.*

We use *enough* after an adverb or adjective.

I didn't get up early ***enough****.*

18 **In negative sentences, adverbs often come before *not*.**

I certainly will not worry about it.
OR *I will certainly not worry about it.*

An adverb does not usually come between a verb and the object, or before an *-ing* form.

Jamie likes the Allosaurus best. NOT ~~*Jamie likes best the Allosaurus.*~~
She started working late. NOT ~~*She started late working.*~~

▶ **See Units 45 and 46 for adverbs which are used to link sentences, e.g. *also, however, then, therefore.***

Practice

A Match the sentence beginnings to the correct endings.

1 The man was thought to be highly
2 I totally
3 Hayley did not take her work very
4 I had completely
5 I found the exam fairly
6 I could hardly
7 I see her quite
8 Drew looks like he's really

a believe what I was seeing.
b forgotten about that evening.
c enjoying himself.
d dangerous.
e often.
f agree with you.
g easy.
h seriously.

B Rewrite the sentences, putting the adverbs in brackets in the correct places. Sometimes more than one answer is possible.

1 She didn't move out of her parents' house when she got married. (even)
She didn't even move out of her parents' house when she got married.
She didn't move out of her parents' house even when she got married.

2 Hi! I was talking about you! (just)

3 He's leading the competition by one point. (only)

4 The TV series is very popular with teenagers. (mostly)

5 Mandy works at the weekends. (mainly)

6 You can come to a class on Wednesday evening or on Friday morning. (either)

7 It's very busy at the weekends, so she has to work. (hard)

C Make sentences by putting the words in the correct order. Sometimes more than one answer is possible.

1 carefully / they / present / chose / the
They chose the present carefully.

2 a / I / to / quickly / asked / doctor /see

3 doesn't / sometimes / until / he / wake up / 10.00

4 gone / we / should / have / never

5 began / he / quietly / crying

6 L.A. / wanted / I / always / to / see / have

7 done / I / not / have / normally / would / that

8 will / soon / dark / it / be

D Rewrite each sentence so that it has a similar meaning, using the word in brackets.

1 She gave her son a gentle kiss on the cheek. (kissed)
She kissed her son gently on the cheek.

2 Poppy gave me a friendly smile. (smiled)

3 She's a very fast runner. (runs)

4 After a long time, I passed my driving test. (eventually)

5 He is almost never late. (hardly)

6 I'm quite good at chess. (well)

7 She was too ill to leave hospital. (enough)

E Complete the sentences with appropriate adverbs or adverb phrases of manner, place or time. Use two adverbs or adverb phrases in each sentence.

1 The children were playing noisily outside.

2 We had a great time .

3 I always sleep .

4 The police arrived .

5 He wrote the words .

6 The teacher was already talking, so we sat down .

F Rewrite the texts about more unusual jobs, putting the adverbs in brackets in appropriate places. There is more than one possible answer.

1 If you can't remember how to open your safe, Sal Schillizzi can help. By listening to the lock, Sal will be able to open the safe. He learnt his skills in the US Army.
(in the 1950s, maybe, quickly)
If you can't remember how to open your safe, maybe Sal Schillizzi can help. By listening to the lock, Sal will be able to open the safe quickly. He learnt his skills in the US Army in the 1950s.

2 Jeffrey Bleim has enjoyed diving. Now he works as a golf ball diver. In one day he collects 5,000 balls from lakes on golf courses. That's 35,000 balls.
(always, in Florida, often, weekly)

3 Ellen Sirot is a foot model. She wears a lot of make-up, but on her feet. Before she goes to sleep, Ellen puts lots of cream on her feet. She sleeps with her feet in plastic bags and wears high heels.
(every night, never, only)

4 When she was three, Francie Berger started playing with LEGO bricks and she has stopped. When she left college, she got a job as a model maker with LEGO. She can build models with as many bricks as she wants.
(never, soon, today)

MY TURN!

Answer the question in six different ways using *will* / *won't* and the adverbs *definitely*, *probably* or *maybe*. Use the phrases from the box or your own ideas.

go to the beach / park	go to bed early	go on the computer	go shopping	have fun
listen to music	meet my friends	read a magazine	talk on the phone	

If you have a free evening today, what will you do?

Example: *I probably won't go shopping.*

1 ....
2 ....
3 ....
4 ....
5 ....
6 ....

MY TEST!

Circle the correct option.

1 She can jump very .... a highly b higher c high
2 I can .... a hardly wait b wait hardly c wait hard
3 He sat down very .... a heavy b heavly c heavily
4 I .... anything to eat tonight. a won't probably have b won't have probably c probably won't have
5 I .... it. a very love b absolutely love c love completely

My Test! answers: 1c 2a 3c 4c 5b

The passive 1

The new metal was called bronze.

The metals copper and tin **have been used** for thousands of years. Copper was one of the first metals which **was discovered by** man. Copper is a soft metal and people soon found out that if they heated the copper and mixed it with tin, a much harder metal **was produced**. The new metal **was called** bronze. This harder metal **could be made** into weapons and tools.

Metals **can be made** better and stronger by mixing two or more of them together. The new mixture **is called** an alloy. When steel **is mixed** with certain other metals, stainless steel **is formed.** Stainless steel is very useful because it is strong and does not rust. Kitchen tools **are** often **made** of stainless steel.

Once metals **have been taken** out of the ground, they **will not be replaced**. For this reason, many metals today **are recycled**. In this photo, used metal **is being heated**. When it is hot, it **can be made** into new products.

?

1 What is an alloy?
2 What alloys are mentioned in the text?

Answers: 1 A mixture of two or more metals
2 Bronze, steel and stainless steel

The passive 1

1 Make the passive with *be* and the past participle.

present simple	Many metals **are recycled**.
present continuous	The metal **is being heated**.
past simple	The new metal **was called** bronze.
past continuous	While the copper **was being heated**, the tin was mixed in.
present perfect	These metals **have been used** for thousands of years.
past perfect	They **hadn't discovered** bronze yet.
will	The metals **will not be replaced**.
be going to	**It's going to be recycled.**
modal verbs + *be* + past participle	Metals **can be made** better and stronger.
+ *have / has been* + past participle	Bronze **may have been discovered** by accident.

TIP

Use *was / were born* NOT ~~*is / are born*~~.
*My grandfather **was born** in Australia.*

2 Use the passive to focus on the process or result of an action rather than the agent (who or what does the action), or when the agent is 'people in general'.
*A harder metal **was produced**.*
*The new metal **was called** bronze.*
(= People called it bronze.)

TIP

There are a few verbs describing events or actions which often use *get* instead of *be* in passive sentences. These are common in informal conversation.
get married, get involved, get stuck
*He is going to **get married** in the autumn.*

3 We can mention the agent in a passive sentence using the preposition *by*. We can use *with* to talk about an object used by the agent. Using *by* and *with* often puts greater emphasis on the agent.
*It was one of the first metals which was discovered **by man**.*
*They broke the rock **with a hammer**.*

TIP

You can find passives in many newspaper reports. The verb *be / get* is often left out in the headline.
STRANGE ANIMAL FOUND AT STEEL FACTORY
(= *A strange animal **was / has been found** at a steel factory.*)

Practice

A <u>Underline</u> the correct option.

1 Shellfish *open* / *<u>are opened</u>* with a knife.
2 Who *invented* / *was invented* the Internet?
3 This metal *is calling* / *is called* steel.
4 People *have known* / *have been known* about these metals for years.
5 The money *was collecting* / *was being collected* when we arrived.
6 That old coat *should throw away* / *should be thrown away*.
7 How *are you made* / *do you make* bread?
8 She *has not invited* / *was not invited* to the party.

B Rewrite these sentences using the passive.

1 QUIET AREA. We do not allow mobile phones.
QUIET AREA. Mobile phones are not allowed.
2 Someone may request ID.
....
3 You must show tickets at the door.
....
4 If you leave a bag in the station, someone will take it away and someone may destroy it. ....
....
5 We do not accept credit cards.
....
6 Please do not make too much noise, or we will ask you to leave.
....
7 You must wear hard hats.
....
8 You should carry ID at all times.
....

C Complete the text, using the words in brackets in an appropriate form of the passive.

Today, aluminium [1] ......is...... so widely ......used...... (use) that it is hard to imagine a world without it. It is a strong but light metal which [2] .... (can / shape) into drinks cans and window frames. It is a common metal for building cars and aeroplanes. NASA's space shuttles [3] .... (could not / build) without it – each space shuttle is 90% aluminium.
Large amounts of aluminium [4] .... (only / produce) for around 100 years, but the metal [5] .... (discover) a long time before that, possibly as much as 2,000 years before. Aluminium comes from bauxite, a rock which [6] .... (find) in hot places such as rainforests. The bauxite [7] .... (take) to a factory where it [8] .... (heat) to produce aluminium. It took many years to find a process for getting the metal out of the bauxite. As a result, when aluminium [9] .... (first / produce), the price of the metal was higher than that of gold.
It is an expensive process because large amounts of electricity
[10] .... (need). For this reason, a lot of aluminium
[11] .... (reuse). Never throw a drinks can away – it
[12] .... (can / recycle) easily.

D What is being done in each picture? Complete the sentences using the verbs from the box and a passive form.

clean ~~open~~ repair show study take

1 The new supermarket ...is being opened...

2 The road ....

3 The floor ....

4 The film ....

5 The mice ....

6 She ....

E Complete these short newspaper reports using the verbs in brackets in the active or passive form. Then write a suitable headline for each report using the passive. Sometimes more than one answer is possible.

NEWS IN BRIEF

INCREASE BLAMED ON INTERNET SHOPPING

There [1] ...has been... (be) an increase in the number of city centre shops which [2] .... (close) recently. The increase [3] .... (blame) on Internet shopping.

....

Drivers in Newport [4] .... (waste) petrol when they wait in traffic jams. Plans [5] .... (put forward) to encourage drivers to turn off their engines. Drivers [6] .... (could / ask) to pay up to £100 for keeping their engines on.

....

A man [7] .... (arrest) in Newport city centre yesterday. He [8] .... (try) to steal a CCTV camera from outside a car park. The man [9] .... currently .... (question) by police.

....

Twenty-eight-year-old film director, Max Tobin, [10] .... (get) married in secret last week. The well-known director [11] .... (born) and [12] .... (bring up) in Newport. He recently [13] .... (make) a film about local boy, Tom Lewis.

F Write six sentences about this film using the facts below. Use the passive where appropriate.

Star Wars Episode V: The Empire Strikes Back
1980
Director: Irvin Kershner
Story for the first six *Star Wars* films by: George Lucas
Mark Hamill (actor) = Luke Skywalker
OSCAR® for best sound
Filming: in Norway and the Elstree Studios in London
Following film: *Return of the Jedi*

Example: *Star Wars: The Empire Strikes Back was made in 1980.*

1 ....

2 ....

3 ....

4 ....

5 ....

6 ....

MY TURN!

What *can* (*not*) or *should* (*not*) be done with these things? Write two sentences for each item, using both modal verbs.

1 a rusty spoon

2 a plastic fork

3 an old shoe

4 a copper pan

5 a used toothbrush

6 bitter chocolate

7 dry bread

8 an old-fashioned mobile phone

Example: 1 *It can be cleaned. It should not be used for eating.*

MY TEST!

Circle the correct option.

1 Your request is .... considered. a being b been c be
2 When .... ? a discovered penicillin? b was penicillin be discovered? c was penicillin discovered?
3 I could see that a lot of work .... on the house. a had done b had been done c has been doing
4 She looked round to see if she .... followed. a was be b was been c was being
5 When will the results .... ? a be announced b announce c being announced?

My Test! answers: 1a 2c 3b 4c 5a

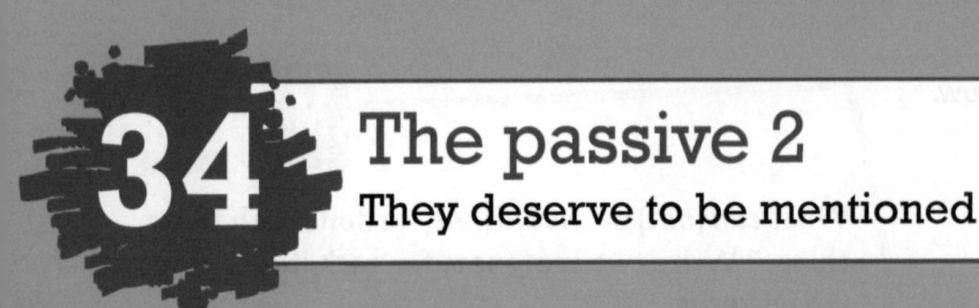

34 The passive 2

They deserve to be mentioned.

WE ARE eco MAGAZINE

Every month we look at buildings which support the environment. Here are three buildings which we think deserve **to be mentioned** this month.

Kurilpa Bridge is a 470-metre-long footbridge in Brisbane, Australia. The bridge has 84 solar panels which supply the power which **is needed** for the lights on the bridge at night. Over 36,000 people **are thought** to use the bridge every week.

The Eden Project in south-west England **has been designed** as a centre to educate the public about the environment. A number of domes contain plants from all around the world. Eden's designers didn't want the domes **to be made** out of glass but instead **had them built** out of a new and lighter material. The opening of the Eden Project in 2001 was a great success and thousands of visitors now enjoy **being welcomed** at the centre every week.

The Terminus Hoenheim-Nord is in Strasbourg, France. This tram station is the work of architect Zaha Hadid. The new tramline in Strasbourg **has been created** to reduce pollution in the city. Zaha Hadid **was given** The Pritzker Prize for Architecture in 2004.

? In what ways do these projects support the environment?

Answer:
Kurilpa bridge has solar panels which supply power.
The Eden Project educates the public about the environment.
The new tramline in Strasbourg reduces pollution in the city.

The passive 2

1 **Verbs with two objects, e.g. *bring, give, buy, allow,* have two passive forms.**
They gave her sister the prize. (active)
She ***was given*** *the prize.* (passive)
The prize ***was given*** *to her.* (passive)

▶ See Unit 27 for more verbs which take two objects.

2 **Verbs which take a *to*-infinitive are followed by *to be* + past participle in the passive.**
They didn't want the domes ***to be made*** *out of glass.*

We can use the passive *to*-infinitive after some adjectives.
I was very happy ***to be invited.***

▶ See Unit 29 for a list of adjectives which are followed by the infinitive.

3 **Verbs which take the *-ing* form are followed by *being* + past participle in the passive.**
They enjoy ***being welcomed.***

TIP

We can use some (passive) past participles as adjectives. Many of these describe feelings, e.g. *bored, disappointed, excited, interested, worried.*
I was ***bored*** *by the film.*

▶ See Unit 29 for more past participle adjectives.

4 **Passive forms of *believe, expect, feel, report, say, think, understand* are common in reports, particularly where the speaker is not necessarily agreeing with the statement or there is some uncertainty about the report.**
Over 36,000 people ***are thought to*** *use the bridge every week.*
It is thought that *over 36,000 people use the bridge ...*
There were thought to *be over 36,000 people using the bridge ...*

5 **We use *have* + object + past participle to talk about getting someone else to do something for us.**
The designers ***had*** *the domes* ***built*** *out of a new material.*

We also use *have* + object + past participle to talk about something (usually bad) that has been done by someone else.
I ***had*** *my mobile phone* ***stolen.***

6 **In informal language we can replace *have* + object + past participle with *get* + object + past participle.**
I ***got*** *my TV* ***fixed.***
I ***got*** *my mobile phone* ***stolen.***

7 ***Need* + *to be* + past participle has a passive meaning but we can also use *need* + *-ing*.**
The roof ***needs to be fixed.***
The roof ***needs fixing.***

Practice

A Complete the news stories with the appropriate form of the verbs in brackets.

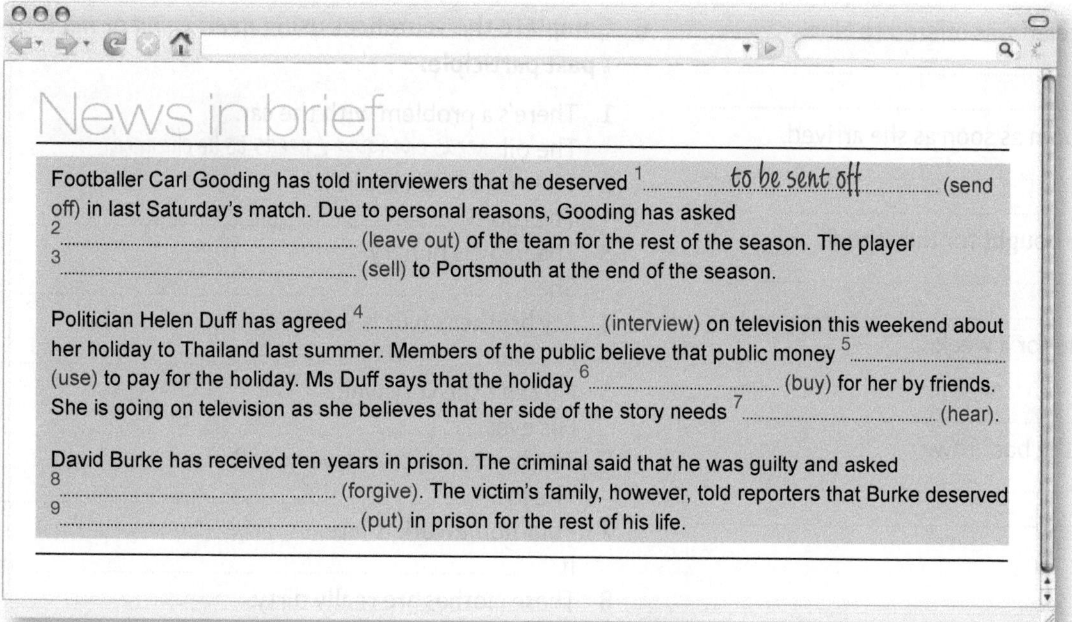

News in brief

Footballer Carl Gooding has told interviewers that he deserved 1 ......to be sent off...... (send off) in last Saturday's match. Due to personal reasons, Gooding has asked 2 .... (leave out) of the team for the rest of the season. The player 3 .... (sell) to Portsmouth at the end of the season.

Politician Helen Duff has agreed 4 .... (interview) on television this weekend about her holiday to Thailand last summer. Members of the public believe that public money 5 .... (use) to pay for the holiday. Ms Duff says that the holiday 6 .... (buy) for her by friends. She is going on television as she believes that her side of the story needs 7 .... (hear).

David Burke has received ten years in prison. The criminal said that he was guilty and asked 8 .... (forgive). The victim's family, however, told reporters that Burke deserved 9 .... (put) in prison for the rest of his life.

B Complete each sentence b so that it means the same as sentence a, using the passive.

1 a She likes people to call her Trixie.
  b She *likes to be called Trixie.*
2 a A dentist checks my teeth every six months.
  b I ....
3 a How would you like other people to remember you?
  b How would you .... ?
4 a People think it is extremely poisonous.
  b It ....
5 a Did anyone leave a parcel for me?
  b Was .... ?
6 a I asked them to tell me the results.
  b I asked ....
7 a Someone needs to fix my car.
  b My car ....
8 a Dogs enjoy it when someone takes them for a walk.
  b Dogs enjoy ....
9 a We expect the championship to be the best ever.
  b The championship ....
10 a I remember someone telling me I would fail.
  b I remember ....

C Rewrite each sentence so that it has a similar meaning, using another passive.

1 The patients were given the wrong medicine.
  The wrong medicine was given to the patients.
2 You will be offered an appointment as soon as possible.
3 There wasn't any food left for me.
4 The last place in the team was offered to Neal.
5 She was shown the room as soon as she arrived.
6 New computers were bought for the school.
7 The car was lent to me for a week.
8 I was found a seat in the back row.

D Look at this actor. Make up eight sentences about him, using the verbs *hate, like, love, prefer, hope, want* and the phrases in the box.

~~interviewed~~ involved in film work left on his own photographed remembered for ... surrounded by friends taken seriously told what to do

1 *He doesn't like being interviewed.*
2
3
4
5
6
7
8

E Complete the sentences using *need* + *-ing* or *need to be* + past participle.

1 There's a problem with the car.
  The oil *needs changing / needs to be changed.*
2 The hotel room is dirty.
  The room ....
3 The baby is hungry.
  She ....
4 My brother's hair is very long.
  His hair ....
5 He can't see very well.
  His eyes ....
6 The key doesn't work very well.
  The lock ....
7 Your homework is late.
  It .... now.
8 These clothes are really dirty.
  They ....

F **Write sentences about what the people are *having* or *getting done*.**

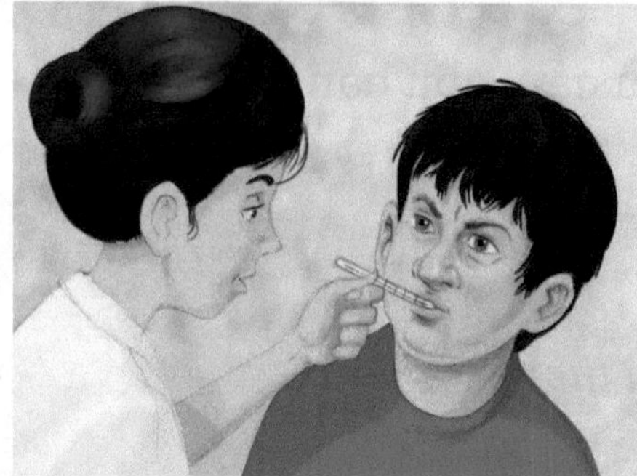

1 *She's having her roof fixed.*
2 ....
3 ....

4 ....
5 ....
6 ....

MY TURN!

Write three things that need doing.

Example: *The hole in my jumper needs repairing.*

1 ....
2 ....
3 ....

Write three things you (or someone you know) have (or has) had done recently.

Example: *My grandmother has had her car fixed.*

4 ....
5 ....
6 ....

MY TEST!

Circle the correct option.

1 The door of the building will need .... **a** to be made larger **b** being made larger **c** making larger
2 He .... by himself. **a** built his flat **b** had his flat built **c** got his flat built
3 The architect Antoni Gaudi did not like .... and there are few pictures of him. **a** taking his photograph **b** having his photograph taken **c** photographing
4 New brick houses .... the workers. **a** were built **b** were built to **c** were built for
5 The stadium .... in the summer. **a** expects to finish **b** expected to be finished **c** is expected to be finished

My Test! answers: 1a 2a 3b 4c 5c

35 Zero, first and second conditionals

If you think you can, you can.

If you don't know where you're going, any road will take you there.

Lewis Carroll

If you don't think about the future, you won't have one.

John Galsworthy

If I walked across a river, the newspapers would say, 'President can't swim.'

Lyndon Johnson

PRESIDENT CAN'T SWIM

If you're tired of London, you're tired of life.

Samuel Johnson

If we didn't have winter, spring wouldn't be so nice.

Anne Bradstreet

Even if you do learn correct English, who will you speak it to?

Clarence Darrow

If you love your job, you will never have to work again in your life.

Confucius

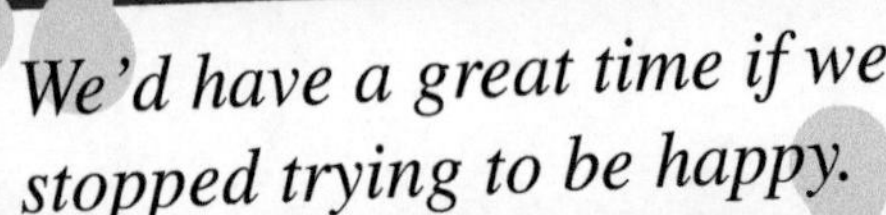

We'd have a great time if we stopped trying to be happy.

Edith Wharton

If you think you can, you can. If you think you can't, you're right.

Markus Ash

? Who said ...

1 journalists always find something bad to say?
2 London is a very interesting place?
3 you should believe in yourself?

Answers: 1 Lyndon Johnson 2 Samuel Johnson 3 Markus Ash

Zero, first and second conditionals

1 **There are two parts to conditional sentences.**

zero conditional	*if* + present simple	present simple	***If** you**'re** tired of London, you**'re** tired of life.*
first conditional	*if* + present simple	*will* + infinitive without *to*	***If** you **love** your job, you **will** never **have to** work again.*
second conditional	*if* + past simple	*would* + infinitive without *to*	*Spring **wouldn't** be so nice **if** we **didn't have** winter.*

TIP

We can use one part of a conditional sentence in a reply.

What would you do if you couldn't swim?
I'd learn!

2 **When *if* comes at the beginning of the sentence, we need a comma in the middle.**
If you think you can't, you're right.

3 **Use the zero conditional to talk about things that are generally true.**
I go to bed early if I don't feel well.
If it rains, you get wet.

4 **Use the first conditional to talk about something that we think is possible in the future, and its result.**
If I see the book, I'll buy it.
Will you tell me if Anna phones?

5 **Both parts of a first conditional sentence talk about the future, even though a present tense is used after *if*. We do not usually use *will* after *if*.**
If you read this book, you will learn many new things.
NOT ~~*If you will read this book ...*~~

6 **Use the second conditional for events and situations which are unlikely, imaginary or impossible in the present and future.**
What would you do if there was a fire? (something unlikely)
If I walked across a river, the newspapers would say ... (something impossible)

7 **We often use *if* + *were* instead of *was* after the pronouns *I, she, he, it* and singular nouns. This is more common in formal language and American English.**
*I wouldn't be surprised if it **were** true.*
*If your father **were** here, he would be shocked.*

TIP

We often use *If I were you ... I would (not)* ... for advice and suggestions.

***If** I **were you, I'd** wear the blue skirt.*

8 **We can use other modals instead of *will*.**
*If you think you can, you **can**.*
*It **might** break if you did that.*

▶ See Unit 37 for variations on conditionals.

9 **We can use *unless* to mean *if ... not* in the zero and first conditional. You can't use *unless* before a past tense.**
I run every morning if it isn't cold. OR *I run every morning unless it's cold.*
I will be disappointed if he doesn't come.
NOT ~~*I would be disappointed unless he came.*~~

10 **We can use *as / so long as* and *provided / providing* (*that*) with a similar meaning to *if*.**
*I don't care **as long as** it's free.*
*It's easy **providing** you read the instructions.*

11 **We can talk about imaginary situations with *imagine* (*that*) and *suppose / supposing* (*that*) in separate sentences.**
***Imagine** that you were famous. Would you be happy?*
***Suppose** she said no. What would we do then?*

TIP

Use *What if ...?* for suggestions and speculations. A present tense sounds more certain than a past tense.

***What if** we **drive** there?*
***What if** we **found** life on Mars?*

▶ See Unit 46 for *if* vs. *in case*, and other linking words.

Practice

A Match the pairs.

1	If I feel sad,	a	I'd ask for some help.
2	If I felt sad,	b	I phone my friend Sally.
3	If it snows tomorrow,	a	I'll make a snowman.
4	If it snowed in June,	b	I'd be very surprised.
5	If you are neighbours,	a	you already know each other.
6	If you were neighbours,	b	you would see each other every day.
7	I'll go to London	a	if I had a ticket.
8	I'd go to London	b	if you come too.
9	Water doesn't boil	a	if the kettle is broken.
10	The water won't boil	b	if it is heated to only 80°.
11	What would you do	a	if you're wrong?
12	What will you do	b	if you were me?

B Underline the correct option.

1 I *will* / *would* buy it if I have enough money.
2 It *will* / *would* be great if we could travel in time.
3 My dad gets angry if I *am* / *will be* late.
4 *Will* / *Would* you be at home if he comes?
5 If I *know* / *knew*, I'd tell you.
6 If it *doesn't* / *wouldn't* work, bring it back to the shop.
7 It *would be* / *is* great if you had the time.
8 What if it *breaks* / *will break*?
9 It will be finished soon *unless* / *if* there are more problems.
10 I wouldn't do that *unless* / *if* I were you.

C Complete the sentences so that they are true for you.

1 If I saw a mouse, I'd scream!
2 If the weather is nice tomorrow, ...
3 ...., I always feel happy.
4 If it was my friend's birthday, ...
5 ...., I'll tell all my friends.
6 If today was Saturday, ...
7 .... unless you study hard.
8 I can stay out late on Saturdays as long as ....

D Write sentences in the second conditional about the story. Look at the next sentence to find out what verb to use.

It is late at night. You are in bed. You hear a strange noise.
1 If I heard a strange noise, I'd get up.
You get up. The window is open.
2 If the window was open, I'd close it.
You close the window. You feel frightened.
3 ....
You go to your parents' room. Their room is empty.
4 ....
You call their mobiles. They are switched off.
5 ....
You are worried. You sit down on the bed.
6 ....
You think what to do next. You close your eyes.
7 ....
You fall asleep. You hear your alarm clock.
8 ....
You wake up. It was all a dream!

E Circle the correct option.

What [1]... life be like if we didn't have paper books? Imagine if there [2]... no bookshops or libraries. Some people think that this is the future if the use of electronic books [3].... Paper is heavy, expensive and bad for the environment; you need a lot of trees if you [4]... to make all those books.

Electronic books are also more convenient, [5]... you have the hardware. For example, [6]... you don't know a word, you can find the translation very quickly. Also, you can download new books very easily. So, is this the end of paper books?

Maybe not. Some people just prefer paper books. This is not surprising. Suppose you [7]... in front of a computer screen for eight hours. [8]... you like to look at another screen if you were relaxing at home? Also, paper books are probably better for your eyes. [9]... you want to get bad eyes, don't spend too much time looking at computer screens.

The future will tell if this [10]... right, but there will probably always be a place for paper books like this one.

1 ⓐ would b does c will d can
2 a were b would be c will be d are
3 a would continue b will continue c continues d continue
4 a would want b want c will want d wanted
5 a as long b suppose c unless d provided
6 a unless b would c if d provided
7 a will work b work c would work d must work
8 a Will b Do c Would d Could
9 a Unless b If c Suppose d Imagine
10 a were b will be c would be d is

F Write replies to the questions using conditionals.

1 Can you come on Tuesday?
I'll come if my dad says yes.
2 Could you lend me 10 euros?
....
3 Why won't you tell me what happened?
....
4 Do you think you can find the way there by yourself?
....
5 What are you going to do in the summer holidays?
....
6 What makes you angry?
....

MY TURN!

Answer the questions.

1 What do you do if you get a cold?
If I get a cold, I drink lots of tea with honey and lemon.
2 Where would you go if you could travel in time?
....
3 What will you tell your best friend if he / she phones now?
....
4 What can people do if they feel lonely?
....
5 If you could invite someone famous to your party, who would it be?
....
6 What would you ask / say to that famous person?
....

MY TEST!

Circle the correct option.

1 If the library is closed, I .... home. a will go b would go c go
2 My eyes get tired if I .... a lot. a read b will read c would read
3 .... you write your autobiography if you were famous? a Will b Would c Should
4 If you .... the book, you .... the film. a will like ... like b would like ... will like c like ... will like
5 *The Life of Lewis Carroll* isn't very interesting .... biographies. a if you will enjoy b unless you enjoy c unless you will enjoy

My Test! answers: 1a 2a 3b 4c 5b

36 Third conditional, *I wish*, *If only*

I wish I had heard those songs.

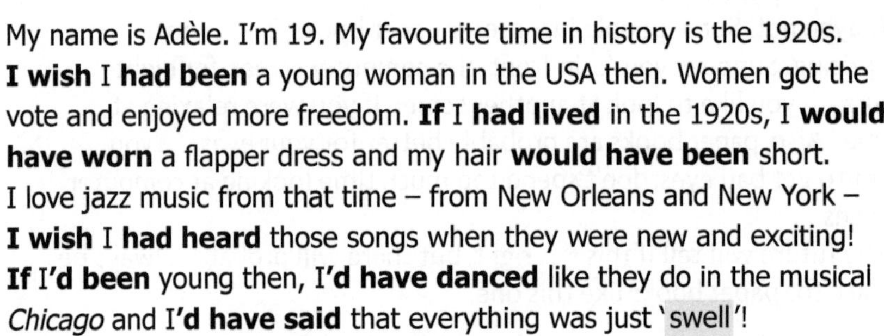

My name is Adèle. I'm 19. My favourite time in history is the 1920s. **I wish** I **had been** a young woman in the USA then. Women got the vote and enjoyed more freedom. **If** I **had lived** in the 1920s, I **would have worn** a flapper dress and my hair **would have been** short. I love jazz music from that time – from New Orleans and New York – **I wish** I **had heard** those songs when they were new and exciting! **If I'd been** young then, I**'d have danced** like they do in the musical *Chicago* and I**'d have said** that everything was just 'swell'!

My name is Ruth. It is 1924 and I am a farmer's wife in the south of the USA. **I wish** we **had** more money to buy new clothes. Times are hard and **I wish** I **were not living** on a farm. Our hut does not have electricity or water. My husband cannot sell the cotton that he has grown. **If only** we **could** sell the cotton, we **would be able** to find somewhere better to live.

?

1 What does Adèle like about the 1920s in the USA?
2 Were the 1920s good years for Ruth? Why / Why not?

Answer: 1 The fashion, the music and the new freedom for women.
2 No. She was a farmer's wife in the south of the USA. Her husband could not sell his cotton.

Third conditional, *I wish*, *if only*

Third conditional

1 Use the third conditional for events in the past which did not in fact happen.

If I ***had lived*** *in the 1920s, I* ***would have worn*** *a flapper dress.* (She didn't live in the 1920s and didn't wear this dress.)

2 Make the third conditional with two clauses

third conditional	*if* + past perfect	*would* + *have* + past participle	***If I had lived*** *in the 1920s, my hair* ***would have been*** *short.*

3 The clause that begins with *if* can come first or second in the sentence. When it comes first, we use a comma after *it*.

If I had lived then, I'd have said everything was just 'swell'.

I would have danced all the time if I'd been young then.

TIP

In third conditional sentences, we can shorten both *had* and *would* to *'d*

If ***I'd*** *lived in the 1920s,* ***I'd*** *have worn a flapper dress.*

I wish and *if only*

4 Use *I wish* or *if only* with the past perfect to talk about regrets.

I wish / If only I had heard *those songs when they were new.* (= It's a pity that I didn't hear those songs then.)

After *wish*, we sometimes use *were* instead of *was*.

I wish I ***was*** */* ***were*** *taller.*

5 Use *I wish* or *if only* with the past tense to talk about events and situations which you would like to be true now.

I wish *we had more money.* (We don't have a lot of money.)

If only *we could sell the cotton.* (We can't sell the cotton.)

TIP

***wish* or *if only*?**

Wish **is usually used with *I* (*I wish* ...) and is more common than *If only* ... .**

If only **expresses a stronger regret.**

Practice

A <u>Underline</u> the correct option.

1 I wish I had my own room. (I *have* / <u>*don't have*</u> my own room.)
2 He wishes he had got up earlier. (The man got up *late* / *early*.)
3 I wish I was good at dancing. (I'm *bad* / *good* at dancing.)
4 If I'd taken the train, I would have got there on time. (I *took* / *didn't take* the train. I *got* / *didn't get* there on time.)
5 I wish my cousins didn't live so far away. (My cousins live *far away* / *near*.)
6 I wish I could say sorry. (I *can* / *can't* say sorry.)
7 There wouldn't have been an accident if she had driven more carefully. (She *drove* / *didn't drive* carefully. There *was* / *wasn't* an accident.)
8 I wish I hadn't given the company my phone number. (I *gave* / *didn't give* the company my phone number.)
9 If they hadn't helped me, the job would have taken a long time. (They *helped* / *didn't help* me. The job *took* / *didn't take* a long time.)

B Complete the third conditional sentences with the correct form of the verbs in the box.

~~be~~ be call go eat listen lose see

1 If I hadn't been a teacher, I *'d have been / would have been* a footballer.
2 If we'd known what was happening, we .... the police.
3 If you .... to the instructions, you'd have known what to do.
4 If the children .... more breakfast, they wouldn't have been hungry.
5 You .... me if you'd waited a bit longer.
6 We'd have gone swimming if it .... sunny.
7 If we .... the match, I would have been so upset.
8 I .... to the party if I hadn't been ill.

C **What are these people thinking? Complete the sentences, starting with *I wish* or *If only*.**

1 I wish it wasn't .... raining.

2 ....
to buy those jeans.

3 .... you .... here.

4 .... we
.... on holiday.

D **Complete each sentence b so that it has a similar meaning to sentence a.**

1 a It's a pity we're not in the same class.
  b I wish we were in the same class.
2 a We should have left earlier.
  b If only ....
3 a Unfortunately I didn't hear the phone and didn't speak to her.
  b If ....
  ....
4 a They're sorry they can't come tonight.
  b They wish ....
5 a It's a shame that they didn't have enough time and the room wasn't finished.
  b The room ....
  ....
6 a I'd love to be sitting nearer the front.
  b I wish ....
  ....
7 a I can't understand why she didn't go to Australia with her friends and have a good time.
  b If she ....
  ....
8 a Oh dear. I've already sent that email.
  b If only ....

E **Read the short biography of F Scott Fitzgerald and, in your notebook, write six regrets that you think he might have had for himself or his wife.**

F Scott Fitzgerald was a writer in the 1920s. His novels are about the colourful lives of the young rich in the USA.

F Scott Fitzgerald started writing as a schoolboy. His first and most well-known novel, *The Great Gatsby*, was published in 1920. The novel was a big success. Fitzgerald and his new wife, Zelda Sayre, were immediately famous but they were soon in financial trouble.

Fitzgerald's later novels did not make as much money as the first. He often had to stop work on his novels and write short stories for magazines in order to make money. He did not particularly enjoy writing the short stories. Fitzgerald's marriage with his wife was very difficult. Many people consider that he did not write as much as he could because of this. Zelda became very ill later in life and spent long periods of time in hospital.

Fitzgerald died believing that he had been a failure. However, people consider him to be one of the best writers of the 20th century. It is a great pity that he did not see the success his novels later found.

Example: I wish I had written more.

F Sometimes things can have unexpected results. Write third conditional sentences about the following situations.

1 I broke my leg in a football match. While I was in hospital I started writing a book. It's just been published and is very successful.
If I hadn't broken my leg, I wouldn't have become a successful writer.

2 My friend told me a good place to buy a new mobile phone, but I couldn't find the shop. Instead I found a different shop and managed to get a really good phone for half the price!
....

3 It was an icy night and I was driving home. The car got stuck. Luckily, a really nice man stopped and pushed the car for me. He's now my husband!
....

4 I didn't want to go to college when I left school, so I travelled for a year instead. When I was in China, I was really interested in the history. When I came back I started studying History at college and I really love it.
....

5 My boss told me to leave my job. On the way home I decided to start my own business. My business is doing really well.
....

6 My parents didn't have enough money to buy a house in the city. We moved to the country instead. Now I love it here and have lots of new friends.
....

7 I didn't pass my Maths exam. I took the exam again and studied really hard. I found out I really liked Maths and now I want to be a Maths teacher.
....

MY TURN!

Write two things that you are glad happened as they did, and two that you are sorry happened as they did.

Example: *I'm glad I came to live here. If I hadn't come to live here, I wouldn't have met all my great friends.*

....
....
....

Write about some things you would like to have or to be able to do.

Example: *I'm not good at singing. I wish I could sing.*

....
....
....

MY TEST!

Circle the correct option.

1 I wish I .... meet people with the same interests. **a** could **b** can **c** –
2 I wish I .... been born 100 years ago. **a** would **b** had **c** have
3 I would have loved Fitzgerald's books if I .... lived then. **a** had **b** have **c** would have
4 If he hadn't loved his wife, he .... have left. **a** had **b** hadn't **c** 'd
5 I wish I .... working on a farm. **a** am not **b** not **c** wasn't

My Test! answers: 1a 2b 3a 4c 5c

Variations on conditionals

We can change the world if people listen to us.

Some young people live in difficult situations. Here are what some young people say on a website.

Education is very important but there are still many places where parents are too poor to send their children to school. **How can their children study if they're hungry**?
Zeina (12) Lebanon

When I was 12, I was already a soldier. I couldn't think for myself. **If someone told me what to do, I did it**. Children should never be in that situation.
Alhaji (14) Sierra Leone

Parents and children should talk to each other more. Too many parents don't understand their own children. **If you're reading this, you know that this is a problem**.
Diana (17) Romania

We can change the world if people listen to us.
Jebanzeb (12) Pakistan

Who thinks ...
1 communication between children and parents could be better?
2 all children should go to school?

Answers: 1 Diana 2 Zeina

Variations on conditionals

1 **Different combinations of tenses are possible in conditional sentences. Here are some possible patterns.**

If + past simple + past simple
*If someone **told** me something, I **did** it.*

If + present simple + present continuous
*If she **says** that, she's **not telling** you the truth.*

If + present continuous + present continuous
*I'm **not going** outside **if** it's **raining**.*

If + present continuous + present simple
*If you're **reading** this, you **know** that this is a problem.*

If + past simple + present perfect
*If Jack really **did** that, he's **made** a big mistake.*

2 **Modals other than *will* may be in conditional sentences.**
*How **can** their children study if they're hungry?*
*If you want to discuss similar topics, you **should** go ...*

3 **We don't usually use *if* + *will*.**
*If you **see** him tomorrow ...* NOT ~~*If you will ...*~~

We don't usually use *if* + *would*
*If you **go** into town ...* NOT ~~*If you would ...*~~

We can use *if* + *will* / *would* in sentences which are not conditionals, e.g. requests.
*If you **will** / **would** sit down, please.*

4 **We can use *if* + *should* and / or *happen to* when we want to show that something is unlikely.**
*If the situation **should** change, I will write to you.*
*Buy some if you **happen to** find them.*

5 **We can use *if* + present + imperative.**
*If you **need** more information, **contact the office**.*

6 **We can use *if it* + *wasn't* / *weren't* / *hadn't* + *for* to show that one thing changes the situation completely.**
***If it wasn't for** my bad leg, I could play in the match.*
*I would never have joined the army **if it hadn't been** for my uncle.*

7 **Instead of using *if*, we can put *had*, *should* or *were* + pronoun / noun first in the sentence. This is more formal.**
***Had I realised** the danger, I would not have given her my number.*
***Should your temperature** increase, phone a doctor at once.*

TIP

We can use *then* in the main part of a conditional sentence for emphasis.
*If you don't understand, **then** ask me.*
*As long as your parents know, **then** that's all right.*

Practice

A Tick the sentence closest in meaning to the conditional.

1 If it's 11 o'clock, Sandra is sleeping.
 a Sandra will sleep at 11 o'clock.
 b It is 11 o'clock now so Sandra is asleep. ✓
 c Sandra wants to sleep at 11 o'clock.

2 I went to Kim if I had a question.
 a In the past I asked Kim for advice.
 b In the future I will ask Kim for advice.
 c Now I ask Kim for advice.

3 See me if you've done page 26.
 a Speak to me before you finish page 26.
 b Speak to me as you do page 26.
 c Speak to me after page 26 is finished.

4 If you should find my gloves, put them in the cupboard.
 a There is a good chance of finding my gloves.
 b There is a small chance of finding my gloves.
 c There is no chance of finding my gloves.

5 If it hadn't been for John, the party would have been a disaster.
 a John saved the party.
 b John made the party a disaster.
 c John didn't go to the party.

6 If you will tell Mike, that'll be great.
 a Mike will be glad to hear you.
 b It is possible for you to tell Mike.
 c Please tell Mike.

B **Underline the correct option.**

1. If you <u>*are going*</u> / *will go* to the shop, please get some eggs.
2. If Boris *is working* / *works*, who is looking after the children?
3. Susan never complained if I *would be* / *was* late.
4. If you *would* / *should* have any problems, bring it back to the shop.
5. If you *would* / *may* come this way, please.
6. It wouldn't have broken if it *had been* / *hadn't been* for the storm.
7. *Would* / *Should* there be any more questions, write to me.
8. If that's true, *so* / *then* Karina was right!

C **Make conditional sentences by putting the words in the correct order. The first word is <u>underlined</u>.**

1. wanted / it / I / bought / <u>if</u> / something / I
   If I wanted something, I bought it.
2. Dad / driving / gets / <u>Mum</u> / if / nervous / is
   ....
3. <u>if</u> / staying / meet / in / you / are / let's / London
   ....
4. I / joke / a / if / laughed / <u>nobody</u> / told
   ....
5. too / now / we / it / be / might / go / late / don't / <u>if</u>
   ....
6. she / <u>if</u> / needs /party / Clare / is / the / a / dress / going / nice / to
   ....

D **Complete the sentences using the verbs in brackets.**

1. If I ....felt.... bad, I drank lots of hot tea. (feel)
2. If I'm travelling overnight I usually .... my suitcase. (take)
3. .... it been Sunday, there would have been fewer cars. (have)
4. Please remind Betty if you .... to see her tonight. (happen)
5. If the pilot .... this plane, then who is?! (not fly)
6. What would life be like if it .... for mobile phones? (not be)
7. People can learn a lot if they .... (read)
8. If you've answered all the questions, you .... the test. (finish)

E **Complete the dialogue with the words in the box.**

are can't could happen should then wasn't were ~~will~~ would

Interviewer: I'm here at UNICEF today to interview John Edwards about the work he does. Welcome, John. If you [1] ....will.... sit down, please. First, what does UNICEF actually do?

John: The most important thing is giving information. We [2] .... do anything if people don't know what is happening. By people, I mean everyone: children, parents, teachers, politicians, you and me .... If people knew the terrible things happening to children around the world, they [3] .... be shocked.

Interviewer: For example?

John: Many young children have to work. If it [4] .... for the money they make, their families would be hungry. I [5] .... give you many examples, if you have time, of the difficult and dangerous jobs which some children do.

Interviewer: If you [6] .... a child in that situation, what should you do?

John: Contact us. In most countries such work is illegal. [7] .... there be an accident, the employer, and maybe parents, would be in a lot of trouble. [8] .... I a politician, I would make very strong laws to stop young children working. Also, if you [9] .... to hear of stories like this, contact us, and the police.

Interviewer: Thank you, John. If you want to know about the work of UNICEF, [10] .... go to their website.

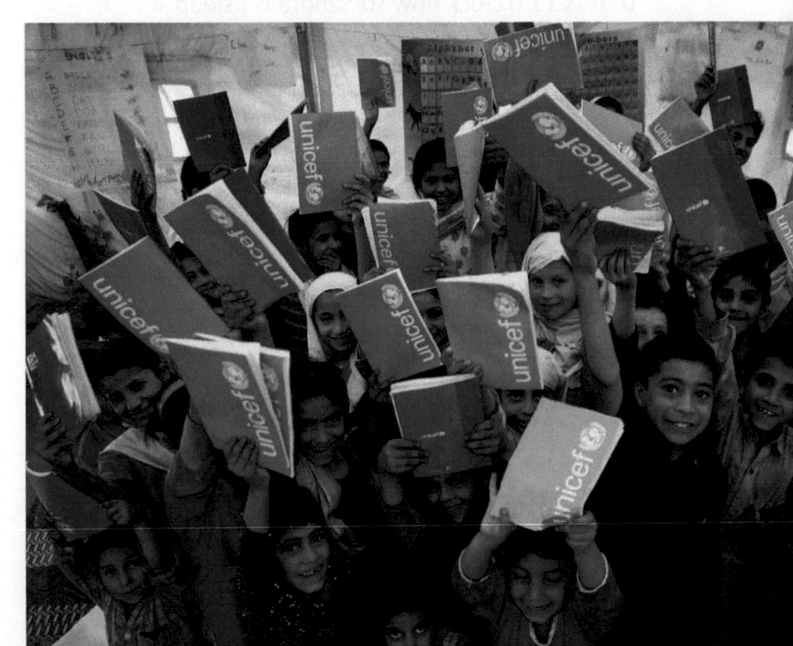

F Complete the sentences.

1 If someone is making a child work, and you know about it, then *phone the police*.

2 The little boy cannot stop work unless ....

3 Write to UNICEF if ....

4 If a child is working all day, ...

5 .... if it wasn't for greedy companies.

6 If a child happens to need money badly, ...

MY TURN!

Write sentences using conditionals for these situations.

1 You need to get your mum a present but you don't have any money.
If I don't have any money, it is going to be difficult to buy anything!
If my mum is hoping for a nice present, she's making a big mistake.

2 It is raining. You need to go out. You don't have an umbrella.

3 Your parents can't decide where to go on holiday.

4 You borrowed your friend's bike and broke it. Your friend doesn't know yet.

5 You have a big match tomorrow but you don't feel very well.

6 You found some money in the classroom. You don't know who lost it.

MY TEST!

Circle the correct option.

1 If you were hungry, you .... study properly. a won't b couldn't c didn't
2 We can't teach children if they .... to school. a didn't go b wouldn't go c aren't going
3 If Alhaji .... a mistake, he got into big trouble. a made b will make c makes
4 If it .... for UNICEF, many children would have very difficult lives. a was b wasn't c isn't
5 .... I in Alhaji's situation, I don't know what I would do. a Am b Be c Were

My Test! answers: 1b 2c 3a 4b 5c

Review: comparatives and superlatives; the passive; conditionals

A Complete each sentence using the word in brackets in the correct form.

1 Angelique is one of *the best* singers I've ever heard. (good)
2 Si Yee looks a lot .... than she did yesterday. (happy)
3 I used to think mathematics was very difficult but I find it much .... nowadays. (easy)
4 Excuse me. Do you know where .... bank is? (near)
5 Ten o'clock is quite late. Could you come a little .... than that? (early)
6 What's .... mistake you've ever made? (big)
7 The first level of this computer game isn't hard but it gets a lot .... (complicated)
8 I love the taste of coffee, but I know that tea is a much .... drink. (healthy)
9 The roads had ice on them and we had to drive as .... as possible. (careful)
10 Water is cheap here but in some countries it's .... than cola. (expensive)
11 There were lots of well-known artists in the 20th century but Picasso was probably .... of them all. (famous)
12 We've had lots of rain recently. In fact, it's .... summer I can remember. (wet)

B Circle the correct option.

Kolo: Have you [1]... heard of Aconcagua?
Sylvia: Yes, it's a mountain in South America, isn't it?
Kolo: Yes, it's in Argentina – well, on the border with Chile too. It's the [2]... mountain in the world outside Asia. It's 6,962 metres.
Sylvia: I see.
Kolo: Yes, I've been reading about it and they say it's [3]... easy to climb, so you don't have to be an experienced climber to get up it.
Sylvia: Really?
Kolo: Yes, several hundred people do it [4]... .
Sylvia: I imagine you need to be [5]... strong and healthy, though.
Kolo: Oh yes, and you have to prepare very [6]... , because it can be dangerous. You go up in a group with experienced climbers.
Sylvia: How long does it take?
Kolo: Usually about ten days, I think. You can't go any [7]... than that because you have to get used to the air up there. There isn't much oxygen, you see.
Sylvia: Yes, I can imagine. I'm sure that's really [8]... .
Kolo: Yes, but not impossible. The [9]... person to reach the top was 87 years old.
Sylvia: Wow!
Kolo: So, I'm sure we could do it. In fact, I think I [10]... try and do it myself one day in the future.

1 a never b sometimes ⓒ ever d often
2 a higher b highest c high d highly
3 a highly b absolutely c obviously d fairly
4 a the year b for a year c yearly d by year
5 a pretty b practically c hardly d nearly
6 a careful b carefully c care d carefuly
7 a quick b quickest c quicker d quickly
8 a hard b hardly c harder d hardest
9 a elder b older c old d oldest
10 a definitely will b will definitely c definitely won't d won't definitely

C Make the sentences passive.

1 We won't see the film in cinemas until the autumn.
The film *won't be seen in cinemas until the autumn.*
2 I hate it when someone cuts my hair.
I ....
3 What questions did they ask you in the exam?
What questions .... ?
4 They're showing the event live on TV.
The event ....
5 They didn't allow her to leave.
She ....
6 People are treating many of the injured in hospital.
Many of the injured ....
7 A police officer was questioning the men.
The men ....
8 Someone had used a stone to break the car windows.
The car windows ....

9 The woman gave the journalists false information.
False information ....

10 People should have reported the problem before.
The problem ....

D Complete the sports stories using passive forms of the verbs in brackets.

It has [1] *been announced* (announce) that Jorge Gomez, the manager of Real Madrid, is to leave the club. He [2] .... (say) to have [3] .... (offer) the job of managing the Irish national team. It [4] .... (think) that the exact date for Mr Gomez's move will [5] .... (agree) later this week.

Monica Serban, the Romanian 1,500 metre runner, [6] .... (expect) to return to racing at the European Games next month. Yesterday, she told journalists: 'I haven't raced internationally for over a year. Last year I [7] .... (tell) I had to have an operation on my knee and my training programme wasn't right and needed to [8] .... (change), but I now feel fitter and stronger than ever.'

The Scottish tennis player, Andrea Finlay, [9] .... (report) to be moving to France. In the past, she has said that she hates [10] .... (follow) by journalists in her home town. Friends say she wants to [11] .... (leave) in peace so that she can work hard on her training. More details about this [12] .... (announce) later today.

E Circle the correct option.

1 If you want to be successful in life,
 ⓐ you have to work hard.
 b you would plan things carefully.
2 If you had a lot of money,
 a how will you spend it?
 b what would you spend it on?
3 Let's see the new Superman film unless
 a you didn't like that kind of film.
 b you've already seen it.
4 You will be late
 a as long as you hurry.
 b unless you leave now.
5 We're not going out
 a if it's snowing.
 b if there will be snow.
6 I really wish
 a I can have more time.
 b I had more time.
7 Please ask Lee to call me
 a if you happen to see him.
 b if you saw him.
8 Phone a doctor
 a if you felt ill.
 b if you feel very ill.
9 If you like this CD,
 a why don't you buy it?
 b I'd buy it for you.
10 If you'd come with us yesterday,
 a you would have a good time
 b you would have enjoyed yourself.

F Underline the correct option.

1 If I were / am you, I'd be careful what I said to Sonya.
2 Get a taxi if you *get / will get* lost.
3 I wish I *can / could* stay a bit longer.
4 If you *happen / happened* to see Mike, phone me at once.
5 I really wish my sister *wouldn't / doesn't* sing in the shower.
6 Sarah *wouldn't learn / wouldn't have learned* Spanish if she hadn't lived in Madrid.
7 Trevor has agreed to help *as long as / supposing* it doesn't take too long.
8 *Provided / Supposing* you saw a ghost, what would you do?
9 If only Jill *had asked / asked* me before she bought it.
10 You *won't / wouldn't* know if I hadn't told you.

38 Indirect statements

They said their son was flying.

When Mr and Mrs Green phoned the police and **said that their six-year-old son was flying away in a balloon**, it became big news. Their story was **that Mr Green had made a** balloon in his garden and **that their son, Kevin, had got inside the balloon and flown away**.

The police followed the balloon for three hours. When the balloon came down, they found nobody inside. The police **thought that this was very strange** and started to look for Kevin. They found him in his parents' garage. Kevin **said he had been hiding**.

Many people now **believed that the whole balloon story was false**. Newspapers **wrote that Mr and Mrs Green (ex-actors) had done this** to get on TV. Finally, Mr Green **admitted that it was all a joke**. He **said he was sorry** and **promised that he wouldn't do anything so stupid again**. The police **didn't think it was very funny** – it had cost two million dollars to try and save the boy.

?

Put the events in order.

a The police found Kevin. ☐
b Mr Green said, 'I'm sorry.' ☐
c The police found the balloon. ☐
d Mr Green phoned the police. ☐
e Mr Green made a balloon. ☐

Answers: 1e 2d 3c 4a 5b

Indirect statements

1 **If the main verb is in the present, there is no change of tense in the indirect statement.**
Mr Green says that he is sorry.
My opinion is that it was a big mistake.

2 **When the main verb is in the past, the verb in the indirect statement usually moves into the past.**

direct statement	indirect statement
present simple ➜	past simple
'It seems strange.'	They thought that it **seemed** strange.
present continuous ➜	past continuous
'I am watching TV.'	She said that she **was watching** TV.
past simple ➜	past perfect
'I made a balloon.'	He told police that he **had made** a balloon.
past continuous ➜	past perfect continuous
'It wasn't raining.'	The weather report showed that it **hadn't been raining**.
present perfect ➜	past perfect
'We've lied.'	They told everyone that they **had lied**.
present perfect continuous ➜	past perfect continuous
'I've been hiding.'	He said that he **had been** hiding.
can ➜	*could*
'I can fly a balloon.'	Mrs Green said that she **could** fly a balloon.
will ➜	*would*
'I won't do this again'	He repeated that he **wouldn't** do this again.
may ➜	*might*
'We may be famous!'	The Greens thought that they **might** be famous.
be going to and *have to* ➜	*was / were going to* and *had to*
'We have to find the boy.'	They knew that they **had** to find the boy.

Past modal verbs (*would, could,* etc.) do not change.
The police said that they ***would*** *like an apology.*

3 **The verb in the indirect statement does not need to change if the information is still true or relevant now.**
Mr Green was sure that balloons ***are*** *safe.*
People did not know that the earth ***is*** *round.*

TIP

Indirect statements can show what people think, not what they actually say.
She didn't believe that it was possible.

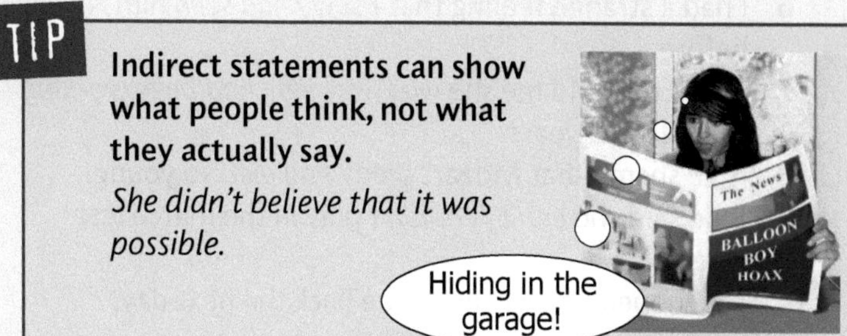

4 **Indirect statements can also come after adjectives and nouns.**
It's ***sad that some people will do anything*** *to get on TV.*
I love the ***idea that he was hiding in the garage****!*

5 ***That*** **often links the main verb of the sentence to the indirect statement.** ***That*** **can be left out, especially in conversation and informal language.**
The police ***didn't think*** *(****that****)* ***it was*** *funny.*
*It is lucky (****that****)* ***Kevin didn't get*** *into the balloon.*

6 **Pronouns and time and place expressions may change for indirect statements.**
we ➜ *they*
now ➜ *then*
next week ➜ *the week after*
this morning ➜ *that morning*
tomorrow ➜ *the next day*
ago ➜ *before*
here ➜ *there*

*'****We*** *will do it* ***tomorrow****.'* ➜ *They said* ***they*** *would do it* ***the next day****.*
*'****I*** *can do it* ***now****.'* ➜ *He said* ***he*** *could do it* ***then****.*

7 **Many verbs which introduce indirect statements are followed by *to*-infinitives, e.g,** ***advise, agree, ask, promise, tell.***
Kevin ***agreed to hide*** *in the garage and* ***promised not to tell*** *the police.*

Practice

A **Underline the correct option.**

1 I thought it *is* / *was* easy.
2 John shouted that he *wanted* / *has wanted* some help.
3 There is a legend that King Arthur *lives* / *lived* here.
4 You said you *were driving* / *had driven* home when it happened.
5 Remember that forest fires *are* / *were* dangerous.
6 I had a strange feeling that I *saw* / *had seen* him before.
7 Mrs Jones told me she *was working* / *had been working* there for 25 years.
8 It's a shame that Mozart *died* / *had died* so young.
9 Julie said she *can't* / *couldn't* play in the match last week.
10 Jake hoped he *will* / *would* be back the next day.

B **Write a dialogue using the underlined information in the text.**

Martin called Carol and said [1]he had a problem. He told Carol that his friend [2]Dave wasn't speaking to him because [3]they had had a big argument.

Carol thought [4]Martin needed to see Dave again. She knew that [5]Dave had been feeling terrible since their argument.

Martin replied that [6]he had tried to call Dave the day before; [7]he had just put the phone down. Martin was sure [8]that Dave wasn't his friend any more.

Carol said [9]she couldn't understand it. She advised Martin [10]to write Dave an email the next day.

Martin: 1 I have a problem.
2 ....
3 because ....
Carol: 4 ....
5 ....
Martin: 6 ....
7 but ....
8 ....
Carol: 9 ....
10 ....

C **Complete the sentences with indirect statements.**

1 He said it had been a long night.

2 My sister dreamed ....

3 He thought ....

I'm a genius!

4 Dracula said ....

I've got toothache!

5 Tom wrote ....

6 She was confident ....

I can do it!

D **Complete each sentence b to make a direct or indirect statement like sentence a, using the word in brackets.**

1 a 'Sam, it's five o'clock.' (told)
b Mary told Sam it was five o'clock.
2 a 'I'm reading a book.' (said)
b She .... a book.
3 a 'Liz has asked him.' (thought)
b I ....
4 a Andrea told Tim she would go the next day. (leave)
b 'Tim, ...'
5 a 'What! Nobody knows!' (strange)
b It was ....
6 a Richard had the idea that everybody disliked him. (nobody)
b 'I'm sure ....'
7 a 'You have to!' (said)
b My boss ....
8 a Brian told Maya that he had done it four weeks before. (month)
b 'Maya, I ....'

E Complete the text using the correct forms of the words in the box.

be beat ~~bring~~ can get hear hide invent may change play will make

In 1770, Wolfgang von Kemplen visited the queen of Austria. He said that he [1] *had brought* her a very unusual present: a machine which could play chess. The queen didn't believe that von Kemplen [2] .... serious, but the machine really did play chess. She thought that someone [3] .... inside the machine, but she opened it and found nothing.

The chess machine travelled all over the world. Von Kemplen understood that he [4] .... a lot of money from his machine and he was proud that it [5] .... even very good players. Napoleon and Benjamin Franklin both played and lost! People believed that von Kemplen [6] .... a real chess machine and they hoped he [7] .... another one. Newspapers wrote that technology [8] .... the laws of nature.

But there *was* someone inside the machine. People didn't know that all the time a little man [9] .... for the machine. The secret was discovered but the machine was still popular. Finally, the machine went to a museum in America. In 1854, there was a fire in the museum and the machine was destroyed. One man thought that he [10] .... the machine shouting for help in the fire. Today the museum has a working model of the original machine.

F Complete the sentences with indirect statements.

1 My friend didn't buy me a birthday card.
I thought *that she had forgotten about my birthday / she was angry with me*.

2 A stranger stopped me and asked me for ten euros.
I said ....

3 They are planning to open a new shopping centre near where I live.
I don't like the idea ....

4 No one knows if there is life on other planets.
I think ....

5 The film we saw last night was all right.
My opinion was ....

6 I found an interesting blog about strange pets.
I went on the blog and wrote ....

MY TURN!

Write at least four things that you heard, thought, read or said recently.

1 *I told my sister that I loved her new dress.*

2 ....

3 ....

4 ....

5 ....

6 ....

MY TEST!

Circle the correct option.

1 The newspapers wrote that Mr and Mrs Green .... the truth. a not to tell b don't tell c weren't telling
2 Mr Green said that he .... the story that his son was in the balloon. a had invented b invents c has invented
3 Journalists couldn't believe that Kevin .... at home all the time. a is b was c has been
4 Mrs Green said she .... to write a book about the story one day. a has wanted b had been wanting c wants
5 They promised that this .... again. a wasn't happening b wouldn't happen c may not happen

My Test! answers: 1c 2a 3b 4c 5b

Indirect questions

If you are wondering why glaciers are interesting …

File Edit View Favourites Tools Help

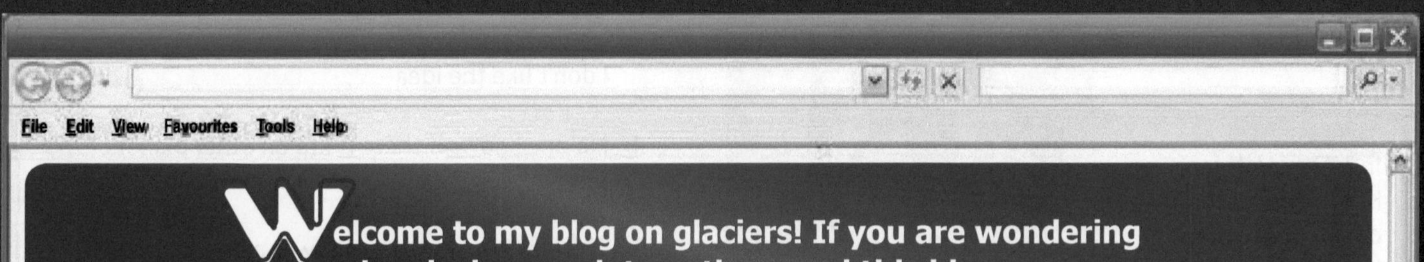

Maria (14, Spain) **asks what a glacier is**.

A glacier is a large piece of moving ice. Glaciers cover 10% of the Earth's surface.

Kylie (13, New Zealand) asks **the question how quickly glaciers move**.

Fairly slowly, usually less than 100 metres a year. Big glaciers move more quickly: some glaciers in Greenland move more than one kilometre a year.

Ming-Ji (13, Korea) wants to **know if icebergs are glaciers**.

No, icebergs are pieces of glaciers (sometimes very big pieces!) which break off from glaciers into the sea.

Djalma (15, Brazil) **asks why glaciers are important**.

Glaciers give us 75% of our fresh water. They are very important for the climate. If the Antarctic glaciers melt, sea water will rise 65 metres.

Henry (14, Tanzania) **asks whether there are any glaciers in Africa**.

Yes, in some mountains. There are also glaciers on Mars!

?
True or False?
1 Greenland has some big glaciers.
2 Glaciers are made from sea water.

Answers: 1 True 2 False

Indirect questions

1 **For indirect questions, the word order is question word + subject + verb. There is no auxiliary *do* or question mark.**
Maria asks ***what a glacier is.*** NOT *~~... what is a glacier?~~*
I wonder ***who Djalma saw.*** NOT *~~... who did Djalma see?~~*

2 **If the main verb is in the present, there is no change of tense in the indirect question. When the main verb is in the past, the verb in the indirect question usually moves into the past.**
A lot of people ***wonder why I am interested in glaciers.***
I asked my dad why he looked so sad.
NOT *~~... why he looks ...~~*
We ***wondered where she had gone.***
NOT *~~... where she has gone ...~~*

▶ See Unit 38 for more information on the change of tenses in indirect speech.

3 **Indirect questions can also come after nouns and adjectives.**
Kylie asks ***the question how quickly glaciers move.***
It is ***uncertain who did it.***

4 **For indirect yes / no questions, use *if* or *whether*.**
Ming-Ji wants to know ***if / whether*** *icebergs are glaciers.*
Henry asks ***if / whether*** *there are any glaciers in Africa.*

5 **Usually, *if* and *whether* are both possible.**
I don't know ***if / whether*** *it is true.*
But we can use only *whether* after prepositions and before *to*-infinitives.
It's a question ***of whether*** *we need it.* NOT *~~... of if ...~~*
Claire wondered ***whether to phone*** *him.*
NOT *~~... if to phone ...~~*

We say *whether or not*, NOT *~~if or not~~*.
I asked ***whether or not*** *that was OK.*

6 **If the subject of the indirect question is the same as in the main part of the sentence, we can use a *to*-infinitive.**
Maria doesn't know ***where to see glaciers.***
He asked ***what to write.***

We say *know how to*, NOT *~~know to~~*.
Scientists don't ***know how to*** *stop climate change.*
NOT *~~... know to stop ...~~*

Practice

A Match the situations to the indirect questions.

1 You have been waiting for a bus for one hour. — d
2 You need to borrow 200 euros from your dad.
3 Somebody has taken your favourite pen without asking you.
4 You have a test tomorrow but you know nothing.
5 Your aunty has given you a book on gardening for your birthday.
6 There was a very exciting film on TV but you missed the end of it.
7 Your friend wants to wear a bright green dress to the party.
8 You are at a great party but your mum rings and tells you to come home.

a I don't know what to say to her.
b I wonder whether my friend Louise can help me.
c I want to know why she chose this present for me.
d I doubt if it is coming.
e I'll ask if I can stay for another hour.
f I'm not sure if he will say yes.
g I'll find out who took it.
h I'm interested in what happened next.

B Make sentences by putting the words in the correct order. The first word is underlined.

1 me / was / date / what / asked / it / she
She asked me what date it was.

2 birthday / wonder / is / when / I / Jack's

....

3 care / what / say / Liz / doesn't / I

....

4 Simon / nobody / his / knows / exam / passed / if

....

5 happened / where / it / me / told / she

....

6 asked / I / all / right / the / whether / was / doctor

....

7 do / is / Charles / what / thinking / to

....

8 of / money / where / the / get / problem / is / the / we / there

....

C Complete the sentences with indirect questions.

1 'Six o'clock.'
I wanted to know what time it was.

2 'February 15th.'
I asked ....

3 'I'm not feeling very well.'
I wondered ....

4 'Yes, it should be great!'
I asked ....

5 'My friend Sam.'
I was interested to know ....

6 'No, I don't have enough money.'
Do you know ....

D Circle the correct option.

A hundred years ago, a team of explorers found a glacier in Antarctica. They weren't sure [1]..., so they named it the Mertz Glacier after the explorer Xavier Mertz. Although the Mertz Glacier is one of the biggest glaciers in the world, many people can't even say [2]... .

Xavier Mertz (1883–1913) was part of a team which wanted to find out [3]... Antarctica. There weren't even any maps of Antarctica at that time. They needed to know [4]... this very big continent, and [5]... possible to get from Antarctica to South Australia.

In November 1912, Mertz and two men, Ninnis and Mawson, were on a long difficult journey across the ice. There was a scream. At first, Mertz didn't understand [6]... . Then he saw that Ninnis had fallen through the ice. Even worse, he had fallen with most of their food. Mertz had no idea [7]... and asked Mawson [8]... to wait for help. Mawson told him they had to continue.

The two men were soon tired and hungry. On 7 January, 100 miles from their camp, Mertz asked [9]... . He wasn't sure [10]... . Sadly, Mertz soon died. Mawson managed to get back to camp safely and went on many more Antarctic journeys.

1 a what is it called (b) what to call it c what was it called
2 a who was Mertz b who Mertz was c what did Mertz
3 a was what in b what it was c what was in
4 a how do you cross b how was crossed c how to cross
5 a if it was b was it c what was it
6 a if happened b was what happening c what had happened
7 a what to do b if to do c what he did
8 a if b whether or not c if or not
9 a if he had stopped b why to stop c to stop
10 a how he continued b he could continue c if to continue

E Write indirect questions for what they are saying or thinking.

1 He is asking if he can have an ice cream.

2 ....

3 ....

4 ....

5 ....

6 ....

F Complete the indirect questions.

It was midnight. Jill was in bed [1]but her husband Jack wasn't home. Jill phoned Jack [2]but there was no answer. Then she called Jack's friend Tom [3]about Jack. Tom knew nothing. Two hours later Jack came home. Jill wanted [4]an explanation. Jack said he would tell her in the morning. Then they both went to sleep.

Jill woke up very early because of [5]a strange noise. [6]Had Jack heard it too? she thought. Jack then got up and went downstairs. The noise stopped but then there was a very bright light. [7]Jill was confused and frightened. Jack came back to the bedroom. He was carrying two spacesuits. [8]Jill was very surprised.

[9]Jack asked and Jill agreed to put on the spacesuit. They went outside and Jill saw the spaceship. Jill kissed Jack and answered [10]his question by saying that yes, she was happy. At last they were going back to Earth.

1 Jill didn't know ......where Jack was......
....
2 Jill wondered ....
....
3 Jill asked ....
....
4 Jill wanted to know ....
....
5 Jill didn't know ....
....
6 Jill wondered ....
....
7 Jill didn't understand ....
....
8 Jill wondered ....
....
9 Jack asked Jill ....
....
10 Jack wanted to know ....
....

G Write indirect questions about these people.

1 James Bond
I'd ask him if he liked detective stories.

2 Your favourite sports star
....

3 William Shakespeare
....

4 Xavier Mertz
....

5 Your favourite actress
....

6 The cleverest person in the world
....

MY TURN!

Complete the sentences with your own ideas.

1 I need to ask someone ......if they can look after my dog while I'm on holiday.
2 I've always wanted to know ....
....
3 In my opinion, it is doubtful if ....
....
4 It's very bad manners to ask ....
....
5 Most teenagers have no idea ....
....
6 Does anybody know the reason why ....
.... ?

MY TEST!

Circle the correct option.

1 She doesn't even know .... a what an iceberg is b what is an iceberg c if an iceberg is
2 I wonder .... the biggest glacier in the world. a where can you see b where you can see c you can see
3 The teacher asked .... geology. a if I liked b what I liked c if I did like
4 There's some doubt about .... glaciers will exist in 1,000 years. a if b that c whether
5 Scientists are not sure why .... so quickly. a move some glaciers b some glaciers move c do some glaciers move

My Test! answers: 1a 2b 3a 4c 5b

40 Defining relative clauses

The companies who connect people to the Internet

? Do you know your ISPs from your USBs?

Test your computer knowledge by matching the computer words to their definitions.

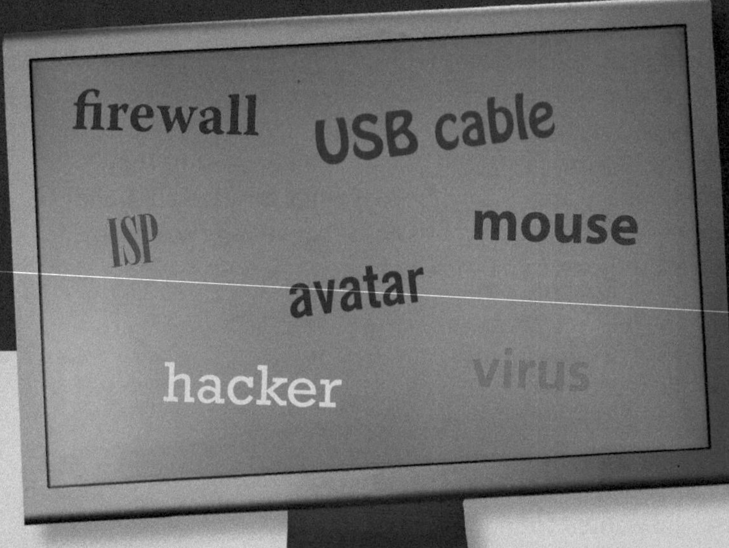

1 The companies **who** connect people to the Internet are called ***s.

2 A *** is something we use to move around the computer screen.

3 A *** is **what** you use to move photos from your digital camera to your computer.

4 An *** is a picture of yourself or a favourite character **whose** picture you use. The picture represents yourself in games and discussions on the Internet.

5 A *** is a small computer program **which** is designed to damage your computer files.

6 A *** is someone **who** uses or changes the information in other people's computer systems.

7 A *** protects your computer. It stops information **which** you don't know about coming into your computer.

Answers: 1 ISP 2 mouse 3 USB cable 4 avatar 5 virus 6 hacker 7 firewall

Defining relative clauses

1 **A relative clause gives us information about a noun. A defining relative clause says which person, thing, animal or idea we are talking about.**

*A hacker is someone **who uses or changes the information in other people's computer systems.***

2 **Many relative clauses begin with the relative pronouns *who, which* or *that*.**

Use *who* to refer to a person. Use *which* to refer to a thing, an animal or an idea.

Use *that* instead of *who* or *which* in informal language.

*A computer programmer is a person **who** / **that** designs computer programs.*
*A virus is a small computer program **which** / **that** is designed to damage your computer files.*

We can use *who* or *which* to refer to groups of people.

*The companies **who** / **which** connect people to the Internet are called ISPs.*

3 **We can leave out the relative pronouns *who, which* or *that* when they are the object of the relative clause.**

*This is something **(that)** we use to move around the computer screen.*

4 **If there is a preposition, it usually goes at the end of a relative clause.**

*... information **(which)** you don't **know about** ...*

In more formal language, we can use the preposition directly in front of the relative pronoun.

*... information **about which** you know nothing ...*

5 **When the relative pronoun is the object of the relative clause, or comes after a preposition, we do not need to repeat it.**

This is something that we use to move around the computer screen.
NOT ~~*This is something that we use it to move ...*~~
The teacher (who) I was telling you about.
NOT ~~*The teacher who I was telling you about her.*~~

6 **If *who* comes after a preposition or is the object of the relative clause, we can use *whom* instead. This is only used in more formal language.**

*... the woman **to whom** the prize was given ...*
*... someone **whom** Theo had met years before ...*

7 **Use *when* or *where* as relative pronouns after nouns which refer to a time or a place. We can often use a preposition + *which* with a similar meaning.**

*The room **where** the exam is taking place is ready.*
*(= the room **in which** the exam is taking place)*
*I don't like days **when** it gets dark early.*

8 **Use *why* (or *that*) after the noun *reason*.**

*That's the reason **why** / **that** I came.*

9 **Use *what* to mean 'the thing(s) which'.**

*A USB cable is **what** you use to move photos from your digital camera to your computer. (= **the thing which** you use)*

10 **Use *whose* + noun to mean *of whom, of which. Whose* can refer to people, animals or things.**

*We are an organisation **whose aim** is to make computer training available to everyone. (= the aim of which)*

TIP

We can often use *with* instead of:

– **a relative clause with *whose***
*a friend **whose** brother lives nearby = a friend **with** a brother **who** lives nearby*
– **a relative clause using *who* / *which* and *have***
*an old computer **which has** a lot of problems = an old computer **with** a lot of problems*

11 **There is no comma before a defining relative clause.**

*The companies **who connect people to the Internet** are called ISPs.*
NOT ~~*The companies, who connect people to the Internet are called ISPs.*~~

Practice

A **Underline the correct option. Sometimes both options are possible.**

1 This is the place where / *which* I live.
2 April is the month *in which* / *when* she was born.
3 The giant panda lives in forests *which* / *where* are being cut down.
4 The letter should only be read by the person *to who* / *to whom* it is addressed.
5 He's a lovely man *who has* / *with* a lot of friends.
6 The 1950s and 60s were the years *when* / *where* the Cold War was at its worst.
7 That's the reason *that* / *why* we moved.
8 I don't know *what* / *that* you mean.

B **Complete the email by putting relative clauses a–h in the correct places.**

Delete Reply Reply All Forward Print

I had a letter from Lily Wylie recently. You remember me talking about my Uncle Ray, don't you? He's the uncle [1] ......g...... . He grew up in Glasgow with my dad and my Uncle Colin. Uncle Ray left home when he was quite young. That was in the 1950s [2] .... He got on a ship [3] .... and lived there for the rest of his life. When he arrived in Canada, he stayed with a couple, Mr and Mrs Bennett, [4] .... They had one child. She's my cousin, but I've never met her. Uncle Colin stayed in Glasgow in the house [5] .... and opened a shop [6] .... Uncle Ray and Uncle Colin never saw each other again. Anyway, I had a letter from Lily recently. She's the daughter of the cousin [7] .... She's going to be over here [8] .... and I think she would like to meet you!

a I've never met
b when you could leave school at 15
c when you're next at home
d where he was born
e that sold fish
f which was going to Canada
g ~~who moved to Canada~~
h whose daughter he later married

C **Complete the sentences with *who, which* or *that*. (More than one relative pronoun is possible in each sentence.) Then put brackets around the pronouns which can be left out.**

1 It's the 5.00 train ...(which / that)... you need to catch.
2 The man .... is sitting in the corner is not well.
3 The reporter asked her a lot of questions .... she couldn't answer.
4 You can pick any strawberries .... are red.
5 There are not many people .... would like his job.
6 How could a person .... I love have done this?
7 Look! It's the actor .... played Sam.
8 Chelsea is the football team .... my brother supports.

D **Complete the sentences by putting the words in the correct order.**

1 were / about / you / boy / telling / the / me
Is that ...the boy you were telling me about... ?
2 of / that / something / I'm / proud
It's not ....
3 joke / laughing / understand / were / at / the / they
I didn't ....
4 book / film / which / on / the / the / based / is
I've read ....
5 books / for / looking / which / found / you / the / were
Have you .... ?
6 old / across / came / which / were / very / they
The clothes ....
7 yesterday / to / the / listening / you / were / song
What was .... ?
8 died / to / was / married / has / she
The actor ....

E Join the sentences using relative pronouns.

1 The stories talk of a princess. Her hair is like gold.
The stories talk of a princess whose hair is like gold. /
The stories talk of a princess who has hair like gold.

2 This is the film. The Coen brothers are most famous for this film.

3 That's the guy. You go to school with his son.

4 The people should come to the front of the class. I read out their names.

5 You will never guess. I've just been talking to someone.

6 Why don't we visit that museum? You were looking at their website.

7 There are some shoes in this shop. I'd really like them.

8 Suddenly Dawn saw the man. She had bought the car from him.

F In your notebook, write definitions for at least four of the computer words, using the words in brackets.

1 a webmaster (create)
A webmaster is someone who creates a website.
2 a chatroom (send / receive)
3 a cybercafé (use)
4 an email (send)
5 a laptop or a notebook (carry)
6 screen (look at)
7 Bill Gates (start)

MY TURN!

Complete the sentences with relative clauses to make them true for you.

1 I can't imagine a time *when there were no computers.*

2 I've never been to a country .

3 I'd like to meet someone .

4 I prefer watching films .

5 I don't like people .

6 I never buy clothes .

7 I always remember places .

8 I love days .

MY TEST!

Circle the correct option.

1 I need to find someone .... can fix my computer. a who b which c –
2 An inbox is the place .... your emails arrive. a when b where c why
3 I don't know ....
a what about you were worrying b about what you were worrying c what you were worrying about
4 That is the guy .... I went to school with. a who the wife b whose wife c the wife of who
5 A console is .... you need to play a video game on the TV or your computer. a what b which c that

My Test! answers: 1a 2b 3c 4b 5a

41 Non-defining relative clauses

'I thought it was dumb, which shows he's smarter than I am!'

When Mike Hayes started university at Illinois in the United States, he found he did not have enough money to pay for his studies. Hayes came up with an idea. He wrote to Bob Greene, **who** was a famous writer for the *Chicago Tribune*, and asked every reader of the letter to send him a penny. The newspaper has millions of readers, **many of whom** sent in a penny. Money was received from every state in the USA, as well as Mexico, Canada and the Bahamas, **where** the paper is also read. Eventually, Mike raised $28,000, **which** was the amount he needed for his studies. Hayes, **who** went on to get his degree in food science, says the idea worked because 'I didn't ask for a lot of money. I just asked for money from a lot of people.' Hayes's father, Bill, says, 'When Mike first told me about his idea, I thought it was dumb, **which** shows he's smarter than I am!'

?

1 Why did Mike Hayes write to the *Chicago Tribune*?
2 Was the idea dumb?

Answers: 1 To ask all the readers for a penny. 2 No

Non-defining relative clauses

1 **A non-defining relative clause gives us additional information about a person, thing, animal or idea.**
Hayes, who went on to get his degree in food science, says the idea worked.

▶ See Unit 40 for information on defining relative clauses.

2 **If we take the non-defining relative clause out of a sentence, the sentence will make sense without it.**
Hayes, ~~who went on to get his degree in food science,~~ says the idea worked.

We can use brackets ( ) or dashes – ... – instead of commas (,) before and after non-defining relative clauses.
Hayes (who went on to get his degree in food science) says the idea worked.

3 **Use commas with a non-defining relative clause.**
*Eventually, Mike raised $28,000, **which was the amount he needed for his studies.***
*Bob Greene, **who was a famous writer for the** Chicago Tribune, asked every reader of the letter to send a penny.*

4 ***Who, whose, which, where*** **and** ***when*** **are common relative pronouns in non-defining relative clauses.**
*Money was received from every state in the USA, as well as Mexico, **where the paper is also read.***

5 **We cannot leave out the relative pronoun in non-defining relative clauses.**
*Bob Greene, **who** he wrote to, thought it was a great idea.* NOT *~~Bob Greene, he wrote to ...~~*

6 **We can use** ***which*** **to refer to a whole statement.**
*I thought the idea was dumb, **which** shows he's smarter than I am!* (*which* refers back to *I thought the idea was dumb*)

TIP

We do not use ***that*** **as a relative pronoun in a non-defining clause.**
*Bob Greene, **who** was a famous writer for the Chicago Tribune, asked every reader to send Mike a penny.* NOT *~~Bob Greene, that was a famous writer for the Chicago Tribune, asked ...~~*

7 **After words like** ***all, both, many, neither, some, first, last,*** **numbers and superlatives (e.g.** ***the best, the worst*****), we can use** ***of which*** **or** ***of whom.***
*The newspaper has millions of readers, **many of whom** sent in a penny.*
*There are a number of newspapers in Chicago, the **most popular of which** is probably the* Chicago Tribune.

8 **If there is a preposition, it usually goes at the end of a relative clause.**
*Bob Greene, who he wrote **to**, thought it was a great idea.*

In more formal language we can use the preposition directly in front of the relative pronoun, as in defining relative clauses.
*She did not mention John again, **for which** I was grateful.*

9 **If** ***who*** **comes after a preposition or is the object of the relative clause, we can use** ***whom*** **instead. This is only used in more formal language.**
*The people, **to whom** the land actually belonged, were asked to leave.*

Practice

A Underline the correct option.

1 Mario Testino has taken some great photos, some of *which / that* are in this book.
2 Toby, *whose / who his* parents wanted him to be a doctor, became a musician instead.
3 I missed the game on Saturday, *what / which* was a shame.
4 They had four children, the eldest of *who / whom* was just ten years old.
5 They called their daughter Emiko, *which / that* means 'smiling child'.
6 Everyone came except for Cameron, *who / which* was not very well.
7 Most people had not heard of Usain Bolt before the Beijing Olympics, *where / which* he won three gold medals.
8 I met Dale last year, *when / who* he was working at the holiday centre.

B Complete the sentences with the correct relative pronouns.

1 The actor, ...who.... is now only 26, has already starred in a number of well-known films.
2 The city centre hospital, ... my mum worked, is closing at the end of the year.
3 In the summer, ... the tourists are here, there are lots of jobs in bars and restaurants.
4 The dog, ... had followed her along the road, didn't seem to have a home.
5 At this hotel, ... he often came to stay, Proust wrote his most famous book.
6 The team, ... manager left last January, have not been playing well.
7 He has never spoken to me about it, ... I think is really strange.
8 The money was won by a couple, ... later gave it away.

C Complete these sentences with the correct relative pronouns and prepositions.

1 The running club is going to several races this year including the New York Marathon, ...which.... I'm taking part ....in.... .
2 I was so embarrassed in the restaurant yesterday! My uncle didn't like the food, ... he kept complaining ....
3 There was a bad accident here yesterday. The old woman, ... house the car crashed ...., was later taken to hospital.
4 There are many hotels in the city, the best .... is probably the Victoria.
5 I can't work at the cinema on Saturday. They will need someone to collect the tickets at the door, ... I'm usually responsible ....
6 Tomorrow my mum is going to stay with my aunt, ... she is always worrying ....
7 Thankfully the neighbours, ... dog we've been looking ...., are coming back from holiday tomorrow.
8 The pop band sang in front of around 20,000 people, most .... seemed to be young girls.

D Rewrite each sentence to include the information in brackets.

1 The Taj Mahal was built by Emperor Shah Jahan for his wife. (It is in northern India.)
The Taj Mahal, which is in northern India, was built by the Emperor Shah Jahan for his wife.
2 There are 132 rooms and 35 bathrooms in the White House. (The President of the United States lives there.)
3 Vincent Van Gogh was born in the Netherlands in 1853. (His most famous work is probably *Sunflowers*.)
4 Landing on the planet Mars was finally achieved in 1976. (Scientists had always dreamed of this.)
5 The Sydney Opera House was designed by Danish architect, Jorn Utzon. (Its roof looks like the sails of many boats.)
6 Che Guevara fought in the Cuban Revolution. (He died in 1967.)
7 The idea of using sound waves to find illness was put forward in the middle of the 20th century. (We now know this as ultrasound.)
8 The Russian winter lasts from late October to April. (Temperatures typically drop to –25ºC.)

E Rewrite this story, changing the underlined sentences into relative clauses.

I love this story. I think about it when things are difficult. It is a true story. The beginning of the film *Good Will Hunting* is based on it. The story is about a young maths student, George Dantzig. He studied at the University of California, Berkeley, in the USA. One day Dantzig arrived late for a class and copied down two maths problems from the board. He thought these were for homework. The problems took him longer than usual to solve. Dantzig found both of them difficult. A few weeks later he was woken early by someone at the front door. Dantzig had forgotten all about the homework now. He opened the door to find his teacher with the homework in his hand. His teacher was very excited. The homework had in fact been two examples of famous unsolved maths problems and Dantzig had just solved them! Dantzig believed this was an example of positive thinking. Dantzig's father was a mathematician. If he had known these were unsolved problems, he would never have been able to do them!

I love this story, which I think about when things are difficult.

F Add more information to this story using relative clauses.

One day a man was taking some apples to the town, [1] *which was several kilometres away*. He put all the apples into bags on his donkey, [2] .... On the way he met a boy, [3] .... , and his donkey.
'How long will it take to get to the town?' asked the man, [4] ....
'If you go quickly, it will take you a long time,' said the boy. 'But if you go slowly, you will get there quicker.'
The man thought the boy was being silly, [5] ....
'I'll get there before you!' he said.
The man and his donkey went very quickly along the road. They went so fast that the apples started to fall out of the bags. The man, [6] .... , stopped for a rest. Suddenly he saw the bags, [7] ....
'Where are all the apples?' he cried.
The man went back to pick up all the apples. It took a long time. Night fell and it was dark when the man finally got to the town. He saw a hotel, [8] .... , and went in.
The boy, [9] .... , was staying there too.
'Ah,' said the boy. 'I told you to go slowly!'

MY TURN!

Write a simple sentence about each of the topics below.

1. A friend: ....
2. Your school: ....
3. Your favourite thing: ....
4. Someone in your family: ....
5. Your hometown: ....
6. The month you were born: ....
7. Somewhere you went on holiday: ....
8. Your favourite subject: ....

Example: 1 *Charlie lives in my street.*

Now add one more piece of information in a relative clause to each sentence and write it in your notebook.

Example: *Charlie, who I've known for years, lives in my street.*

MY TEST!

Circle the correct option.

1. The hotel is on a fantastic beach, ... the sand is almost black. **a** where **b** which **c** that
2. They had three sons, all of .... became lawyers. **a** which **b** whom **c** who
3. The teacher did not give me a very good mark, ... I did not understand. **a** that **b** what **c** which
4. Mike Hayes, ... idea it was, raised $28,000. **a** whom **b** who **c** whose
5. The club meetings, ..., are on Tuesday evenings.
   a I look forward to which **b** which I look forward to **c** that I look forward to

My Test! answers: 1a 2b 3c 4c 5b

42 Word formation 1: verbs and adjectives (affixes)

Scrabble – the international game

Scrabble is a game where you need to build words from letters. It's not difficult to **under**stand the basic rules of Scrabble but players need to be very skil**ful** if they want to score a lot of points and **out**play each other.

PRE DE ABLE LESS

Look for 'affixes', groups of letters which go before (**pre**fixes) or after words (suffixes) and make them bigger.

For example, prefixes like **mis**, **sub**, **over** and **un** are very use**ful** because you can make words like **mis**hear, **sub**standard, **over**eat and **un**interesting.

MISHEAR
SUBSTANDARD

Suffixes like **ize / ise**, **ent** and **ive** are also great.

DIFFERENT
MODERNIZE
IMAGINATIVE

Remember that you can also put affixes together in one word.

UNSOCIABLE
OVERCOMPLICATE

Scrabble is an **inter**national game with versions in many languages. There are **pro**fessional games and **con**tests, but most people play for fun. Scrabble can also be very help**ful** for building your vocabulary. Look at the website www.scrabble.com to **dis**cover more about this great game.

?

1 In the word *unhappy*, is *un* a prefix or a suffix?
2 Do suffixes come at the start or end of words?

Answers: 1 A prefix 2 At the end

Word formation 1: verbs and adjectives (affixes)

Prefixes

1 Prefixes change the meaning of a word.

I played John, but lost.
*I **out**played John, and won.*

2 These prefixes change verbs and / or adjectives:

prefix	meaning	examples
co-	together	***co**exist, **co**operate*
de-	change, reverse	***de**form, **de**forest*
dis-, in- (il- / im- / ir-), un-	not	***in**active, **im**possible, **un**happy*
inter-	between	***inter**view, **inter**national*
mis-	wrongly, badly	***mis**take, **mis**understand*
out-	do something better than	***out**do, **out**play*
over-	more, too much	***over**eat, **over**-excited*
post-	after	***post**graduate, **post**-war*
pre-, ante-	before	***pre**view, **ante**rior*
pro-	for, in favour of	***pro**-democracy, **pro**-freedom*
re-	again	***re**build, **re**sell*
semi-	half, partly	***semi**circular, **semi**conscious*
tele-	from far away	***tele**phone, **tele**work*
trans-	across	***trans**port, **trans**atlantic*
under-, sub-	less, not enough	***under**estimate, **sub**standard*

Instead of *in-*, use *im-* before *m* and *p*, *il-* before *l*, and *ir-* before *r*.

*in- + mature ➜ **im**mature*
*in- + legal ➜ **il**legal*
*in- + responsible ➜ **ir**responsible*

TIP

The prefix *en-* changes nouns and adjectives into verbs.
***en**danger, **en**large*

3 Most prefixes don't have hyphens (-). Add a hyphen only if it is needed to show a change of meaning, or make the meaning clearer.

***re**mark* = to say something
***re**-mark* = to mark again

TIP

New words created with prefixes in English usually have a hyphen until they become very common. For example, today *email* is spelled without a hyphen.

Some words can be spelled both with and without a hyphen.

cooperative /kəʊˌɒp.ᵊr.ə.tɪv/
▶ ***adjective*** (UK ALSO **co-operative**) *willing to help or do what people ask: I've asked them not to play their music so loudly, but they're not being very cooperative.*

Suffixes

4 Suffixes usually change the type of word as well as its meaning; *heart* is a noun but *heartless* is an adjective; *hard* is an adjective but *harden* is a verb.

*A skil**ful** player has a lot of skill.*
*If you length**en** a word, you increase its length.*

5 These suffixes change verbs or nouns into adjectives:

suffix	meaning	examples
-able	can be done	*do**able**, work**able***
-al	related to	*accident**al**, critic**al***
-ant, -ent	related to	*import**ant**, depend**ent***
-en	made of	*gold**en**, wood**en***
-ful	full of, related to	*harm**ful**, use**ful***
-ic	related to	*hero**ic**, poet**ic***
-ish	like / people or language of	*green**ish**, Span**ish***
-ive	related to	*creat**ive**, effect**ive***
-less	without	*home**less**, speech**less***
-like	like	*business**like**, child**like***
-ous	related to	*fam**ous**, nerv**ous***
-y	like / having	*funn**y**, wind**y***

6 These suffixes change nouns or adjectives into verbs.

suffix	examples
-ate	*cre**ate**, demonstr**ate***
-en	*deaf**en**, strength**en***
-ify	*horr**ify**, simpl**ify***
-ise / ize	*modern**ise**, revolution**ize***

TIP

Many verbs can be spelled with both *-ise* and *-ize*, but *-ize* is more common today, especially in American English.

*a computer**ised** / computer**ized** system*

Some verbs are only spelled with *-ise*, even in American English, e.g. *advertise, revise*.

Practice

A Match the pairs.

1 This rice is overcooked. — a Just put it in the microwave.
2 This rice is precooked. — b Throw it away!

3 It's harmful. — a Don't touch it!
4 It's harmless. — b Don't worry.

5 She's semiconscious. — a She is moving her eyes.
6 She's unconscious. — b She can't hear you.

7 Wanda is overpaid. — a She is looking for another job.
8 Wanda is underpaid. — b She has a bigger salary than me.

9 Brad is very forgetful. — a He forgot what time the play started.
10 Brad's acting was unforgettable. — b I think he is brilliant.

B Add affixes to the words.

1 Federer o u t played Nadal and won the match.
2 Switch off your computer and then _ _ start it.
3 It was a cold and wind_ day.
4 You can save money by _ _ _-booking two weeks before you go.
5 That music is too loud. It will deaf_ _ you!
6 If the pasta is _ _ _ _ _ _ cooked, it will be very hard, so put it back in the pan.
7 They supported the president and his _ _ _-government army.
8 It is expensive to advert _ _ _ on TV.
9 It was all done in a very business_ _ _ _ way.
10 Julia is a very like _ _ _ _ girl. She's popular with everyone.

C Complete the crossword with verbs and adjectives.

Across

2 Strong winds can be very ....
4 Running will .... your legs.
5 Horror films .... me. I can't watch them!
7 .... footballers get very high salaries.
9 Jack really .... his parents when he didn't go to university.
10 If something is .... , it is not good enough.
11 'To .... the wheel' means to make something that already exists.
12 English is an .... language.

Down

1 I .... it at first but then I listened again and everything was clear.
3 The opposite of 'valuable'.
6 The piano and the guitar are examples of .... instruments.
8 My alarm clock was broken, so I .... this morning.

D Write a word with an affix that means the same as each definition.

1 across the Atlantic transatlantic
2 to make modern ....
3 by chance ....
4 to get too hot ....
5 to do an exam again ....
6 with no hope ....
7 to see before ....
8 the language spoken by the Finns ....

E Complete the text with the correct prefixes and / or suffixes.

English spelling is [1]fam ous for being [2]illogic........ . Many words are not written as they sound. G. B. Shaw liked to [3]demonstr........ how you could [4]........nounce the (non-word) 'ghoti' as 'fish': *gh* is pronounced like *f* in *laugh*; *o* is pronounced like *i* in *women*; *ti* is pronounced like *sh* in *station*. He argued that our spelling system is very [5]........effective and he wanted to [6]........form the system. Shaw invented a different system but people used to [7]critic........ it and call his system [8]........workable.

Since Shaw, there have been attempts to [9]reorgan........ the system of English spelling but none have really been [10]success........ . Noah Webster, a [11]........-spelling reform dictionary writer, managed to [12]simpl........ some spellings in American English, for example the *-or* instead of *-our* suffix: *color* (*colour*), *honor* (*honour*).

Actually, it is not true that English words are [13]unpronounce........ . In fact, over 90% of words are completely [14]........dictable in how they are read. English is not so [15]chaot........ ! Maybe this is the reason why attempts to [16]revolution........ spelling have not been popular.

F Guess the meanings of these words from their affixes.

1 co-write
to write together
2 telesales
....
3 interlock
....
4 blueish
....
5 deplane
....
6 unprintable
....

MY TURN!

Make up six new English verbs and adjectives using affixes (then check if they really exist!).

1 co-study – to study for a test with a friend
(Not a real word – yet!)
2 hellish – very bad
(Yes, it exists.)
3 ....
4 ....
5 ....
6 ....
7 ....
8 ....

MY TEST!

Circle the correct option.

1 We should ....play the game if you think it was unfair. a out b over c re
2 Scrabble is use........ if you want to improve your spelling. a ful b less c able
3 Sandra ....reacted when she couldn't make a word and started crying. a over b under c mis
4 It is very effect........ to make words with uncommon letters of the alphabet. a al b ive c y
5 It is a big disadvantage to be ....literate today. a im b in c il

My Test! answers: 1c 2a 3a 4b 5c

43 Word formation 2: nouns (affixes)

You need imagination, self-confidence …

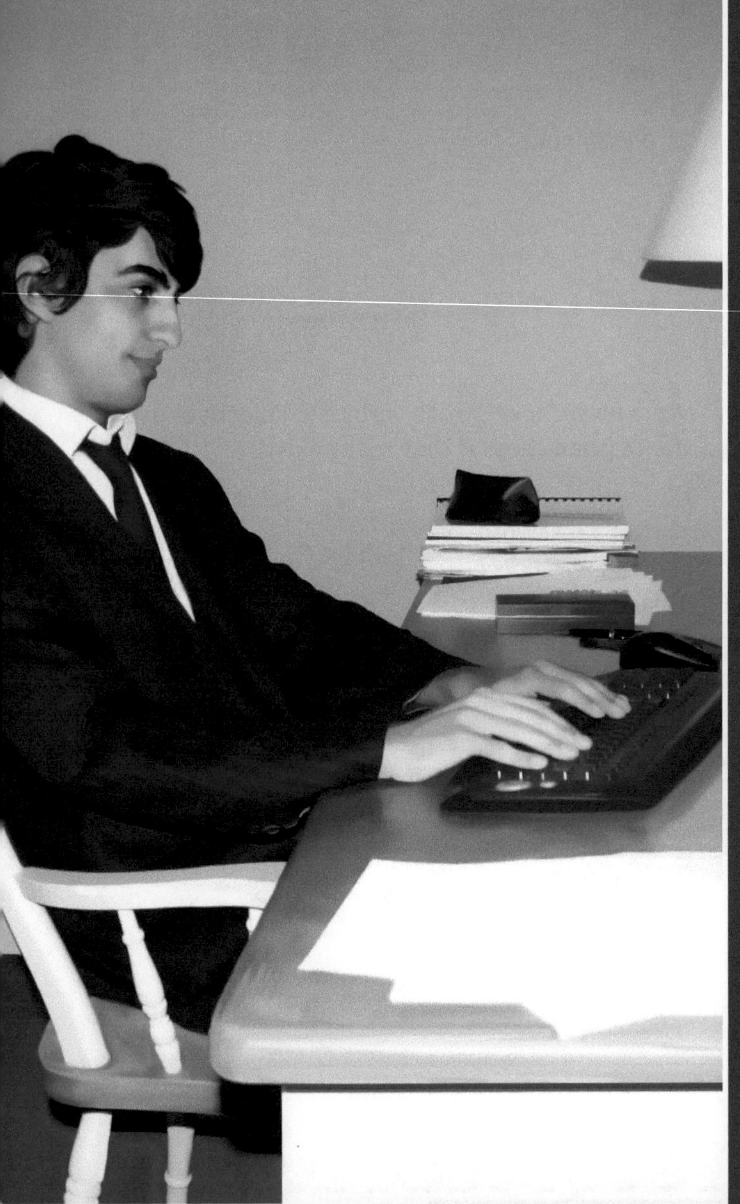

Are you thinking of starting your own business when you leave school? Here are five things you need to be successful.

1. Imagi**nation**

Think of a good idea, then do some **re**search to see if it will work.

2. **Self**-confide**nce**

Every business is a risk but you need to believe in yourself. Always remember that if you don't do it, someone else will. Have some optim**ism**!

3. **Co**operation

You can't do everything. Make contacts and get help. Relation**ships** are very important in business.

4. Good time manage**ment**

Time is money. Don't waste time going to different places yourself. Using **e**mail or the **tele**phone will save your time, and legs!

5. Professional**ism**

Be the best at whatever you do. You may not make **mega**-money but you will definitely get a lot of enjoy**ment** and **self**-satisfaction. So, start thinking and planning now. Your business might not be the next **Micro**soft, but perhaps it could be a **mini**-Microsoft!

?

Are these good (G) or bad (B) ideas according to the text?

1 Making sure you do everything yourself.
2 Travelling a lot.
3 Taking risks.

Answers: 1B 2B 3G

Word formation 2: nouns (affixes)

Prefixes

1 Prefixes add to or change the meaning of the original word to make new nouns.

A plant grows outside.
*A **trans**plant is a medical operation.*

2 The following prefixes can be used with nouns the same way they are used with verbs and adjectives.

prefix	meaning	examples
co-	together	***co**operation, **co**-star*
dis-, in-, un-	not	***dis**ease, **in**action, **un**happiness*
re-	again, back	***re**construction, **re**turn*
tele-	from far away	***tele**phone, **tele**vision*
trans-	across	***trans**action, **trans**plant*
under-, sub-	below, too little	***under**wear, **sub**way*

▶ See Unit 42 for prefixes used with verbs and adjectives.

3 The following prefixes usually come with nouns only.

prefix	meaning	examples
auto-	self	***auto**biography, **auto**graph*
cyber-	computer	***cyber**space, **cyber**war*
non-	not	***non**sense, **non**-smoker*
e-	electronic, Internet	***e**mail, **e**-sales*
ex-	former	***ex**-footballer, **ex**-husband,*
mega-	very big	***mega**byte, **mega**-star*
micro-	very small	***micro**chip, **micro**scope*
mini-	small	***mini**cab, **mini**-Olympics*
mono-	one	***mono**poly, **mono**rail*
self-	personal	***self**-confidence, **self**-study*
semi-	half	***semi**-professional, **semi**colon*

Suffixes

4 Suffixes add to or change the meaning of the original word to make new nouns.

A relation is someone in your family.
*A relation**ship** is connections between people.*

5 These suffixes make a new noun from the original word.

suffix	meaning	examples
-ant, -ent	a person who acts or works as	*assist**ant**, stud**ent***
-ar, -er, -or	a person who works as	*manag**er**, audit**or***
-ess	female	*lion**ess**, wait**ress***
-ful	quantity	*bag**ful**, hand**ful***
-hood	relations	*brother**hood**, child**hood***
-ism	belief, practice	*Darwin**ism**, rac**ism***
-ist	person with a belief or skill	*biolog**ist**, pian**ist***
-ology	study of	*ge**ology**, psych**ology***
-phobia	fear of	*claustro**phobia***

6 These suffixes are added to verbs and adjectives to make nouns.

suffix	examples
-age	*bagg**age**, break**age***
-al	*arriv**al**, refus**al***
-ance, -ancy, -ence, -ency	*brilli**ance**, resid**ency***
-ation, -ition, -sion	*imagin**ation**, compet**ition***
-(e)ry	*bak**ery**, ent**ry***
-ity	*rar**ity**, similar**ity***
-ment	*disappoint**ment**, enjoy**ment***
-ness	*sad**ness**, weak**ness***
-ship	*hard**ship**, relation**ship***

7 Another way of making nouns is compounding: adding words to each other. Compund nouns can be written with or without a hyphen, or as a single word.

business suit, tablecloth	noun + noun
mother-in-law	noun + preposition + noun
go-ahead	verb + adverb

Practice

A Write at least one word from the box next to each affix.

~~achieve~~ agree bag comfort confidence count enjoy found graduate ground hand help importance lion play popular relax rest similar steward treat trust vision wear

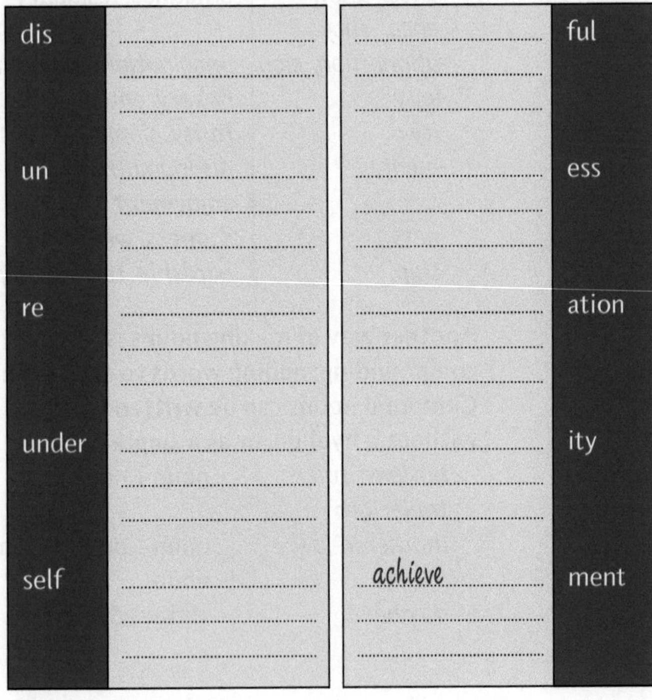

B Add prefixes to these words to make nouns.

1 vision *television*
2 production
3 trust
4 circle
5 biography
6 chip
7 smoker
8 wear

Now do the same by adding suffixes.

9 wait
10 neighbour
11 assist
12 guitar
13 hard
14 spoon
15 weak
16 millionaire

C Add affixes to each word to make at least three nouns.

1 vision
television, revision, revisionism, visionary
2 form
3 market
4 manage
5 play
6 rule

D Look at the affixes and work out what these words mean.

1 refusal
when you say 'no'
2 misinterpretation
3 microsecond
4 monosyllable
5 sociology
6 submarine
7 tigress
8 applicant

E Complete the advertisement with the correct affixes.

Calling all young business people!

After the incredible [1]popular.....ity..... of last year's contest, we are starting a second [2]compet.............. for teenagers who have a great business idea. The first prize, 10,000 euros to help start your business, will again be given in a special [3]present.............. by Donald Fish. Sir Donald is [4]..............- president of the World Bank and is now in [5]retire.............. in Florida.

Last year's [6]winn.............. was Rachel Thomas, 16, from Skegness who started an [7].............. - book company on her home computer. It wasn't easy. First, Rachel is not an IT [8]special.............. . Second, she had a big [9]..............agree.............. with her parents about her business plans. However, Rachel had the [10]..............fidence and [11]commit.............. to make her dream come true, and even her parents are happy now!

Remember, we are not looking for amazing [12]original.............. , something that will make you a business [13].............. - star, just projects which show [14]imagin.............. and real [15]useful.............. .

To apply, you first need to

F Guess each noun from its definition, then underline the prefix and / or suffix.

1 You feel this emotion when what you hoped for did not happen. ....disappointment....
2 Scientists use this instrument to look at small things. ....
3 A situation where all the business is controlled by one company. ....
4 A path which lets you walk under a busy road. ....
5 What you feel when you aren't happy. ....
6 This punctuation mark ; ....
7 Somebody who makes and checks financial documents. ....
8 You take part in this to win something. ....

MY TURN!

Make up six new English nouns using affixes (then check if they really exist!).

1 cyber-teacher – a robot teacher (Not reality – yet!)
2 ....
3 ....
4 ....
5 ....
6 ....

MY TEST!

Circle the correct option.

1 A good manag.............. works hard and plays hard. a or b ar c er
2 ....working (doing your job away from the office) is getting popular. a Ex b Tele c Mis
3 It is ....sense to say that money brings you happiness. a non b dis c in
4 In my child.............. I dreamed about opening a chocolate shop. a hood b ness c ment
5 A completely original business idea is a rar.............. . a aty b ety c ity

My Test! answers: 1c 2b 3a 4a 5c

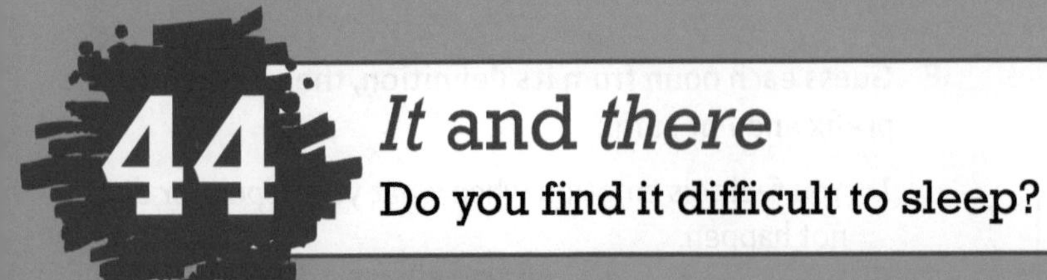

44 *It* and *there*

Do you find it difficult to sleep?

Do you often feel worried or unwell? Are you unusually quiet, angry or sad? Do you **find it difficult to** sleep or eat?
If you answered yes to any of these questions, you could be showing signs of stress.

What is stress?

Stress is the body's way of preparing us for an emergency situation, such as a car accident. **It is important that** the body reacts quickly. **There are** a number of physical reactions; for example, the heart beats faster and the body produces more glucose for energy. **There's no doubt** this is a good thing in an emergency situation. But situations such as difficulties at home can also produce stress. Over a long period of time, **it** can make a person tired and weaken the body.

What can I do about it?

- **It's very easy to** do too much. Try giving up one activity per week.
- Don't stay up late doing homework. **It's not worth it**. You'll feel more tired and **find it harder** to learn new information.
- Be positive. **There are** some things you can't do anything about. **There's no point** worrying because **it's rainy** or you **don't like it** when exams start.
- Know when **it's time to** stop. Make sure **there's** enough time for having fun!

?
1 What can long-term stress do to the body?
2 What should you make time for?

Answers: 1 Make it tired and weak. 2 Having fun.

It and *there*

It

1 **Use *it* + *be* to identify or describe something which has already been mentioned or which is already known to exist.**

*What's that noise? **It's** my phone ringing.*
*What colour's your car? **It's** blue.*

2 **Use *it* + *be* for facts or situations which have already been mentioned or which are already known about.**

*The heart beats faster and the body produces more glucose. **It's** the body's way of preparing us for an emergency situation.*

3 **We can sometimes use *it* to refer to a person.**

*Who's that over there? **It's** Mrs Evans.*
NOT ~~*She's Mrs Evans.*~~

And on the phone: *Hello! **It's** Lara.* NOT ~~*I'm Lara.*~~

4 **Use *it* + *be* to describe days, dates, distances, temperatures, times, weather and the current situation.**

***It's** rainy.*
***It's** five miles away.*
***It's** Friday already.*

> **TIP**
> **We can also use *this* / *that* instead of *it* to refer back to a fact or situation. *This* / *that* give more emphasis.**
> *Long-term situations, such as difficulties at home, can also produce stress.*
> ***It* / *This** can leave a person feeling tired.*

5 **We can use *it* when the subject of a sentence is a *to*-infinitive.**

It's very easy to do too much.
NOT usually ~~*To do too much is very easy.*~~

> **TIP**
> **In informal language, we can sometimes use the verb + *-ing* instead of the *to*-infinitive.**
> ***It** was great seeing you.* (= It was great to see you.)

6 **We can use *it* when the subject of a sentence is a clause.**

***It** was a shame that she gave up.*
NOT usually ~~*That she gave up was a shame.*~~

7 **Use *it* as a subject in certain expressions.**

***It** doesn't matter. / **It** doesn't matter if ...*
***It's** no use. / **It's** no use + -ing ...*
***It's** no good. / **It's** no good + -ing ...*
***It's** (not) worth it. / **It's** (not) worth + -ing ...*
***It** seems* (+ adjective) *that ...*
***It** looks as if ...*
***It's** time* (*for* + object) *to ...*

8 **We can use a past tense verb or *to*-infinitive after *It's time*. Both refer to the present.**

***It's time** I stopped. / **It's time** to stop.*

9 **Use *it* with *take* + *to*-infinitive to talk about time that is needed.**

*It **takes** (him) an hour **to get ready**.*

10 **Use *it* as an object in certain expressions.**

*couldn't believe **it** when ...*
*like / love / hate **it** when ...*
*find **it** difficult / hard / impossible / easy to ...*
*make **it** clear that ...*

There

11 **Use *there is* / *there are* to show that something is present or exists.**

*Make sure **there's** enough time for having fun.*
***There are** some things you can't do anything about.*

> **TIP**
> **When we are speaking, we often use *there's* with plural subjects.**
> ***There's a lot of things** I want to tell you.*

12 **Use *there's* with pronouns such as *nothing* and *someone*.**

***There's nothing** to worry about.*

13 **Use *there* in the following expressions:**

***There's** no point / use (in) ...*
***There's** no need for* (+ noun) / ***There's** no need to ...*
***There's** no doubt (that) ... / **There's** no doubt about* (+ noun)
***There's** no danger / sign of* (+ noun)
***There's** no guarantee / way (that) ...*

Reporting with *it* and *there*

14 ***It* and *there* are common in reports with the passive of the verbs *believe, expect, feel, report, say, think, understand*.**

***It is thought** that 70% of visits to doctors are due to stress.*
***There were thought** to be 20,000 people there.*

▶ See Unit 34 for more information on reporting using the passive of the verb.

Practice

A Match the sentences to the replies.

1 What have you got in that bag?
2 Who's your teacher this year?
3 Can you see Mark?
4 Have you enjoyed the training?
5 Can you see any seats?
6 Sorry, I can't find that number.
7 Look! It's really late!
8 Was that the bell?

a Yes, it's time we went home.
b Yes, there's some at the front.
c It doesn't matter. Jay will have it.
d No, there's no sign of him.
e Yes, there's someone at the door.
f It's a surprise.
g It's Miss Collins.
h Yes, but there's no guarantee of a job at the end of it.

1 ...f... 2 .... 3 .... 4 ....
5 .... 6 .... 7 .... 8 ....

B Circle the correct option. Sometimes more than one option is possible.

1 It is best .... honest.
 (a) to be (b) that you are c be
2 .... safe to drink the water?
 a Is there b Is it c Is she
3 Thanks again – it has been lovely .... to you.
 a that talk b talking c to talk
4 She's a great dancer. It's a shame ....
 a that she's giving up b she to give up c give up
5 .... no need to get upset.
 a It's b There are c There's
6 She didn't phone to say where she was. .... was very worrying.
 a This b There c It
7 .... reported to be fewer than 2,000 Giant Pandas left in the world.
 a It is b There are c There's
8 I hate .... when you talk to me like that.
 a it b this c there

C Complete the sentences with *it* or *there*.

1 How long does ...it... take to get to the airport?
2 Who were you talking to last night? .... was Tina.
3 Go straight on. ....'s a post box on the corner of the street.
4 .... seems strange that walking to school is now often quicker than going by car.
5 A: What can you do at the sports centre?
 B: ....'s lots of different exercise classes.
6 ....'s nearly my birthday!
7 I knew something had happened to her. .... was just a feeling I had.
8 This year .... has been a big increase in crime in this area.

D Complete the text with the words in the box.

clear doubt important impossible matter nothing point ~~thought~~

Bullying is a problem which affects millions of teenage students. It is [1] ...thought... that nearly half of all teenagers have suffered from cyber-bullying: on mobile phones or the Internet.

What can you do if it happens to you?

Be positive. Don't think this is your fault and there's [2] .... you can do about it.

- Walk away. If you walk away or ignore someone's rude messages, you are making it [3] .... that you just don't care. He or she will soon get bored.
- Don't reply. There's no [4] .... trying to fight back or reply to the messages. It'll only make things worse.
- It's [5] .... to build your confidence. It doesn't [6] .... if it's karate or computers – join a club and do something you enjoy.
- There's no [7] .... talking to someone will help you. Talk to an adult you can trust.
- Think carefully about sharing personal information or photos. Once you've put a photo or message online, it can be [8] .... to delete.

E Write two sentences using *it* and two sentences using *there* for each picture. Use the labels to help you.

1 It's night. 2 ....

3 There are some stars. 4 ....

5 .... 6 ....

7 .... 8 ....

9 .... 10 ....

11 .... 12 ....

F Rewrite each sentence so that it has a similar meaning, using the word in brackets.

1 There was no point. (worth)
It wasn't worth it.
2 It's not necessary for you to know. (There's)
....
3 It's time for you to leave. (left)
....
4 There's no use in talking to him. (good)
....
5 I needed three hours to finish it. (me)
....
6 People say there are 500,000 words in the English language. (said)
....
7 I'm definitely not going on my own. (way)
....
8 The winner is certain. (doubt)
....
9 I was really surprised when they walked in the room. (couldn't)
....

MY TURN!

Complete the sentences about your feelings and experience of learning English. Use a different structure in each sentence.

1 It's a good idea to watch the news in English.
2 .... understand people on the phone.
3 .... visiting an English-speaking country is helpful.
4 .... make mistakes.
5 .... understand a joke in English.
6 .... people talk too fast.
7 .... learning long lists of vocabulary.
8 .... remember new words.

MY TEST!

Circle the correct option.

1 .... been very cold at night. a It b It's c There
2 It's good .... to someone who understands. a that talk b to talk c talk
3 I find .... hard to study when I'm tired. a I'm b it c there
4 .... doubt in my mind. a There are no b It's no c There's no
5 .... lots of people at the party. a There were b They were c It was

My Test! answers: 1b 2b 3b 4c 5a

Linking words 1: addition, contrast and time

Once you have read one ...

There are many reasons to read detective stories. **First of all,** you know that lots of things will happen **and** the story will move quickly, especially as the detective is usually in danger. **Then** there's the fun of being a detective at the same time as the characters. And **finally,** there is the satisfaction of a solved crime.

If you're new to detective stories, try the Alex Rider series by Anthony Horowitz.
Though only 14, Alex Rider is no ordinary teenager. **After** his uncle is mysteriously killed, Alex is thrown into the world of spies. **While** most kids worry about spots and homework, Alex is just trying to stay alive!

There are six books in the series. **Once** you have read one, you'll want to read the others. The characters are easy to believe in, the stories are original and, **above all,** the situations Alex gets into are really cool!

Gavin Martin (aged 15)

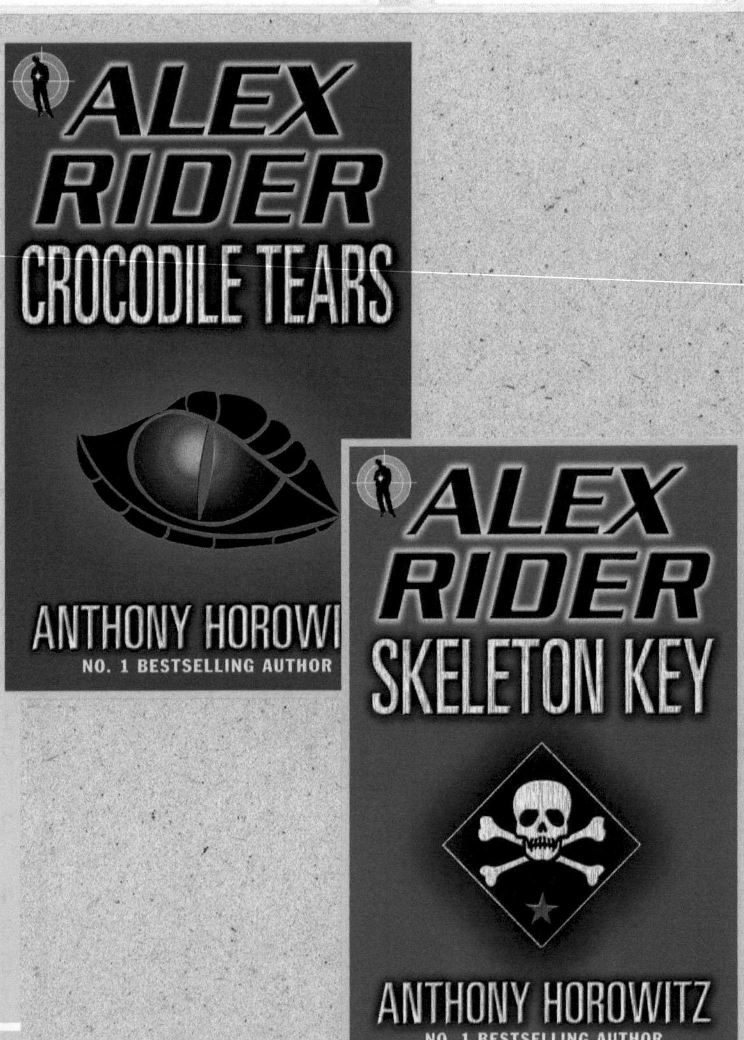

?
1 What does the writer think is fun about detective stories?
2 When does Alex Rider become a spy?

Answers: 1 Being a detective at the same time as the characters. 2 After his uncle is mysteriously killed.

Linking words 1: addition, contrast and time

Addition

1 **Use *and, too, as well* and *also* to connect words, phrases or sentences.**
*You know that lots of things will happen **and** the story will move quickly.*

2 ***Too* and *as well* are usually used at the end of a sentence. *Also* can come in the middle.**
*She writes great stories. She draws the pictures **too**. / She **also** draws the pictures.*

3 Use ***in addition, besides, furthermore, moreover*** or ***what's more*** to introduce a sentence with more information. ***What's more*** is informal.

He was cold and hungry. ***What's more****, he didn't know the way home.*

4 Use the phrase ***above all*** to suggest that something is more important than other things you have mentioned.

Above all*, the situations Alex gets into are really cool!*

5 Use ***equally, likewise*** and ***similarly*** at the beginning of a sentence to introduce information which is similar in some way.

There are a lot of Sherlock Holmes stories. ***Similarly****, there are many films.*

Contrast

6 We can use ***but, (and) yet, however*** and ***nevertheless*** to contrast information.

The government knew of the problems, ***yet*** *they didn't publish the report until now.*

7 We can also use ***although, though, in spite of*** + noun or ***despite*** + noun to contrast ideas.

Although *he is only 14, /* ***Despite*** *his young age, Alex Rider is no ordinary teenager.*

> **TIP**
>
> Use ***though*** in informal language at the beginning of a sentence to mean 'although' or at the end to mean 'however'.
>
> ***Though*** *only 14, Alex Rider is no ordinary teenager.*
> *We had a great time at the beach. It was very windy,* ***though****.*

> **TIP**
>
> We can't use ***in spite of*** to join sentences. Instead we use the phrase ***in spite of the fact that***.
>
> *I was really happy* ***in spite of the fact that*** *I hadn't won.* NOT ~~*... in spite of that I hadn't won.*~~

8 Use ***on the one hand ... on the other hand, while, whereas*** and ***in / by contrast*** to compare contrasting ideas.

The footballer dislikes being seen in public. His wife, ***in contrast****, clearly loves it!*

We can use ***on the other hand*** without ***on the one hand***.

Todd wasn't sure if Terry was telling the truth. I, ***on the other hand****, had no doubts at all.*

9 Use ***on the contrary*** when you add information to support a negative statement.

The government has not managed to improve standards in schools. ***On the contrary****, more students are failing their exams.*

We also use it to contradict a suggestion made by another person.

A: You probably know this already.
B: ***On the contrary****, I had no idea!*

Time

10 Use ***as, when*** or ***while*** to talk about two things happening at the same time.

He was still working ***when*** *I went to bed.*
While *most kids worry about spots and homework, Alex is just trying to stay alive.*

11 Use ***after, before, when, as soon as*** and ***once*** to talk about two things that happen one after the other.

I phoned him ***when / after*** *I got home.* (= I got home. Then I phoned him.)

12 Use ***since*** to talk about when something began and ***for*** to talk about how long it went on.

I've lived here ***since*** *last year / I got married / for a year.*

▶ See Units 5 and 26 for the use of *since* and *for*.

13 We use ***until*** to talk about the time when something stops happening and something else starts.

He didn't know anything about all this ***until*** *his uncle died /* ***until*** *last year.*

Use ***by the time*** to mean at the time when or before something else happens.

I'll be rich ***by the time*** *I'm 30.*

14 Use the following adverbs or adverbial phrases to describe the order of events or the sequence of points in an argument: ***first(ly), second(ly) (etc.), first of all, next / then, afterwards / after that, before, finally / eventually / lastly, later.***

First of all*, you know that lots of things will happen.*
Then *there is the satisfaction of a solved crime.*

Use ***before*** and ***afterwards*** (not ***after***) as adverbs.

I finish college next summer. ***Afterwards*** (NOT ~~*After*~~), *I'm going travelling for a year.*

15 Use ***meanwhile*** to talk about what happens between two events or at the same time as another event.

The parents went out. ***Meanwhile****, at home, the children ...*

Practice

A Match the sentences.

1 There are some good coats in that shop at the moment. [d]
2 I don't think you need your own car. [ ]
3 The new riverside centre would bring more cafés and restaurants to the town. [ ]
4 Since the new manager arrived, the team has won a few matches. [ ]
5 Windsurfing is exciting and not particularly dangerous. [ ]
6 Don't tell anyone your number. [ ]
7 More teenagers are taking up dance classes as a result of recent TV shows. [ ]
8 The organisation helps governments to provide food and clean water for their people. [ ]

a It also trains health workers and supplies medicines.
b In addition, the players are training harder.
c Besides, we can't afford to buy one.
d What's more, they're half price this week!
e Moreover, the development would create valuable jobs.
f Similarly, don't give this information over the Internet.
g Likewise, there has been increased interest in classes from older people.
h Above all, it is fun.

B Make sentences by putting the words in the correct order. More than one answer is possible.

1 you / until / I / home / sleep / were / couldn't
I couldn't sleep until you were home. / Until you were home, I couldn't sleep.
2 go / before / lunch / let's / have / we
....
3 arrived / had / we / a / when / surprise / we
....
4 afterwards / dinner / they / a / had / watched / and / film
....
5 home / time / the / we / midnight / it / was / by / got
....
6 start / once / you've / can / eating / finished / we
....
7 getting / dressed / noticed / he / something / as / was / strange / he
....
8 boiling / the / water / add / next
....

C Complete the sentences in an appropriate way.

1 We had a lovely day in spite of the fact that it was raining.
2 I haven't read *The Lord of the Rings*. ...., though.
3 We don't really have time. On the other hand, ...
4 My friends want to go snowboarding. However, ...
5 Simon is very confident, whereas ....
6 The buildings around the edge of the city are mostly modern. In contrast, ...
7 It was cold but ....
8 The teacher spoke a bit quickly. ...., nevertheless.

D Complete the student's presentation using the linking words in the box.

after also as before ~~but~~ in spite of meanwhile what's more

I want to talk to you about my favourite book. It's *Noughts and Crosses* by Malorie Blackman. My aunt gave me this book for my birthday. I don't read many books, [1] but I couldn't stop reading this! It's the first in a series of books. I've just started reading the second book which is [2] .... great!
The story is about Sephy, a Cross (I won't tell you what that means. You'll find out [3] .... you've read the first few pages.). Ever since she was little, Sephy's best friend has been Callum, who is a Nought. [4] .... they get older, this becomes a problem because in their world Noughts and Crosses don't mix. [5] .... this, Sephy and Callum try to stay friends. Their parents, [6] ...., try to make them understand the rules of their world.
Malorie Blackman has written a very exciting story. [7] ...., you'll feel you've known the characters for years. Of course, this means you share their feelings, so make sure you have some tissues with you [8] .... you start reading!

E Complete this formal letter of complaint by underlining the correct option. Sometimes both options are possible.

Customer Complaints
In Your Dreams Holidays

I am writing to complain about a holiday that I spent in your hotel in August of this year.

I have several reasons for complaining. [1]*Firstly / First of all*, the information I received about the hotel was incorrect. The adverts talked about a swimming pool and a golf course. In August of this year, [2]*however / in addition*, the swimming pool had not yet been built. [3]*Equally / Likewise*, the golf course was still unfinished.

[4]*Then / After* there was the room. [5]*Although / Despite* this had a sea view as advertised, the view was spoilt by building works in front of the hotel. [6]*On the other hand / Furthermore*, the noise of the building woke us up early every morning.

[7]*Lastly / Secondly*, we were so disappointed by the holiday that we left early.

[8]*Despite / In spite of* our complaints, the hotel manager was rude and refused to give us any money back.

I am therefore writing to request an immediate refund. If we do not receive this within seven days, we will send our story and photos to the newspapers.

Yours sincerely,

Y Mee

Mr Y Mee

F Complete each sentence b so that it has a similar meaning to sentence(s) a, using the word in brackets. You may need to leave out some words, put the words in a different order or add another sentence.

1 a I had a sandwich. Then I got on the train. (before)
  b I *had a sandwich before I got on the train.*
2 a He had an injury. He still finished the race. (despite)
  b He ....
3 a She was singing. She was packing her bags at the same time. (while)
  b She ....
4 a I'll stay here. I'll leave at 9.00. (until)
  b I ....
5 a She cleans during the week and helps in the café at weekends. (too)
  b She ....
6 a It started raining. I immediately went inside. (as soon as)
  b I ....
7 a She was not unreasonable and listened carefully to everything. (contrary)
  b She ....
8 a The team played with ten men. It was surprising that they managed to win easily. (yet)
  b The team ....

MY TURN!

Think of a book you enjoyed reading. In your notebook, write paragraphs about the story events, the characters and why you enjoyed it. Use the questions and the linking words to help you.

1 The story (*when, while, and, at first, then, finally*)
What's the name of the book? What happens at the beginning of the story? What are two other things that happen?
2 The characters (*although, but, however, also, as well*)
Who is your favourite character? What do you like about this character? What weakness does the character have? Who else do you like?
3 Why did you like it? (*above all, what's more*)
Which adjective or phrase best describes the book? Can you think of two other reasons why you liked it?

MY TEST!

Circle the correct option.

1 .... I could stop her, she had left the room. a Before b After c When
2 TV adverts should be allowed, ... not in the middle of a film! a and b but c in contrast
3 The book was interesting. It was very long, ... a although b too c though
4 Anthony Horowitz has .... written *The Power of Five* series. a though b too c also
5 Alex trains as a spy. .... he is sent to the home of millionaire Herod Sayle. a After b While c Afterwards

My Test! answers: 1a 2b 3c 4c 5c

46 Linking words 2: reason, purpose and result

Why? Because the roads were bad.

John McAdam (1756–1836) is famous for improving roads. Road transport became very important in the early 1800s **because** England was a busy industrial centre, **so** people and goods were moving all over the country. However, **in order to** move things quickly, they needed better roads.

Therefore, McAdam tried out a new type of road. The new roads were built with a lot of small stones **so that** they were stronger. There was also a small rise, called a 'camber', in the middle of the road, **in order that** rain could run off the road. McAdam made the first of his roads in 1816. **As** these roads were very successful, he built them in America in the 1830s.

At the end of the 19th century, cars came onto the roads. Cars are heavy, so roads needed to be stronger. The basic McAdam roads were covered with a thick black material called tar **so that** they would hold cars. The new surface was called 'tarmac'.

? True or False?

1 There were no roads in England before 1816.
2 Tarmac made roads stronger.

Answers: 1 False 2 True

Linking words 2: reason, purpose and result

Reason

1 Use *because, since* and *as* to give a reason. *Because* is the most common and the most informal.
The roads were bad ***because*** *they were very old.*
He knew a lot about roads ***since*** *he was an engineer.*
As *these roads were very successful, he built more.*

As can also mean 'in the same way as'.
The workers made the road ***as*** *McAdam told them to.*

2 The part of the sentence with the reason usually comes last but it can come first.
I went by car ***because*** *it was quicker.*
Since *it was quicker, I went by car.*

3 Only *because* can come by itself in short answers.
A: Why did you go by car? *B:* ***Because*** *it was quicker.*
NOT ~~*Since ...*~~

Some prepositions also give a reason, e.g. *because of, due to, owing to, on account of*. *Because of* is the most common and informal.
Roads were better ***because of*** *McAdam.*

4 *For* meaning *because* is very formal and old-fashioned. *For* never comes first in the sentence.
Engineering is a difficult subject, ***for*** *it is necessary to study very hard.*

5 *Seeing that* and *now* (*that*) are informal.
Seeing that *it's Monday, you should be at school.*
Now *he has a car, he's happy.*

6 Use *in case* + present tense for reasons for things that might happen in the future.
I'll stay at home ***in case*** *Jack phones.*
Carry it carefully ***in case*** *it breaks.*

Use *in case* only if you are describing a future possible reason for doing something, not for a future possible situation.
Take a sandwich ***in case*** *you get hungry.*
I'll stay at home ***if*** *it rains.* NOT ~~*... in case it rains.*~~

► See Units 35, 36 and 37 for more information on *if*.

Purpose

7 *In order to / that* and *so that* show purpose. We often use modal verbs after *in order that* and *so that*.
In order to *move things quickly, they needed better roads.*
The roads were rebuilt ***so that*** *they would be stronger.*

8 *For* + *-ing* shows purpose.
Tar is ***for making*** *roads stronger.*

To-infinitives also show purpose.
He drove faster ***to get*** *there on time.*

Result

9 *So* (*that*) also shows a result. If it comes in the middle of a sentence, there is a comma before it.
So *McAdam became rich and famous.*
It was snowing heavily, ***so*** *there was no way we could get there.*

10 The adverbs *therefore, thus, accordingly, hence* and *consequently* are formal ways of showing a cause, reason and result. These words usually go at the beginning of a sentence and are separated by a comma.
Therefore, *McAdam tried out a new type of road.*
There were more cars. ***Consequently,*** *roads became worse.*

Practice

A <u>Underline</u> the correct option.

1 I'm wet *because / so that* it's raining.
2 *As / For* it's already ten o'clock, we really need to finish.
3 I did it *because / in order that* you told me to!
4 *Now / In order* that Jo knows, she feels happier.
5 Remind him *because / so that* he won't forget.
6 Lesley was excited *because / because of* the party.
7 A: Why did you come?
B: *Because / As* I wanted to see Justin.
8 I was tired, *because / so* I went to bed early.
9 There's a great place *since / for* cycling in the park.
10 *Therefore, / In order that* we have a serious problem.
11 Phone me *if / in case* you get there.
12 Take a good book to read *if / in case* the plane is late.

B Match the pairs.

1 I saved some money because — b I didn't spend much.
2 I needed some money so that — a I could buy my gran a present.

3 John did it quickly as / a he could finish on time.
4 John did it quickly in order that / b he didn't have much time.

5 Claudia wasn't feeling well because / a she ate something bad.
6 Claudia wasn't feeling well, so / b she phoned the doctor.

7 Now you know English, / a you should study French.
8 In order to know English / b you need to study hard.

9 Hide your money if / a someone steals it.
10 Hide your money in case / b you know a safe place.

C Complete each sentence b so that it means the same as sentence a, using the word in brackets.

1 a Jack felt bad and stayed at home. (because)
b Jack stayed at home ......because he felt...... bad.
2 a It might rain so take your umbrella. (case)
b Take your umbrella ....
3 a I flew because it saved time. (order)
b I flew .... time.
4 a Since it's Friday, you can stay out later. (seeing)
b ...., you can stay out later.
5 a These shoes are specially designed so that you can run on grass. (ideal)
b These shoes are .... on grass.
6 a Bad driving is the main cause of road accidents. (of)
b Most road accidents happen ....
7 a Sally must feel great because her exams are over. (now)
b .... have finished, she must feel great.
8 a Mike and Sarah went early in order to get a ticket. (so)
b Mike and Sarah went early .... could get a ticket.

D Join the sentences using different linking words. More than one answer is possible.

1 James was 15. He still went to school.
Since James was 15, he still went to school.
2 Nicky is angry. Don't speak to her.
....
3 It's your birthday. You can go home early.
....
4 Lisa bought some fruit. She wanted to make a cake.
....
5 The Internet is working now. Check your email.
....
6 Luke is training hard. He wants to get on the school team.
....
7 Leona didn't understand. She didn't know Spanish.
....
8 It's a lovely day. It would be nice to have a picnic.
....

E Complete the text with appropriate linking words.

Route 66 is a famous road which once went 3,940 km from the east to the west of the USA. It was built in 1926 [1] *because* there was no road transport across the country. Many poor farmers travelled along Route 66 in the 1930s [2] .... to move to California. They went [3] .... they could find work there.

The road was very useful [4] .... people driving on business. Therefore, many shops, restaurants and hotels opened along Route 66 [5] .... drivers could take a break on their journeys. The first McDonald's restaurant opened on Route 66.

A new, bigger road was built next to Route 66 and [6] .... the famous road became, sadly, less important. In 1985, Route 66 was taken off the road map [7] .... it was no longer an official state road. The road was broken up, [8] .... it became a system of smaller roads. [9] .... it is no longer possible to drive along Route 66 today. However, there is a Route 66 museum and even a Route 66 fan club [10] .... the road is still very famous.

F Complete the sentences using linking words.

1 *Now that he has explained*, everyone understands.
2 Jake apologised to his teacher ....
3 ...., let's begin the game.
4 Julie is saving money ....
5 Alex started laughing ....
6 Tomorrow is Vicky's birthday, ...

G Complete the sentences with your own ideas.

1 Sally worked hard since *she had a test the next day*.
2 Jim was tired because ....
3 It was a lovely day, so ....
4 Be careful with that glass in case ....
5 As ...., Sam didn't have breakfast.
6 Now ...., you can relax.
7 The supermarket made their prices cheaper in order that ....

MY TURN!

Write about the purpose of these things or the reason for using them.

1 Cars
We need cars in order to move around. /
We use cars because we want to get to places quickly.
2 Music
3 Friends
4 Money
5 Language
6 School

MY TEST!

Circle the correct option.

1 Transport was difficult .... roads were bad. a because b for c so that
2 .... it was 1830, there were no cars. a For b So c As
3 He built better roads .... people could travel more quickly. a in order b so that c for
4 Tar is .... making roads stronger. a for b because c since
5 Transport got better. ...., prices went down. a Because b So that c Therefore

My Test! answers: 1a 2c 3b 4a 5c

R6 Review: indirect speech; relative clauses; word formation; *it* and *there*; linking words

A You are interviewing Sophie Dickens, who writes novels for teenagers. Rewrite Sophie's answers as indirect statements, using the words in brackets. Sometimes more than one answer is possible.

1 'OK. I'll answer some of your questions.' (agreed)
Sophie *agreed to answer some of my questions.*

2 'I'll be as open and honest as I can.' (promised)
She ....

3 'I know what my readers are interested in.' (knew)
She ....

4 'Tell me what you think about my last book.' (asked)
She ....

5 'It's true some readers didn't like the ending of my last book.' (admitted)
She ....

6 'In my opinion, it's my best book so far.' (thought)
She ....

7 'I've tried to introduce more humour into my new book.' (said)
She ....

8 'I've been reading about birds in preparation for another writing project.' (told)
She ....

9 'Young writers like you should read as much as possible.' (advised)
She ....

B Underline the correct option.

1 I'm not sure where *we are / are we* going this evening.
2 She asked me *what should she do / what she should do.*
3 Enrico *doesn't know to / doesn't know how to* use a washing machine.
4 Lizzie couldn't decide *whether or not / if or not* to go home.
5 I asked my brother *what was he / what he was* looking at.
6 Amalia asked the little girl how old *she was / was she.*
7 We often talk about *how can we / how we can* improve our environment.
8 I wonder *where my keys are / where are my keys.*
9 There is some doubt about *if / whether* we should go by bus or by train.
10 Can you tell me *how can I / how I can* solve this problem quickly?

C Join the sentences using relative pronouns. Sometimes more than one answer is possible. Then underline the pronouns that can be left out.

1 This is the café. I told you it was good.
This is the café which I told you was good. /
This is the café that I told you was good.

2 There are two people at the door. They want to speak to you.
....

3 That's the house! My dad was born there.
....

4 Martin Amis is a famous author. His father was a writer too.
....

5 Look at that boy. Emily's sitting next to him.
....

6 It was a great day. I'll never forget it.
....

7 I have two good friends. They always come when I need help.
....

8 My cousin goes to a school. They have hardly any rules there.
....

9 This song is about a woman. Her life was very hard.
....

10 This photo is of an old friend. I used to play tennis with her.
....

D Complete the text with new words formed from the words in brackets.

A long time before J R R Tolkien's [1] (die) ....death.... in 1973, his books, [2] (special) .... *The Lord of the Rings*, had become very [3] (fashion) .... in many countries round the world. Since the 1970s, their [4] (popular) .... has continued to grow. Tolkien himself was a very quiet man who was [5] (comfort) .... with all the attention directed at him. He didn't write his books in order to become [6] (fame) .... In fact, he wrote his first book, *The Hobbit*, to read to his children. His books are actually full of things he was interested in, like [7] (tradition) .... ways of life, religion, old stories and languages. His deep love and [8] (know) .... of languages, particularly ancient ones like Old English, Old Icelandic and Old German, helped him to invent new but [9] (believe) .... languages for the characters in his books. Not everyone likes Tolkien's work, and when *The Lord of the Rings* was first published, it received quite a lot of [10] (criticise) .... Far more people, however, expressed admiration for Tolkien's incredible [11] (imagine) .... and [12] (skill) .... storytelling, and they still do.

E Complete the sentences using *it* and *there*.

1 ....There.... is a strange insect in the bathroom. ....It.... is flying around the light.
2 .... is someone at the door. I don't know who .... is.
3 .... is an interesting market in the town square on Saturdays. .... will only take us 20 minutes to get ....
4 .... is easy to buy books on the Internet. .... is no point travelling so far to buy them.
5 .... is a big, black cloud coming towards us. .... looks as if we're going to get wet.
6 .... doesn't matter if you use all the paper. .... is more in the cupboard.
7 .... isn't enough time to cook a big meal now. .... is very easy to make a sandwich instead.
8 .... will be a party for the opening of the new sports centre. .... is reported that several well-known people will be at the party.
9 .... is no good complaining. .... is no more ice cream for anyone.
10 .... is a shame we didn't get to the museum earlier, because .... is such a lot to see.

F Underline the correct option.

Dear Editor,

I am writing [1] *for / to* tell you what I think about the plan to build two new car parks in the city centre. [2] *Although / However* it is true that we have a problem with too many cars parked at the side of the road, building more car parks is not the solution [3] *as / but* this will only encourage more people to drive into the centre. We already have too many cars in the city centre. [4] *So / But,* we should try to stop people driving there, not encourage them. [5] *On the one hand / Moreover,* we need to make big changes [6] *before / whereas* the problem becomes even worse. [7] *Firstly / Similarly*, we need to close some of the city centre streets to traffic. [8] *On the contrary / In addition*, we need to make it very expensive to park cars in the centre. [9] *Next / Finally*, we need a much better bus service [10] *so / in case* more people will be happy to travel by bus. At the moment, the buses are uncomfortable and expensive and, [11] *above all / nevertheless,* they are very slow. [12] *Lastly / On the other hand*, we need to make it safer for people to cycle, [13] *so / then* more special paths for bicycles are needed. Many cities have made changes like these [14] *for / in order to* reduce the amount of traffic in their centres. We should do the same.

Ron James

Verb tenses

	statement	negative	questions
Present simple			
I/you/we/they	work	do not work (I **don't** work)	Do I work?
he/she/it	works	does not work (he **doesn't** work)	Does he work?
Present continuous			
I	**am** working (I**'m** working)	**am not** working (I**'m not** working)	**Am** I working?
you/we/they	**are** working (you**'re** working)	**are not** working (you**'re not** / you **aren't** working)	**Are** you working?
he/she/it	**is** working (it**'s** working)	**is not** working (it**'s not** /it **isn't** working)	**Is** it working?
Past simple			
I/you/he/she/it/we/they	worked	did not work (you **didn't** work)	Did you work?
Present perfect simple			
I/you/we/they	**have** worked (they**'ve** worked)	**have not** worked (they **haven't** worked)	**Have** they worked?
he/she/it	**has** worked (she**'s** worked)	**has not** worked (she **hasn't** worked)	**Has** she worked?
Present perfect continuous			
I/you/we/they	**have been** working (you**'ve been** working)	**have not been** working (you **haven't been** working)	**Have** you **been** working?
he/she/it	**has been** working (he**'s been** working)	**has not been** working (he **hasn't been** working)	**Has** he **been** working?
Past perfect simple			
I/you/he/she/it/we/they	**had** worked (you **had** worked)	**had not** worked (you **hadn't** worked)	**Had** you worked?
Past perfect continuous			
I/you/he/she/it/we/they	**had been** working (she **had been** working)	**had not been** working (she **hadn't been** working)	**Had** she **been** working?

Irregular verbs

infinitive	past simple	past participle
be	was/were	been
beat	beat	beaten
become	became	become
begin	began	begun
bend	bent	bent
bet	bet	bet
bite	bit	bitten
blow	blew	blown
break	broke	broken
bring	brought	brought
broadcast	broadcast	broadcast
build	built	built
burst	burst	burst
buy	bought	bought
catch	caught	caught
choose	chose	chosen
come	came	come
cost	cost	cost
creep	crept	crept
cut	cut	cut
deal	dealt	dealt
dig	dug	dug
do	did	done
draw	drew	drawn
drink	drank	drunk
drive	drove	driven
eat	ate	eaten
fall	fell	fallen
feed	fed	fed
feel	felt	felt
fight	fought	fought
find	found	found
flee	fled	fled
fly	flew	flown
forbid	forbade	forbidden
forget	forgot	forgotten
forgive	forgave	forgiven
freeze	froze	frozen
get	got	got
give	gave	given
go	went	gone
grow	grew	grown
hang	hung	hung
have	had	had
hear	heard	heard
hide	hid	hidden
hit	hit	hit
hold	held	held
hurt	hurt	hurt
keep	kept	kept
kneel	knelt	knelt
know	knew	known
lay	laid	laid
lead	led	led
leave	left	left
lend	lent	lent
let	let	let
lie	lay	lain

infinitive	past simple	past participle
light	lit	lit
lose	lost	lost
make	made	made
mean	meant	meant
meet	met	met
pay	paid	paid
put	put	put
read	read	read
ride	rode	ridden
ring	rang	rung
rise	rose	risen
run	ran	run
say	said	said
see	saw	seen
seek	sought	sought
sell	sold	sold
send	sent	sent
set	set	set
sew	sewed	sewn/sewed
shake	shook	shaken
shine	shone	shone
shoot	shot	shot
show	showed	shown/showed
shrink	shrank	shrunk
shut	shut	shut
sing	sang	sung
sink	sank	sunk
sit	sat	sat
sleep	slept	slept
slide	slid	slid
speak	spoke	spoken
spend	spent	spent
spit	spat	spat
split	split	split
spread	spread	spread
spring	sprang	sprung
stand	stood	stood
steal	stole	stolen
stick	stuck	stuck
sting	stung	stung
stink	stank	stunk
strike	struck	struck
swear	swore	sworn
sweep	swept	swept
swim	swam	swum
swing	swung	swung
take	took	taken
teach	taught	taught
tear	tore	torn
tell	told	told
think	thought	thought
throw	threw	thrown
understand	understood	understood
wake	woke	woken
wear	wore	worn
weep	wept	wept
win	won	won
write	wrote	written

Glossary

afford to have enough money to buy something 19

agriculture the work of growing plants and looking after animals which are then used for food 4

alarm clock a clock that makes a noise to wake you 18

architect someone who designs buildings 7

bilingual using or able to speak two languages 30

boarding school a school where students live and study 28

burglar someone who gets into buildings illegally and steals things 1

CCTV closed circuit television: a system of television cameras filming in shops and public places so that people can watch and protect those places 26

colleague someone that you work with 26

composer someone who writes music 22

copper a soft, red-brown metal 33

crack a line on the surface of something that is damaged 32

crash If a vehicle crashes, it hits something by accident. 7

credit card a small plastic card that allows you to buy something and pay for it later 22

creep to move very quietly and carefully 1

currency the money used in a particular country 3

detective someone whose job is to discover information about a crime 45

disaster a very bad situation, especially something that causes a lot of harm or damage 6

diving the activity or sport of swimming under water, usually using special breathing equipment 32

dumb stupid or silly 41

earthquake a sudden movement of the Earth's surface, often causing damage 6

entrance exam an examination which you take to decide if you can be accepted into a school, etc. 4

erosion where parts of land or buildings disappear because of the effect of the weather 13

estate an area with a lot of buildings of the same type 26

extreme sport a sport that is very dangerous and exciting 29

gang a group of criminals who work together 26

get fit become healthy and strong 18

glove a piece of clothing which covers your fingers and hand 18

graphologist a person who studies handwriting 17

gravity the force that makes objects fall to the ground 10

helmet a hard hat that protects your head 29

hero a very brave man that a lot of people admire 2

high heels women's shoes with heels raised high off the ground 32

homesick feeling sad because you are away from your home 28

hunter a person or an animal that hunts animals for food or for sport 9

hurricane a bad storm with very strong winds 6

ID identification: an official document that shows or proves who you are 33

inflation an increase in prices 3

inhabitant someone who lives somewhere 14

junk food food which is bad for your body but quick to eat 24

kid a child 30

knee pad a piece of soft thick cloth or rubber which is used to protect the knee 29

monument something that is built to make people remember a famous person or something important that happened 32

nuclear bomb a very powerful weapon that explodes using power that is made when an atom is divided 9

online connected to a system of computers, especially the Internet 24

part-time working or studying only for part of the day or the week 24

passenger someone who is travelling in a car, train, etc., but not controlling the car, train, etc. 2

penny a small coin in the US worth one cent; a small coin in the UK (= $\frac{1}{100}$ of a pound) 41

publisher a company or person who prepares and prints books, newspapers, magazines, etc. 19

ranger someone whose job is to look after a forest or a park 6

refund	an amount of money that is given back to you, especially because you are not happy with something you have bought 45
regret	to feel sorry about a situation, especially something that you wish you had not done 19
remote control	a piece of equipment that is used to control something such as a television from a distance 18
robot	a machine controlled by a computer, which can move and do other things that people can do 7
rottweiler	a type of large, powerful dog 1
rust	a dark orange substance that you get on metal when it is wet 33
safe	a strong metal box with locks where you keep money, jewellery, etc. 32
scream	to make a loud, high noise with your voice because you are afraid or hurt 1
security	the things that are done to keep someone or something safe 22
smart	clever 41
solar panel	a piece of equipment that changes light from the sun into electricity 34
sour	having a sharp taste like a lemon, and not sweet 21
speed bump	a small raised area built across a road to force people to drive more slowly 26
spy	someone who secretly tries to find information about a person, country, etc. 22, 45
steel	a very strong metal made from iron, used for making knives, machines, etc. 33
surfer	a person who rides on a wave on a special board 29
survivor	someone who continues to live after almost dying because of an accident, illness, etc. 6
swell	an old-fashioned US English word for 'very good' 36
tin	a soft silver metal 33
trainer	a soft sports shoe 18
tram	an electric vehicle for carrying passengers, mostly in cities, which moves along metal lines in the road 34
try on	to put on a piece of clothing to see if it fits 18
tsunami	an extremely large wave from the sea which causes a lot of damage to buildings, etc. on land and is often caused by an earthquake (= sudden movement of the Earth's surface) under the sea 6
twin	one of two children who are born to the same mother at the same time 30
vaccine	a substance that is given to people to stop them from getting a particular disease 7
virtual	using computer images and sounds that make you think an imagined situation is real 7
windsurfing	a sport in which you sail across water by standing on a board and holding onto a large sail 45
worthless	having no value in money 3
zoology	the scientific study of animals and how they behave 4

Grammar index

Thanks and Acknowledgements

The authors would like to thank Penny Ur for her patience, knowledge and extremely helpful advice. We would also like to thank the editorial team for their encouragement and hard work, especially Alison Sharpe, Lynn Dunlop, Lynn Townsend, Matthew Duffy, Rhona Snelling, Janet Weller, Robert Vernon and Frances Disken. Fiona would like to thank Steve and Ollie for their support.

The authors and publishers would like to thank the following individuals who commented on the materials during the development stage:
Mónica Martina Carrera García, Dany Etienne, Ludmilla Kozhevnikova, Aisha Osman and Anila R Scott-Monkhouse.

The publishers are grateful to the following for permission to reproduce copyright photographs and materials:

Alamy /©Greg Balfour Evans for p. 22(t), /©Philippe Hays for p. 22(b), /©IS317/Image Source for p. 30(cr), /©i love images for p. 30(bl), /©Odilon Dimier/PhotoAlto for p. 34, /©Marvin Dembinsky Photo Associates for p. 38(c), /©yannick luthy for p. 38(b), /©David W. Hamilton for p. 41, /©Marvin Dembinsky Photo Associates for p. 44(cr), /©Middle East for p. 56, /©Frans Lanting Studio for p. 66, /©Mary Evans Picture Library for p. 86(t), /©Mary Evans Picture Library for p. 86(c), /©Dennis Gilbert/The National Trust Photolibrary for p. 86(b), /©Picture Partners for p. 130, /©Chris Luneski for p. 134(b), /©Kumar Sriskandan for p. 138(l), /©David Gordon for p. 142(cr), /©Alan Marsh/First Light for p. 146(cr), /©MATTES René/Hemis for p. 146(br), /©Ton Koene/Picture Contact for p. 160, /©INTERFOTO for p. 167, /©ICP for p. 180; The Art Archive /©Jean Vinchon Numismatist Paris/Alfredo Dagli Orti for p. 14; Corbis /©NOAA for p. 26(t), /©Charles O'Rear for p. 142(bl); Getty Images /©Marko Georgiev for p. 26(b), /© Bettmann for p. 82(tl), /©George Napolitano/FilmMagic for p. 82(cr), /©Kevin Winter for p. 104, /©Norbert Wu/Minden Pictures II for p. 137, /©Dea/G. Nimatallah/De Agostini Picture Library for p. 142(tl), /©Zubin Shroff/Taxi for p. 148, /©Stockbyte for p. 167, /©Jim Brandenburg/Minden Pictures for p. 168, /©Andy Caulfield/Photographer's Choice for p. 199; iStockphoto.com /©Denis Jr. Tangney for p. 18, /©Huchen Lu for p. 30(tl), /©Robert Breme for p. 38(t), /©Cliff Wassmann for p. 57, /©Nick Berrisford for p. 134(t), /©William Blacke for p. 138(r), /©Craig Dingle for p. 146(cl); The Kobal Collection /©Charlie and The Chocolate Factory/Warner Bros. for p. 120(r); NASA /© for p. 44(cl); Rex Features /©Charles Sykes for p. 82(bl), /©ITV for p. 120(l); SKELETON KEY and CROCODILE TEARS by Anthony Horowitz Cover designs © 2010 Walker Books Ltd (p. 192). Boy with torch Logo™ & Alex Rider™ © 2010 Stormbreaker Productions Ltd (p. 192). Reproduced by permission of Walker Books Ltd, London SE11 5HJ.

While every effort has been made, it has not always been possible to identify the sources of all the material used, or to trace all copyright holders. If any omissions are brought to our notice, we will be happy to include the appropriate acknowledgements on reprinting.

Review units written by Tom Bradbury.
Picture research by Suzanne Williams/Pictureresearch.co.uk
Illustrations by David Shephard, Humberto Blanco, Javier Joaquin, Julian Mosedale, Leo Brown, Mark Draisey, Mark Duffin, Roger Penwill, Rory Walker and Tom Croft.

Notes